GW01316147

GETTING STARTED

WELCOME

Thanks for purchasing these training notes for the **AWS Certified Developer Associate** exam from Digital Cloud Training. The information in these Cheat Sheets relates to the latest **DVA-C01** version of the exam blueprint.

The DVA-C01 exam covers a broad set of AWS services and the aim of putting this information together is to provide a centralized, detailed list of the facts you need to know before you sit the exam. This will shortcut your study time and maximize your chance of passing the exam first time.

I hope you get great value from this popular resource that has been well received by our pool of over 70,000 students. Wishing you all the best with your AWS Certified Developer Associate exam.

Neal Davis

AWS Solutions Architect & Founder of Digital Cloud Training

ABOUT THESE TRAINING NOTES

This document does not read like a book or instructional text. We provide a raw, point-to-point list of facts backed by tables and diagrams to help with understanding.

For easy navigation, the information on each AWS service in this document is organized into the same categories as they are in the AWS Management Console.

The scope of coverage of services, and what information is included for each service, is based on feedback from our pool of over 70,000 students as well as our own experience - and may differ between AWS services.

To test your understanding, we have added **110 quiz questions** that you will find at the end of each major chapter. Please note that quiz questions are designed as a tool to review your knowledge of the content that was presented within the section. They do not necessarily represent the AWS exam style or difficulty.

YOUR PATHWAY TO SUCCESS

If you're new to AWS, we'd suggest first enrolling in the online instructor-led AWS Certified Developer Associate Video Course from Digital Cloud Training to familiarize yourself with the AWS platform before returning to the Training Notes to get a more detailed understanding of the AWS services.

To assess where you are at on your AWS journey, we recommend taking the AWS Certified Developer Associate Practice Exams on the Digital Cloud Training website. The **online exam simulator** with 390 **unique questions** will help you identify your strengths and weaknesses. These practice tests are designed to reflect the difficulty of the AWS exam and are the closest to the real exam experience available.

As a final step, use these training notes to focus your study on the knowledge areas where you need to most.

BONUS OFFER

To assess your AWS exam readiness, we have included one full-length practice exam from Digital Cloud Training. These 65 exam-difficulty practice questions are timed and scored and simulate the real AWS exam experience. To gain access to your free practice test on our interactive exam simulator online, simply navigate to the CONCLUSION at the back of this book where you'll find detailed instructions.

CONTACT, SUPPORT & FEEDBACK

We hope you get great value from these training resources. If for any reason you are not 100% satisfied, please message us at feedback@digitalcloud.training.

For technical support, contact us at:

support@digitalcloud.training.

If you enjoy reading reviews, please consider paying it forward. It's the best way you can help us improve our books and help your fellow AWS students make the right choices. We celebrate every honest review and truly appreciate it. You can leave a review at any time at amazon.com/ryp (or your local amazon store, e.g. amazon.co.uk/ryp).

The AWS platform is evolving quickly, and the exam tracks these changes with a typical lag of around 6 months. We are therefore reliant on student feedback to keep track of what is appearing in the exam. Our private Facebook group is a great place to ask questions and share knowledge and exam tips with the AWS community. Please join the discussion and share your exam feedback to our Facebook group:

https://www.facebook.com/groups/awscertificationqa

HOW TO BEST PREPARE FOR YOUR EXAM

The AWS Developer Associate exam is one of three AWS certifications at the associate level. This certification is geared towards those who work in development roles using AWS cloud services. If you don't work as a developer, this might put you off. However, this certification is both accessible and useful to those who do not come from a development background.

DVA-C01 EXAM GUIDE

The AWS Developer Associate certification is intended for those individuals who perform a development role working with AWS services. It is expected that you'll have at least one year of hands-on experience developing and maintaining AWS-based applications. The exam validates the following ability to:

- Demonstrate an understanding of core AWS services, uses, and basic AWS architecture best practices
- Demonstrate proficiency in developing, deploying, and debugging cloud-based applications using AWS

In reality, you don't need to know how to program and you don't actually need to have experience of developer tools to pass this exam. Plenty of students pass this exam using only video-based training, practice tests, and hands-on practice using an AWS free-tier account.

The exam includes 65 questions and has a time limit of 130 minutes. You need to score a minimum of 720 out of 1000 points to pass the exam. The question format of the exam is multiple-choice (one correct response from four options) and multiple-response (two or more correct responses from five or more options).

In the AWS Certified Developer Associate (DVA-C01) exam guide, it is stated that students should have the following knowledge and experience:

- In-depth knowledge of at least one high-level programming language
- Understanding of core AWS services, uses, and basic AWS architecture best practices
- Proficiency in developing, deploying, and debugging cloud-based applications using AWS
- Ability to use the AWS service APIs, AWS CLI, and SDKs to write applications
- Ability to identify key features of AWS services
- Understanding of the AWS shared responsibility model
- Understanding of application lifecycle management
- Ability to use a CI/CD pipeline to deploy applications on AWS
- Ability to use or interact with AWS services
- Ability to apply a basic understanding of cloud-native applications to write code
- Ability to write code using AWS security best practices
- Ability to author, maintain, and debug code modules on AWS
- Proficiency writing code for serverless applications
- Understanding of the use of containers in the development process

DOMAINS, OBJECTIVES AND EXAMPLES

The knowledge required is organized into five "domains". Within each domain, there are several objectives that broadly describe the knowledge and experience expected to pass the exam.

DOMAIN 1: DEPLOYMENT

This domain makes up 22% of the exam and includes the following four objectives:

1.1 Deploy written code in AWS using existing CI/CD pipelines, processes, and patterns
1.2 Deploy applications using Elastic Beanstalk
1.3 Prepare the application deployment package to be deployed to AWS
1.4 Deploy serverless applications

What you need to know

You need to know how to use the AWS Developer Tools such as AWS CodeCommit, AWS CodeBuild, AWS CodeDeploy, and AWS CodePipeline. You'll need to know how to use these tools for creating CI/CD pipelines to deploying code. These tools make it easy for you, so don't be too intimidated by this if you've not worked with CI/CD pipelines before.

You'll definitely need to be confident when to use an appspec.yml file vs a buildspec.yml file. For CodeDeploy, make sure you know the different deployment types such as in-place and blue/green and also the various traffic shifting options including canary, linear, and all-at-once. These are different for each service (Lambda, ECS, EC2 etc.) and you will be tested on this knowledge.

AWS Elastic Beanstalk can feature quite heavily on the exam. You'll need to understand the structure of Elastic Beanstalk and its uses cases. Make sure you understand the difference between web server environments and worker environments. Elastic Beanstalk deployment policies come up often and it's very important to understand the various features and constraints of each policy and when to use them. These include All-at-once, rolling, rolling with additional batch, and immutable.

Serverless is a big topic on the AWS Certified Developer Associate exam. You need to know how to deploy AWS Lambda functions, Amazon API Gateway APIs, Amazon DynamoDB tables, and other serverless services. This can include using AWS CodeDeploy, Amazon CloudFormation, and the AWS Serverless Application Model.

Example Questions

Question: The source code for an application is stored in a file named index.js that is in a folder along with a template file that includes the following code:

AWSTemplateFormatVersion: '2010-09-09'

Transform: 'AWS::Serverless-2016-10-31'

Resources:

  LambdaFunctionWithAPI:

   Type: AWS::Serverless::Function

   Properties:

    Handler: index.handler

    Runtime: nodejs12.x

What does a Developer need to do to prepare the template so it can be deployed using an AWS CLI command?

1. Run the aws cloudformation compile command to base64 encode and embed the source file into a modified CloudFormation template

2. Run the aws cloudformation package command to upload the source code to an Amazon S3 bucket and produce a modified CloudFormation template

3. Run the aws lambda zip command to package the source file together with the CloudFormation template and deploy the resulting zip archive

4. Run the aws serverless create-package command to embed the source file directly into the existing CloudFormation template

Answer: 2. The template shown is an AWS SAM template for deploying a serverless application. This can be identified by the template header: *Transform: 'AWS::Serverless-2016-10-31'*. The Developer will need to package and then deploy the template. To do this the source code must be available in the same directory or referenced using the "codeuri" parameter. Then, the Developer can use the "aws cloudformation package" or "sam package" commands to prepare the local artifacts (local paths) that the AWS CloudFormation template references.

Question: A Developer has completed some code updates and needs to deploy the updates to an Amazon Elastic Beanstalk environment. The environment includes twelve Amazon EC2 instances and there can be no reduction in application performance and availability during the update. Which deployment policy is the most cost-effective choice so suit these requirements?

1. All at once

2. Rolling

3. Rolling with additional batch

4. Immutable

Answer: 3. The "rolling with additional batch" policy will add an additional batch of instances, updates those instances, then move onto the next batch.

Question: A Developer is writing an imaging microservice on AWS Lambda. The service is dependent on several libraries that are not available in the Lambda runtime environment. Which strategy should the Developer follow to create the Lambda deployment package?

1. Create a ZIP file with the source code and all dependent libraries

2. Create a ZIP file with the source code and a script that installs the dependent libraries at runtime

3. Create a ZIP file with the source code and an appspec.yml file. Add the libraries to the appspec.yml file and upload to Amazon S3. Deploy using CloudFormation

4. Create a ZIP file with the source code and a buildspec.yml file that installs the dependent libraries on AWS Lambda

Answer: 1. A deployment package is a ZIP archive that contains your function code and dependencies. You need to create a deployment package if you use the Lambda API to manage functions, or if you need to include libraries and dependencies other than the AWS SDK.

DOMAIN 2: SECURITY

This domain makes up 26% of the exam and includes the following three objectives:

2.1 Make authenticated calls to AWS services
2.2 Implement encryption using AWS services
2.3 Implement application authentication, and authorization

What you need to know

Security is an important topic for all AWS exams and with the AWS Developer Associate certification, you'll need to be familiar with how to develop secure applications and use best practices for secure application development.

You need to understand how and when to use IAM users, groups, and roles. You should be familiar with how delegation works and how to assume roles programmatically. You need to know when to use access keys and when to use instance profiles. You'll also need to be able to read JSON permissions policies and know how to construct them.

The AWS Developer Associate Exam includes quite a few questions on AWS Cognito. You'll need to know when to use Cognito User Pools and Cognito Identity Pools. This can be a confusing topic but you need to be crystal clear on the differences on exam day. Also, make sure you understand Lambda authorizers and how to use them with API Gateway.

For encryption you need to understand the encryption SDK. AWS KMS, AWS CloudHSM, and Amazon S3 encryption come up regularly. Make sure you understand all the options and when and how to use each service. It's important to understand the process of how data is protected with encryption. Encryption at rest vs encryption in-transit comes up too.

If encryption and security make your head spin, fear not! Enroll in my **AWS Certified Developer Associate training course** and you'll learn these complex topics through visual and theoretical lessons and practical learning exercises.

Example Questions

Question: A developer needs to add sign-up and sign-in capabilities for a mobile app. The solution should integrate with social identity providers (IdPs) and SAML IdPs. Which service should the developer use?

1. AWS Cognito user pool
2. AWS Cognito identity pool
3. API Gateway with a Lambda authorizer
4. AWS IAM and STS

Answer: 1. User pools are for authentication (identify verification). With a user pool, your app users can sign in through the user pool or federate through a third-party identity provider (IdP). Identity pools are for authorization (access control). You can use identity pools to create unique identities for users and give them access to other AWS services.

Question: A development team is migrating data from various file shares to AWS from on-premises. The data will be migrated into a single Amazon S3 bucket. What is the SIMPLEST method to ensure the data is encrypted at rest in the S3 bucket?

1. Use SSL to transmit the data over the Internet
2. Ensure all requests use the x-amz-server-side-encryption-customer-key header
3. Ensure all requests use the x-amz-server-side-encryption header
4. Enable default encryption when creating the bucket

Answer: 4. Amazon S3 default encryption provides a way to set the default encryption behavior for an S3 bucket. You can set default encryption on a bucket so that all new objects are encrypted when they are stored in the bucket. The objects are encrypted using server-side encryption with either Amazon S3-managed keys (SSE-S3) or customer master keys (CMKs) stored in AWS Key Management Service (AWS KMS).

DOMAIN 3: DEVELOPMENT WITH AWS SERVICES

This domain makes up 30% of the exam and includes the following four objectives:

3.1 Write code for serverless application

3.2 Translate functional requirements into application design

3.3 Implement application design into application code

3.4 Write code that interacts with AWS services by using APIs, SDKs, and AWS CLI

What you need to know

I'll state it again, you DON'T actually need to be able to write any code. They won't ask you to write any code in the exam. But, you will need to be able to read some code. That doesn't mean you need to understand any specific language, just that you might get asked to identify a structural pattern in the code and what the best practice should be.

For instance, keeping one-off time-consuming tasks outside of the Lambda function handler. Such as:

- Connecting to databases.
- Initializing the AWS SDK.
- Pulling in dependencies or datasets.

You should be familiar with the API actions associated with some of the key services covered in the exam. This includes AWS Lambda, Amazon DynamoDB, AWS Elastic Beanstalk, Amazon S3, Amazon SQS, and others. You can look these up quite easily on the AWS website. It's also a good idea to have some familiarity with the AWS CLI and know the basic commands for key services.

For design, make sure you're familiar with the use cases for serverless services. Serverless applications come up a lot on the exam, as do microservices design patterns such as using Amazon ECS. AWS Lambda, Amazon API Gateway, Amazon DynamoDB, and Amazon S3 are the services that are MOST tested on the exam. But Amazon ECS is definitely important too so make sure you know your launch types and task placement strategies.

The AWS Developer Associate Exam mainly covers API Gateway REST APIs, rather than WebSocket APIs. In the Developer Associate exam, the focus is mainly on method requests/responses, integration requests/responses, mapping templates, stages and stage variables, caches, and throttling. You should also understand usage plans and API keys.

Example Questions

Question: A Developer needs to create an instance profile for an Amazon EC2 instance using the AWS CLI. How can this be achieved? (Select THREE.)

1. Run the aws iam create-instance-profile command

2. Run the CreateInstanceProfile API

3. Run the aws iam add-role-to-instance-profile command

4. Run the AddRoleToInstanceProfile API

5. Run the aws ec2 associate-instance-profile command

6. Run the AssignInstanceProfile API

Answer: 1,3,5. To add a role to an Amazon EC2 instance using the AWS CLI you must first create an instance profile. Then you need to add the role to the instance profile and finally assign the instance profile to the Amazon EC2 instance.

Question: A Developer needs to write some code to invoke an AWS Lambda function using the AWS Command Line Interface (CLI). Which option must be specified to cause the function to be invoked asynchronously?

1. Set the –invocation-type option to Event
2. Set the –invocation-type option to Invoke
3. Set the –payload option to Asynchronous
4. Set the –qualifier option to Asynchronous

Answer: 1. Several AWS services, such as Amazon Simple Storage Service (Amazon S3) and Amazon Simple Notification Service (Amazon SNS), invoke functions asynchronously to process events. To do this using the CLI you can set the –invocation-type option to Event.

DOMAIN 4: REFACTORING

This domain makes up 10% of the exam and includes the following two objectives:

4.1 Optimize application to best use AWS services and features

4.2 Migrate existing application code to run on AWS

What you need to know

The AWS Developer Associate Exam includes scenarios such as optimizing the performance of applications on AWS using features such as caching, auto scaling, and load balancing. Topics you should understand include caching with Amazon DynamoDB DAX, and Amazon ElastiCache, as well as when to use Amazon RDS read replicas and Multi-AZ.

Domain 4 also includes knowing when to use a specific service such as a serverless service over Amazon EC2 or Amazon RDS and how you might refactor services that are being migrated into the cloud using AWS Step Functions or application integration services such as Amazon SQS and Amazon SNS.

Quite a few scenarios come up relating to migrating applications from on-premises to the AWS cloud. These scenarios can test your knowledge of the use cases for different services and the methods of migrating them. The trick is to identify what the key requirements are for the design such as cost-effectiveness, security, resilience, or performance.

Example Questions

Question: A call center application is being refactored into a serverless architecture. The new application includes several AWS Lambda functions that are involved in the automation of support tickets. What is the BEST way to coordinate the complex invocation logic for the Lambda function?

1. Create a State Machine with AWS Step Functions
2. Include the invocation of other Lambda functions within the Lambda code
3. Create a Workflow using the Amazon Simple Workflow Service (SWF)
4. Use the AWS Serverless Application Model (SAM)

Answer: 1. AWS Step Functions makes it easy to coordinate the components of distributed applications as a series of steps in a visual workflow. You can quickly build and run state machines to execute the steps of your application in a reliable and scalable fashion.

Question: A company recently migrated a multi-tier application to AWS. The web tier runs on an Auto Scaling group of Amazon EC2 instances and the database tier uses Amazon DynamoDB. The database tier requires extremely high performance and most requests are repeated read requests. What service can be used to scale the database tier for BEST performance?

1. Amazon CloudFront

2. Amazon ElastiCache

3. Amazon DynamoDB Accelerator (DAX)

4. Amazon SQS

Answer: 3. Amazon DynamoDB Accelerator (DAX) is a fully managed, highly available, in-memory cache for DynamoDB that delivers up to a 10x performance improvement – from milliseconds to microseconds – even at millions of requests per second.

DOMAIN 5: MONITORING AND TROUBLESHOOTING

This domain makes up 12% of the exam and includes the following two objectives:

5.1 Write code that can be monitored

5.2 Perform root cause analysis on faults found in testing or production

What you need to know

The last domain covers knowledge of services such as AWS CloudWatch, and AWS X-Ray. You'll be tested on high-resolution and custom metrics with CloudWatch, namespaces, and dimensions. You should also be familiar with CloudWatch Events, CloudWatch Logs, and CloudWatch Alarms.

X-Ray is useful for root-cause analysis and comes up with a few exam questions. Make sure you know how to use get it working with services such as Amazon EC2, AWS Lambda, and Amazon DynamoDB. You'll need to know some basic terminology including segments, subsegments, annotations, and metadata. You also need to understand how X-Ray works with the SDK.

AWS CloudTrail is used for logging API activity and is therefore used as an auditing tool. CloudTrail comes up in exam questions so you should be familiar with how to create CloudTrail trails and what information is logged. Also, make sure you're absolutely clear on the difference between CloudWatch (monitoring) and CloudTrail (auditing).

Example Questions

Question: An application is instrumented to generate traces using AWS X-Ray and generates a large amount of trace data. A Developer would like to use filter expressions to filter the results to specific key-value pairs added to custom subsegments. How should the Developer add the key-value pairs to the custom subsegments?

1. Add metadata to the custom subsegments

2. Add annotations to the custom subsegments

3. Add the key-value pairs to the Trace ID

4. Setup sampling for the custom subsegments

Answer: 2. You can record additional information about requests, the environment, or your application with annotations and metadata. You can add annotations and metadata to the segments that the X-Ray SDK creates, or to custom subsegments that you create.

Question: An application running on Amazon EC2 is experiencing intermittent technical difficulties. The developer needs to find a solution for tracking the errors that occur in the application logs and setting up a notification when the error rate exceeds a certain threshold. How can this be achieved with the LEAST complexity?

1. Use CloudTrail to monitor the application log files and send an SNS notification

2. Configure the application to send logs to Amazon S3. Use Amazon Kinesis Analytics to analyze the log files and send an SES notification

3. Configure Amazon CloudWatch Events to monitor the EC2 instances and configure an SNS topic as a target

4. Use CloudWatch Logs to track the number of errors that occur in the application logs and send an SNS notification

Answer: 4. You can use CloudWatch Logs to monitor applications and systems using log data. For example, CloudWatch Logs can track the number of errors that occur in your application logs and send you a notification whenever the rate of errors exceeds a threshold you specify.

COMPUTE

AMAZON EC2

GENERAL

Amazon Elastic Compute Cloud (Amazon EC2) is a web service that provides resizable compute capacity in the cloud. It is designed to make web-scale computing easier for developers.

With Amazon EC2 you launch virtual server instances on the AWS cloud.

Each virtual server is known as an "instance".

You are limited to running up to a total of 20 On-Demand instances across the instance family, purchasing 20 Reserved Instances, and requesting Spot Instances per your dynamic spot limit per region (by default).

AWS are transitioning to a vCPU based, rather than instance based, limit. This is currently being rolled out and may not feature on the exam yet.

Amazon EC2 currently supports a variety of operating systems including: Amazon Linux, Ubuntu, Windows Server, Red Hat Enterprise Linux, SUSE Linux Enterprise Server, Fedora, Debian, CentOS, Gentoo Linux, Oracle Linux, and FreeBSD.

EC2 compute units (ECU) provide the relative measure of the integer processing power of an Amazon EC2 instance.

With EC2 you have full control at the operating system layer.

Key pairs are used to securely connect to EC2 instances:

- A key pair consists of a **public key** that AWS stores, and a **private key file** that you store.
- For Windows AMIs, the private key file is required to obtain the password used to log into your instance.
- For Linux AMIs, the private key file allows you to securely SSH (secure shell) into your instance.

Metadata and User Data:

- User data is data that is supplied by the user at instance launch in the form of a script.
- Instance metadata is data about your instance that you can use to configure or manage the running instance.
- User data is limited to 16KB.
- User data and metadata are not encrypted.
- Instance metadata is available at http://169.254.169.254/latest/meta-data/ (the trailing "/" is required).
- Instance user data is available at: http://169.254.169.254/latest/user-data.
- The IP address 169.254.169.254 is a link-local address and is valid only from the instance.
- On Linux you can use the curl command to view metadata and userdata, e.g. "curl http://169.254.169.254/latest/meta-data/".
- The Instance Metadata Query tool allows you to query the instance metadata without having to type out the full URI or category names.

BILLING AND PROVISIONING

On demand:

- Pay for hours used with no commitment.

- Low cost and flexibility with no upfront cost.

- Ideal for auto scaling groups and unpredictable workloads.

- Good for dev/test.

Spot:

- Amazon EC2 Spot Instances let you take advantage of unused EC2 capacity in the AWS cloud.

- Spot Instances are available at up to a 90% discount compared to On-Demand prices.

- You can use Spot Instances for various stateless, fault-tolerant, or flexible applications such as big data, containerized workloads, CI/CD, web servers, high-performance computing (HPC), and other test & development workloads.

- You can request Spot Instances by using the Spot management console, CLI, API or the same interface that is used for launching On-Demand instances by indicating the option to use Spot.

- You can also select a Launch Template or a pre-configured or custom Amazon Machine Image (AMI), configure security and network access to your Spot instance, choose from multiple instance types and locations, use static IP endpoints, and attach persistent block storage to your Spot instances.

- **New pricing model:** The Spot price is determined by long term trends in supply and demand for EC2 spare capacity.

- You don't have to bid for Spot Instances in the new pricing model, and you just pay the Spot price that's in effect for the current hour for the instances that you launch.

- Spot Instances receive a two-minute interruption notice when these instances are about to be reclaimed by EC2, because EC2 needs the capacity back.

- Instances are not interrupted because of higher competing bids.

- To reduce the impact of interruptions and optimize Spot Instances, diversify and run your application across multiple capacity pools.

- Each instance family, each instance size, in each Availability Zone, in every Region is a separate Spot pool.

- You can use the RequestSpotFleet API operation to launch thousands of Spot Instances and diversify resources automatically.

- To further reduce the impact of interruptions, you can also set up Spot Instances and Spot Fleets to respond to an interruption notice by stopping or hibernating rather than terminating instances when capacity is no longer available.

Reserved:

- Purchase (or agree to purchase) usage of EC2 instances in advance for significant discounts over On-Demand pricing.

- Provides a capacity reservation when used in a specific AZ.

- AWS Billing automatically applies discounted rates when you launch an instance that matches your purchased RI.

- Capacity is reserved for a term of 1 or 3 years.
- EC2 has three RI types: Standard, Convertible, and Scheduled.
- Standard = commitment of 1 or 3 years, charged whether it's on or off.
- Scheduled = reserved for specific periods of time, accrue charges hourly, billed in monthly increments over the term (1 year).
- Scheduled RIs match your capacity reservation to a predictable recurring schedule.
- For the differences between standard and convertible RIs, see the table below.
- RIs are used for steady state workloads and predictable usage.
- Ideal for applications that need reserved capacity.
- Upfront payments can reduce the hourly rate.
- Can switch AZ within the same region.
- Can change the instance size within the same instance type.
- Instance type modifications are supported for Linux only.
- Cannot change the instance size of Windows RIs.
- Billed whether running or not.
- Can sell reservations on the AWS marketplace.
- Can be used in Auto Scaling Groups.
- Can be used in Placement Groups.
- Can be shared across multiple accounts within Consolidated Billing.
- If you don't need your RI's, you can try to sell them on the Reserved Instance Marketplace.

	Standard	Convertible
Terms	1 year, 3 year	1 year, 3 year
Average discount off On-Demand price	40% - 60%	31% - 54%
Change AZ, instance size, networking type	Yes via ModifyReservedInstance API or console	Yes via ExchangeReservedInstance API or console
Change instance family, OS, tenancy, payment options	No	Yes
Benefit from price reductions	No	Yes

RI Attributes:

- Instance type – designates CPU, memory, networking capability.
- Platform – Linux, SUSE Linux, RHEL, Microsoft Windows, Microsoft SQL Server.
- Tenancy – Default (shared) tenancy, or Dedicated tenancy.

- Availability Zone (optional) – if AZ is selected, RI is reserved, and discount applies to that AZ (Zonal RI). If no AZ is specified, no reservation is created but the discount is applied to any instance in the family in any AZ in the region (Regional RI).

Comparing Amazon EC2 Pricing Models

The following table provides a brief comparison of On-demand, Reserved and Spot pricing models:

On-Demand	Reserved	Spot
No upfront fee	Options: No upfront, partial upfront or all upfront	No upfront fee
Charged by hour or second	Charged by hour or second	Charged by hour or second
No commitment	1-year or 3-year commitment	No commitment
Ideal for short term needs or unpredictable workloads	Ideal for steady-state workloads and predictable usage	Ideal for cost-sensitive, compute intensive use cases that can withstand interruption

Dedicated hosts:

- Physical servers dedicated just for your use.
- You then have control over which instances are deployed on that host.
- Available as On-Demand or with Dedicated Host Reservation.
- Useful if you have server-bound software licences that use metrics like per-core, per-socket, or per-VM.
- Each dedicated host can only run one EC2 instance size and type.
- Good for regulatory compliance or licensing requirements.
- Predictable performance.
- Complete isolation.
- Most expensive option.
- Billing is per host.

Dedicated instances:

- Virtualized instances on hardware just for you.
- Also uses physically dedicated EC2 servers.
- Does not provide the additional visibility and controls of dedicated hosts (e.g. how instance are placed on a server).
- Billing is per instance.

- May share hardware with other non-dedicated instances in the same account.

- Available as On-Demand, Reserved Instances, and Spot Instances.

- Cost additional $2 per hour per region.

The following table describes some of the differences between dedicates instances and dedicated hosts:

Characteristic	Dedicated Instances	Dedicated Hosts
Enables the use of dedicated physical servers	X	X
Per instance billing (subject to a $2 per region fee)	X	
Per host billing		X
Visibility of sockets, cores, host ID		X
Affinity between a host and instance		X
Targeted instance placement		X
Automatic instance placement	X	X
Add capacity using an allocation request		X

Partial instance-hours consumed are billed based on instance usage.

Instances are billed when they're in a running state – need to stop or terminate to avoid paying.

Charging by the hour or second (by the second with Linux instances only).

Data between instances in different regions is charged (in and out).

Regional Data Transfer rates apply if at least one of the following is true, but are only charged once for a given instance even if both are true:

- The other instance is in a different Availability Zone, regardless of which type of address is used.

- Public or Elastic IP addresses are used, regardless of which Availability Zone the other instance is in.

INSTANCE TYPES

Amazon EC2 provides a wide selection of instance types optimized to fit different use cases.

Instance types comprise varying combinations of CPU, memory, storage, and networking capacity and give you the flexibility to choose the appropriate mix of resources for your applications.

Each instance type includes one or more instance sizes, allowing you to scale your resources to the requirements of your target workload.

Category	Families	Purpose/Design
General Purpose	A1, T3, T3a, T2, M5, M5a, M4	General purpose instances provide a balance of compute, memory and networking resources, and can be used for a variety of diverse workloads
Compute Optimized	C5, C5n, C4	Compute Optimized instances are ideal for compute bound applications that benefit from high performance processors
Memory Optimized	R5, R5a, R4, X1e, X1, High Memory, z1d	Memory optimized instances are designed to deliver fast performance for workloads that process large data sets in memory
Accelerated Computing	P3, P2, G4, G3, F1	Accelerated computing instances use hardware accelerators, or co-processors, to perform functions, such as floating-point number calculations, graphics processing, or data pattern matching
Storage Optimized	I3, I3en, D2, H1	This instance family provides Non-Volatile Memory Express (NVMe) SSD-backed instance storage optimized for low latency, very high random I/O performance, high sequential read throughput and provide high IOPS at a low cost

Options when launching Instances

Choose whether to auto-assign a public IP – default is to use the subnet setting.

Can add an instance to a placement group.

Instances can be assigned to IAM roles which configures them with credentials to access AWS resources.

Termination protection can be enabled and prevents you from terminating an instance.

Basic monitoring is enabled by default (5-minute periods), detailed monitoring can be enabled (1 minute periods, chargeable).

Can define shared or dedicated tenancy.

T2 unlimited allows applications to burst past CPU performance baselines as required (chargeable).

Can add a script to run on startup (user data).

Can join to a directory (Windows instances only).

There is an option to enable an Elastic GPU (Windows instances only).

Storage options include adding additional volumes and choosing the volume type.

Non-root volumes can be encrypted.

Root volumes can be encrypted if the instance is launched from an encrypted AMI.

There is an option to create tags (or can be done later).

You can select an existing security group or create a new one.

You must create or use an existing key pair – this is required.

AMAZON MACHINE IMAGES

An Amazon Machine Image (AMI) provides the information required to launch an instance.

An AMI includes the following:

- A template for the root volume for the instance (for example, an operating system, an application server, and applications).

- Launch permissions that control which AWS accounts can use the AMI to launch instances.

- A block device mapping that specifies the volumes to attach to the instance when it's launched.

AMIs are regional. You can only launch an AMI from the region in which it is stored. However, you can copy AMI's to other regions using the console, command line, or the API.

Volumes attached to the instance are either EBS or Instance store:

- Amazon Elastic Block Store (EBS) provides persistent storage. EBS snapshots, which reside on Amazon S3, are used to create the volume.

- Instance store volumes are ephemeral (non-persistent). That means data is lost if the instance is shut down. A template stored on Amazon S3 is used to create the volume.

NETWORKING

Networking Limits (per Region or as Specified):

Name	Default Limit
EC2–Classic Elastic IPs	5
EC2–VPC Elastic IPs	5
VPCs	5
Subnets per VPC	200
Security groups per VPC	500
Rules per VPC security group	50
VPC security groups per elastic network interface	5
Network interfaces	350
Network ACLs per VPC	200
Rules per network ACL	20
Route tables per VPC	200
Entries per route table	50
Active VPC peering connections	50
Outstanding VPC peering connection requests	25
Expiry time for an unaccepted VPC peering connection	168

IP Addresses

There are three types of IP address that can be assigned to an Amazon EC2 instance:

- Public – public address that is assigned automatically to instances in public subnets and reassigned if instance is stopped/started.
- Private – private address assigned automatically to all instances.
- Elastic IP – public address that is static.

Public IPv4 addresses are lost when the instance is stopped but private addresses (IPv4 and IPv6) are retained.

Public IPv4 addresses are retained if you restart the instance.

Elastic IPs are retained when the instance is stopped.

Elastic IP addresses are static public IP addresses that can be remapped (moved) between instances.

All accounts are limited to 5 elastic IP's per region by default.

AWS charge for elastic IP's when they're not being used.

An Elastic IP address is for use in a specific region only.

You can assign custom tags to your Elastic IP addresses to categorize them.

By default, EC2 instances come with a private IP assigned to the primary network interface (eth0).

Public IP addresses are assigned for instances in public subnets (VPC).

Public IP addresses are always assigned for instances in EC2-Classic.

DNS records for elastic IP's can be configured by filling out a form.

Secondary IP addresses can be useful for hosting multiple websites on a server or redirecting traffic to a standby EC2 instance for HA.

You can choose whether secondary IP addresses can be reassigned.

You can associate a single private IPv4 address with a single Elastic IP address and vice versa.

When reassigned the IPv4 to Elastic IP association is maintained.

When a secondary private address is unassigned from an interface, the associated Elastic IP address is disassociated.

You can assign or remove IP addresses from EC2 instances while they are running or stopped.

All IP addresses (IPv4 and IPv6) remain attached to the network interface when detached or reassigned to another instance.

You can attach a network interface to an instance in a different subnet as long as it's within the same AZ.

The following table compares the different types of IP address available in Amazon EC2:

Name	Description
Public IP address	Lost when the instance is stopped
	Used in Public Subnets
	No charge
	Associated with a private IP address on the instance
	Cannot be moved between instances
Private IP address	Retained when the instance is stopped
	Used in Public and Private Subnets
Elastic IP address	Static Public IP address
	You are charged if not used
	Associated with a private IP address on the instance
	Can be moved between instances and Elastic Network Adapters

Elastic Network Interfaces

An elastic network interface (referred to as a network interface in this documentation) is a logical networking component in a VPC that represents a virtual network card.

A network interface can include the following attributes:

- A primary private IPv4 address from the IPv4 address range of your VPC
- One or more secondary private IPv4 addresses from the IPv4 address range of your VPC
- One Elastic IP address (IPv4) per private IPv4 address
- One public IPv4 address
- One or more IPv6 addresses
- One or more security groups
- A MAC address
- A source/destination check flag
- A description

You can create and configure network interfaces in your account and attach them to instances in your VPC.

You cannot team by adding ENIs to an instance.

eth0 is the primary network interface and cannot be moved or detached.

By default, eth0 is the only Elastic Network Interface (ENI) created with an EC2 instance when launched.

You can add additional interfaces to EC2 instances (number dependent on instances family/type).

An ENI is bound to an AZ and you can specify which subnet/AZ you want the ENI to be added in.

You can specify which IP address within the subnet to configure or leave it be auto-assigned.

You can only add one extra ENI when launching but more can be attached later.

ENIs can be "hot attached" to running instances.

ENIs can be "warm-attached" when the instance is stopped.

ENIs can be "cold-attached" when the instance is launched.

If you add a second interface AWS will not assign a public IP address to eth0 (you would need to add an Elastic IP).

Default interfaces are terminated with instance termination.

Manually added interfaces are not terminated by default.

You can change the termination behavior.

ENHANCED NETWORKING – ELASTIC NETWORK ADAPTER (ENA)

Enhanced networking provides higher bandwidth, higher packet-per-second (PPS) performance, and consistently lower inter-instance latencies.

Enhanced networking is enabled using an Elastic Network Adapter (ENA).

If your packets-per-second rate appears to have reached its ceiling, you should consider moving to enhanced networking because you have likely reached the upper thresholds of the VIF driver.

AWS currently supports enhanced networking capabilities using SR-IOV.

SR-IOV provides direct access to network adapters, provides higher performance (packets-per-second) and lower latency.

Must launch an HVM AMI with the appropriate drivers.

Only available for certain instance types.

Only supported in VPC.

ELASTIC FABRIC ADAPTER (EFA)

An Elastic Fabric Adapter is an AWS Elastic Network Adapter (ENA) with added capabilities.

An EFA can still handle IP traffic, but also supports an important access model commonly called OS bypass.

This model allows the application (most commonly through some user-space middleware) access the network interface without having to get the operating system involved with each message.

Elastic Fabric Adapter (EFA) is a network interface for Amazon EC2 instances that enables customers to run applications requiring high levels of inter-node communications at scale on AWS.

Its custom-built operating system (OS) bypass hardware interface enhances the performance of inter-instance communications, which is critical to scaling these applications.

With EFA, High Performance Computing (HPC) applications using the Message Passing Interface (MPI) and Machine Learning (ML) applications using NVIDIA Collective Communications Library (NCCL) can scale to thousands of CPUs or GPUs.

As a result, you get the application performance of on-premises HPC clusters with the on-demand elasticity and flexibility of the AWS cloud.

EFA is available as an optional EC2 networking feature that you can enable on any supported EC2 instance at no additional cost.

ENI VS ENA VS EFA

When to use ENI:

- This is the basic adapter type for when you don't have any high performance requirements.
- Can use with all instance types.

When to use ENA:

- Good for use cases that require higher bandwidth and lower inter-instance latency.
- Supported for limited instance types (HVM only).

When to use EFA:

- High Performance Computing.
- MPI and ML use cases.
- Tightly coupled applications.
- Can use with all instance types.

PLACEMENT GROUPS

Placement groups are a logical grouping of instances in one of the following configurations.

Cluster – clusters instances into a low-latency group in a single AZ:

- A cluster placement group is a logical grouping of instances within a single Availability Zone.
- Cluster placement groups are recommended for applications that benefit from low network latency, high network throughput, or both, and if the majority of the network traffic is between the instances in the group.

Spread – spreads instances across underlying hardware (can span AZs):

- A spread placement group is a group of instances that are each placed on distinct underlying hardware.
- Spread placement groups are recommended for applications that have a small number of critical instances that should be kept separate from each other.

Partition — divides each group into logical segments called partitions:

- Amazon EC2 ensures that each partition within a placement group has its own set of racks.
- Each rack has its own network and power source. No two partitions within a placement group share the same racks, allowing you to isolate the impact of hardware failure within your application.
- Partition placement groups can be used to deploy large distributed and replicated workloads, such as HDFS, HBase, and Cassandra, across distinct racks.

The table below describes some key differences between clustered and spread placement groups:

	Clustered	Spread
What	Instances are placed into a low-latency group within a single AZ	Instances are spread across underlying hardware
When	Need low network latency and/or high network throughput	Reduce the risk of simultaneous instance failure if underlying hardware fails
Pros	Get the most out of enhanced networking Instances	Can span multiple AZs
Cons	Finite capacity: recommend launching all you might need up front	Maximum of 7 instances running per group, per AZ

Launching instances in a spread placement group reduces the risk of simultaneous failures that might occur when instances share the same underlying hardware.

Recommended for applications that benefit from low latency and high bandwidth.

Recommended to use an instance type that supports enhanced networking.

Instances within a placement group can communicate with each other using private or public IP addresses.

Best performance is achieved when using private IP addresses.

Using public IP addresses, the performance is limited to 5Gbps or less.

Low-latency 10 Gbps or 25 Gbps network.

Recommended to keep instance types homogenous within a placement group.

Can use reserved instances at an instance level but cannot reserve capacity for the placement group.

The name you specify for a placement group must be unique within your AWS account for the Region.

You can't merge placement groups.

An instance can be launched in one placement group at a time; it cannot span multiple placement groups.

On-Demand Capacity Reservation and zonal Reserved Instances provide a capacity reservation for EC2 instances in a specific Availability Zone. The capacity reservation can be used by instances in a placement group. However, it is not possible to explicitly reserve capacity for a placement group.

Instances with a tenancy of host cannot be launched in placement groups.

IAM ROLES

IAM roles are more secure than storing access keys and secret access keys on EC2 instances.

IAM roles are easier to manage.

You can attach an IAM role to an instance at launch time or at any time after by using the AWS CLI, SDK, or the EC2 console.

IAM roles can be attached, modified, or replaced at any time.

Only one IAM role can be attached to an EC2 instance at a time.

IAM roles are universal and can be used in any region.

BASTION/JUMP HOSTS

You can configure EC2 instances as bastion hosts (aka jump boxes) in order to access your VPC instances for management.

Can use the SSH or RDP protocols to connect to your bastion host.

Need to configure a security group with the relevant permissions.

Can use auto-assigned public IPs or Elastic IPs.

Can use security groups to restrict the IP addresses/CIDRs that can access the bastion host.

Use auto-scaling groups for HA (set to 1 instance to just replace if it fails).

Best practice is to deploy Linux bastion hosts in two AZs, use auto-scaling and Elastic IP addresses.

EC2 MIGRATION

VM Import/Export is a tool for migrating VMware, Microsoft, XEN VMs to the Cloud.

Can also be used to convert EC2 instances to VMware, Microsoft or XEN VMs.

Supported for:

- Windows and Linux.
- VMware ESX VMDKs and (OVA images for export only).
- Citrix XEN VHD.
- Microsoft Hyper-V VHD.

Can only be used via the API or CLI (not the console).

Stop the VM before generating VMDK or VHD images.

AWS has a VM connector plugin for vCenter:

- Allows migration of VMs to S3.
- Then converts into a EC2 AMI.
- Progress can be tracked in vCenter.

MONITORING

EC2 status checks are performed every minute and each returns a pass or a fail status.

If all checks pass, the overall status of the instance is **OK.**

If one or more checks fail, the overall status is **impaired.**

System status checks detect (StatusCheckFailed_System) problems with your instance that require **AWS** involvement to repair.

Instance status checks (StatusCheckFailed_Instance) detect problems that require **your** involvement to repair.

Status checks are built into Amazon EC2, so they cannot be disabled or deleted.

You can, however, create or delete alarms that are triggered based on the result of the status checks.

You can create Amazon CloudWatch alarms that monitor Amazon EC2 instances and automatically perform an action if the status check fails.

Actions can include:

- Recover the instance (only supported on specific instance types and can be used only with StatusCheckFailed_System).
- Stop the instance (only applicable to EBS-backed volumes).
- Terminate the instance (cannot terminate if termination protection is enabled).
- Reboot the instance.

It is a best practice to use EC2 to reboot instance rather than the OS (create a CloudWatch record).

CloudWatch Monitoring frequency:

- Standard monitoring = 5 mins
- Detailed monitoring = 1 min (chargeable)

TAGS

A tag is a label that you assign to an AWS resource.

Used to manage AWS assets.

Tags are just arbitrary name/value pairs that you can assign to virtually all AWS assets to serve as metadata.

Each tag consists of a key and an optional value, both of which you define.

Tagging strategies can be used for cost allocation, security, automation, and many other uses. For example, you can use a tag in an IAM policy to implement access control.

Enforcing standardized tagging can be done via AWS Config rules or custom scripts. For example, EC2 instances not properly tagged are stopped or terminated daily.

Most resources can have up to 50 tags.

RESOURCE GROUPS

Resource groups are mappings of AWS assets defined by tags.

Create custom consoles to consolidate metrics, alarms and config details around given tags.

HIGH AVAILABILITY APPROACHES FOR COMPUTE

Up-to-date AMIs are critical for rapid fail-over.

AMIs can be copied to other regions for safety or DR staging.

Horizontally scalable architectures are preferred because risk can be spread across multiple smaller machines versus one large machine.

Reserved instances are the only way to guarantee that resources will be available when needed.

Auto Scaling and Elastic Load Balancing work together to provide automated recovery by maintaining minimum instances.

Route 53 health checks also provide "self-healing" redirection of traffic.

MIGRATION

AWS Server Migration Service (SMS) is an agent-less service which makes it easier and faster for you to migrate thousands of on-premises workloads to AWS.

AWS SMS allows you to automate, schedule, and track incremental replications of live server volumes, making it easier for you to coordinate large-scale server migrations.

Automates migration of on-premises VMware vSphere or Microsoft Hyper-V/SCVMM virtual machines to AWS.

Replicates VMs to AWS, syncing volumes and creating periodic AMIs.

Minimizes cutover downtime by syncing VMs incrementally.

Supports Windows and Linux VMs only (just like AWS).

The Server Migration Connector is downloaded as a virtual appliance into your on-premises vSphere or Hyper-V environments.

ELASTIC LOAD BALANCING

GENERAL ELB CONCEPTS

Elastic Load Balancing automatically distributes incoming application traffic across multiple targets, such as Amazon EC2 instances, containers, and IP addresses.

There are three types of Elastic Load Balancer (ELB) on AWS:

- Classic Load Balancer (CLB) – this is the oldest of the three and provides basic load balancing at both layer 4 and layer 7.

- Application Load Balancer (ALB) – layer 7 load balancer that routes connections based on the content of the request.

- Network Load Balancer (NLB) – layer 4 load balancer that routes connections based on IP protocol data.

Note: The Classic Load Balancer may be phased out over time and Amazon are promoting the ALB and NLB for most use cases within VPC.

The following image provides an overview of some of the key differences between the three types of ELB:

Application Load Balancer

Instance Protocol:
HTTP, HTTPS

Load Balancer Protocol:
HTTP, HTTPS

Application Load Balancer

Internet Client

- Operates at the request level
- Routes based on the content of the request (layer 7)
- Supports path-based routing, host-based routing, query string parameter-based routing, and source IP address-based routing
- Supports IP addresses, Lambda Functions and containers as targets

Network Load Balancer

Instance Protocol:
TCP, TCP_UDP

Load Balancer Protocol:
TCP, TLS, UDP, TCP_UDP

Network Load Balancer

Internet Client

- Operates at the connection level
- Routes connections based on IP protocol data (layer 4)
- Offers ultra high performance, low latency and TLS offloading at scale
- Can have static IP / Elastic IP
- Supports UDP and static IP addresses as targets

Classic Load Balancer

Instance Protocol:
TCP, SSL, HTTP, HTTPS

Load Balancer Protocol:
TCP, SSL, HTTP, HTTPS

Classic Load Balancer

Internet Client

- Old generation; not recommended for new applications
- Performs routing at Layer 4 and Layer 7
- Use for existing applications running in EC2-Classic

The following table provides a more detailed feature comparison:

Feature	Application Load Balancer	Network Load Balancer	Classic Load Balancer
Protocols	HTTP, HTTPS	TCP	TCP, SSL, HTTP, HTTPS
Platforms	VPC	VPC	EC2-Classic, VPC
Health Checks	✓	✓	✓
CloudWatch Metrics	✓	✓	✓
Logging	✓	✓	✓
Zonal fail-over	✓	✓	✓
Connection draining	✓	✓	✓
Load balancing to multiple ports on an instance	✓	✓	
WebSockets	✓	✓	
IP addresses as targets	✓	✓	
Lambda functions as targets	✓		
Load balancer deletion protection	✓	✓	
Path-based routing	✓		
Host-based routing	✓		
HTTP header-based routing	✓		
HTTP method-based routing	✓		
Query string parameter-based routing	✓		
Source IP address CIDR-based routing	✓		
Native HTTP/2	✓		
Configurable idle connection timeout	✓		✓

Feature	Application Load Balancer	Network Load Balancer	Classic Load Balancer
Cross-zone load balancing	✓	✓	✓
SSL offloading	✓	✓	✓
Server Name Indication (SNI)	✓		
Sticky sessions	✓		✓
Back-end server encryption	✓	✓	✓
Static IP		✓	
Elastic IP address		✓	
Preserve source IP address		✓	
Resource-based IAM permissions	✓	✓	✓
Tag-based IAM permissions	✓	✓	
Slow start	✓		
User authentication	✓		
Redirects	✓		
Fixed response	✓		
Custom security policies			✓

Elastic Load Balancing provides fault tolerance for applications by automatically balancing traffic across targets – Amazon EC2 instances, containers and IP addresses – and Availability Zones while ensuring only healthy targets receive traffic.

An ELB can distribute incoming traffic across your Amazon EC2 instances in a single Availability Zone or multiple Availabillty Zones.

Only 1 subnet per AZ can be enabled for each ELB.

Route 53 can be used for region load balancing with ELB instances configured in each region.

ELBs can be Internet facing or internal-only.

Internet facing ELB:

- ELB nodes have public IPs.

- Routes traffic to the private IP addresses of the EC2 instances.

- Need one public subnet in each AZ where the ELB is defined.

- ELB DNS name format: <name>-<id-number>.<region>.elb.amazonaws.com.

Internal only ELB:

- ELB nodes have private IPs.

- Routes traffic to the private IP addresses of the EC2 instances.

- ELB DNS name format: **internal**-<name>-<id-number>.<region>.elb.amazonaws.com.

Internal-only load balancers do not need an Internet gateway.

EC2 instances and containers can be registered against an ELB.

ELB nodes use IP addresses within your subnets, ensure at least a /27 subnet and make sure there are at least 8 IP addresses available in order for the ELB to scale.

An ELB forwards traffic to eth0 (primary IP address).

An ELB listener is the process that checks for connection requests:

- Listeners for CLB provide options for TCP and HTTP/HTTPS.

- Listeners for ALB only provide options for HTTP and HTTPS.

- Listeners for NLB only provide TCP as an option.

Deleting an ELB does not affect the instances registered against it (they won't be deleted; they just won't receive any more requests).

For ALB at least 2 subnets must be specified.

For NLB only one subnet must be specified (recommended to add at least 2).

For CLB you don't need to specify any subnets unless you have "Enable advanced VPC configuration" enabled in which case you must specify two.

ELB uses a DNS record TTL of 60 seconds to ensure new ELB node IP addresses are used to service clients.

By default, the ELB has an idle connection timeout of 60 seconds, set the idle timeout for applications to at least 60 seconds.

Perfect Forward Secrecy (PFS) provides additional safeguards against the eavesdropping of encrypted data, through the use of a unique random session key.

Server Order Preference lets you configure the load balancer to enforce cipher ordering, providing more control over the level of security used by clients to connect with your load balancer.

ELB does not support client certificate authentication (API Gateway does support this).

ELB SECURITY GROUPS

Security groups control the ports and protocols that can reach the front-end listener.

In non-default VPCs you can choose which security group to assign.

You must assign a security group for the ports and protocols on the front-end listener.

You need to also allow the ports and protocols for the health check ports and back-end listeners.

Security group configuration for ELB:

Inbound to ELB (allow)

- Internet-facing ELB:

  - Source: 0.0.0.0/0.

  - Protocol: TCP.

  - Port: ELB listener ports.

sg-6b578e13 | Internet-Facing ELB

Internal-only ELB:

- Source: VPC CIDR.
- Protocol: TCP.
- Port: ELB Listener ports.

sg-754e970d | Internal-Only ELB

Outbound (allow, either type of ELB):

- Destination: EC2 registered instances security group.
- Protocol: TCP.
- Port: Health Check/Listener.

sg-6b578e13 | Internet-Facing ELB

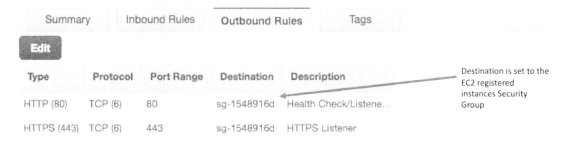

Security group configuration for registered instances:

Inbound to registered instances (Allow, either type of ELB).

- Source: ELB Security Group.
- Protocol: TCP.

- Port: Health Check/Listener.

Outbound (Allow, for both types of ELB).

- Destination: ELB Security Group.
- Protocol: TCP.
- Port: Ephemeral.

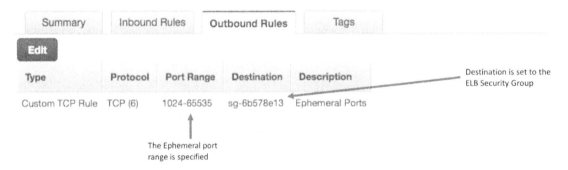

It is also important to ensure NACL settings are set correctly.

Distributed Denial of Service (DDoS) protection:

- ELB automatically distributes incoming application traffic across multiple targets, such as Amazon Elastic Compute Cloud (Amazon EC2) instances, containers, and IP addresses, and multiple Availability Zones, which minimizes the risk of overloading a single resource.

- ELB, like CloudFront, only supports valid TCP requests, so DDoS attacks such as UDP and SYN floods are not able to reach EC2 instances.

- ELB also offers a single point of management and can serve as a line of defence between the internet and your backend, private EC2 instances.

ELB MONITORING

Monitoring takes place using:

- **CloudWatch – every 1 minute**
    - ELB service only sends information when requests are active.
    - Can be used to trigger SNS notifications.
- **Access Logs**
    - Disabled by default.

- Includes information about the clients (not included in CloudWatch metrics).
- Can identify requester, IP, request type etc.
- Can be optionally stored and retained in S3.
- **CloudTrail**
  - Can be used to capture API calls to the ELB.
  - Can be stored in an S3 bucket.

LIMITS

The following table details the default limits for your account on a per-region basis:

Name	Default Limit
Application Load Balancers	20
Network Load Balancers	20
Target Groups	3000
Classic Load Balancers	20

CLASSIC LOAD BALANCER (CLB)

The Classic Load Balancer provides basic load balancing across multiple Amazon EC2 instances and operates at both the request level and connection level.

Operates at layer 4 and layer 7.

Supported protocols: TCP, SSL, HTTP, HTTPS.

CLB does not support HTTP/2.

Load balancers can listen on the following ports:

- [EC2-VPC] 1-65535.
- [EC2-Classic] 25, 80, 443, 465, 587, 1024-65535.

CLB's do not have pre-defined IPv4 addresses but are resolved using a DNS name.

Does not support Elastic IPs.

Supports IPv4 and IPv6.

Within a VPC only IPv4 is supported.

Provides SSL termination and processing.

Sticky Sessions:

- Cookie-based sticky sessions are supported.
- Session stickiness uses cookies and ensures a client is bound to an individual back-end instance for the duration of the cookie lifetime.
- Cookies can be inserted by the application or by the load balancer when configured.

- After cookies expire new requests will be routed by the load balancer normally and a new cookie will be inserted and bind subsequent sessions to the same back-end instance.
- With application-inserted cookies if the back-end instance becomes unhealthy, new requests will be routed by the load balancer normally and a new cookie will be inserted and bind subsequent sessions to the same back-end instance.
- With CLB-inserted cookies if the back-end instance becomes unhealthy, new requests will be routed by the load balancer normally BUT the session will no longer be sticky.

Must have multiple CLBs for multiple SSL certs.

Integrates with Auto Scaling, CloudWatch, CloudTrail and Route 53.

Instances monitored by CLB are reported as InService or OutofService.

Supports domain zone apex records, e.g. example.com.

Wildcard certificates are supported.

Health checks:

- Can be configured for HTTP, TCP, HTTPS, SSL.
- Ping port specifies the port for the health check.
- Ping path specifies the path to check, e.g. /index.html.
- Can define timeout, interval, unhealthy threshold, healthy threshold.

For fault tolerance it is recommended to distribute registered instances across multiple AZs (ideally evenly).

Cross-one load balancing:

- Cross-zone load balancing is enabled by default for CLB and ALB but not for NLB (when created through the console).
- Cross-zone load balancing is NOT enabled by default if the CLB is created from the CLI or API.
- You can enable or disable cross-zone load balancing on the CLB and NLB at any time.
- For the ALB, cross-zone load balancing is always on and cannot be disabled.
- When cross-zone load balancing is enabled, each load balancer node distributes traffic across the registered targets in all enabled Availability Zones.
- When cross-zone load balancing is disabled, each load balancer node distributes traffic across the registered targets in its Availability Zone only.

Connection draining is enabled by default and provides a period of time for existing connections to close cleanly.

When connection draining is in action a CLB will be in the status "InService: Instance deregistration currently in progress".

CLB can take 1 to 7 minutes to detect an increase in load and scale.

If you're anticipating a fast increase in load you can contact AWS and instruct them to pre-warm (provision) additional CLB nodes.

Listeners:

- A CLB listener is the process that checks for connection requests.
- You can configure the protocol/port on which your CLB listener listens.

- Front-end listeners check for traffic from clients to the CLB.
- Back-end listeners are configured with the protocol/port to check for traffic from the CLB to the EC2 instances.
- Front-end and back-end listeners can listen on ports 1-65535.
- Front-end and back-end listeners must be at the same layer (e.g. layer 4 or layer 7).
- There is a 1:1 mapping between front-end and back-end listeners.
- Up to 100 listeners can be configured.
- Supports L4 (TCP, SSL) and L7 (HTTP, HTTPS) listeners.

With packet interception the source IP/port will be from the ELB.

Proxy protocol for TCP/SSL carries the source (client) IP/port information.

The Proxy Protocol header helps you identify the IP address of a client when you have a load balancer that uses TCP for back-end connections.

Ensure the client doesn't go through a proxy or there will be multiple proxy headers.

Also need to ensure the EC2 instance's TCP stack can process the extra information.

X-forwarded-for for HTTP/HTTPS carries the source IP/port information.

To use an HTTPS listener the CLB must have an X.509 SSL/TLS server certificate – this will allow the CLB to terminate the secure session from the client to the CLB.

The session between the CLB and the EC2 instance can be re-encrypted.

You can use a certificate generated by AWS Certificate Manager (ACM) or your own certificate.

If you don't want interception/offloading you can use TCP listeners with certificates on the EC2 instances (traffic is secured end-to-end).

Proxy protocol only applies to L4.

X-forwarded-for only applies to L7.

To filter by source IP use NACLs for proxy protocol (L4) / X-forwarded-for (L7) headers with the EC2 instance's application performing the filtering.

Security

CLB supports a single X.509 certificate.

Two-way authentication with client certificates is not supported on the CLB – you would need to pass through the session using the proxy protocol and have an application that supports client-side certificates.

When using end-to-end encryption use TCP not SSL/HTTPS on the CLB (does not support Session Stickiness).

AWS ACM certificates include an RSA public key – ensure you include a set of ciphers that support RSA in the security policy.

The latest predefined security policy does not include support for SSLv3.

When choosing a custom security policy, you can select the ciphers and protocols (only for CLB).

SSL Security Policy includes:

- Protocol Versions (SSL/TLS)

- Supports TLS 1.0, 1.1, 1.2, SSL 3.0
  - SSL Ciphers
    - Encryption algorithms
    - SSL can use different ciphers to encrypt data
  - Server Order Preference
    - When enabled the first match in the cipher list with the Client list is used

If disabled (default) the first match in the client cipher list with the CLB is used

APPLICATION LOAD BALANCER (ALB)

The Application Load Balancer operates at the request level (layer 7), routing traffic to targets – EC2 instances, containers and IP addresses based on the content of the request.

You can load balance HTTP/HTTPS applications and use layer 7-specific features, such as X-Forwarded-For headers.

Supports HTTPS termination between the clients and the load balancer.

Supports management of SSL certificates through AWS IAM and AWS Certificate Manager for pre-defined security policies.

Server Name Indication (SNI) supports multiple secure websites using a single secure listener.

With Server Name Indication a client indicates the hostname to connect to.

IP addresses as targets allows load balancing any application hosted in AWS or on-premises using IP addresses of the application back-ends as targets.

Need at least 2 availability zones and you can distribute incoming traffic across your targets in multiple Availability Zones.

Automatically scales its request handling capacity in response to incoming application traffic.

Can configure an Application Load Balancer to be Internet facing or create a load balancer without public IP addresses to serve as an internal (non-Internet-facing) load balancer.

Native IPv6 support.

Internal only ALB only supports IPv4.

Content-Based Routing allows the routing of requests to a service based on the content of the request:

- Host-based routing – route client requests based on the Host field of the HTTP header allowing you to route to multiple domains from the same load balancer.

- Path-based routing – route a client request based on the URL path of the HTTP header (e.g. /images or /orders).

Provides support for micro-services and containers with load balancing across multiple ports on a single EC2 instance.

Better performance for real-time streaming.

Deletion protection can be enabled.

Request tracing (allows you to track a request by its unique ID).

Better health checks and CloudWatch metrics.

Integration with Amazon Cognito for user authentication.

Uses a round-robin load balancing algorithm.

Slow start mode allows targets to "warm up" with a ramp-up period.

Health Checks:

- Can have custom response codes in health checks (200-399).

- There are more details provided in the API and management console for health check failures.

- Reason codes are returned with failed health checks.

- Health checks do not support WebSockets.

- Fail open means if no AZ contains a healthy target, the load balancer nodes route requests to all targets.

Detailed access log information is provided and saved to an S3 bucket every 5 or 6 minutes.

ALB does not support back-end server authentication (CLB does).

ALB does not support EC2-Classic (CLB does).

Deletion protection is possible.

Deregistration delay is similar to connection draining.

Sticky Sessions:

- Session stickiness uses cookies and ensures a client is bound to an individual back-end instance for the duration of the cookie lifetime.

- ALB supports load balancer-generated cookies only.

- The name of the cookie is AWSALB.

- The contents of these cookies are encrypted using a rotating key.

- You cannot decrypt or modify load balancer-generated cookies.

- Sticky sessions are enabled at the target group level.

- You can also set the duration for the stickiness of the load balancer-generated cookie, in seconds.

- WebSockets connections are inherently sticky (following the upgrade process).

Monitoring

CloudTrail can be used to capture API calls. Only pay for the S3 storage charges.

CloudTrail records information on API calls only.

To monitor other actions such as time the request was received, the client's IP address, request paths etc. use access logs.

Access logging is optional and disabled by default.

You are only charged for the S3 storage.

ALB logs requests sent to the load balancer including requests that never made it to targets.

ALB does not log health check requests.

Logging of requests is best effort so shouldn't be relied on for auditing.

Target groups

Target groups are a logical grouping of targets (EC2 instances or ECS).

Targets are the endpoints and can be EC2 instances, ECS containers, or IP addresses.

Target groups can exist independently from the ALB.

Target groups can have up to 1000 targets.

A single target can be in multiple target groups.

Only one protocol and one port can be defined per target group.

The target type in a target group can be an EC2 instance ID, IP address (must be a valid private IP from an existing subnet) or AWS Lambda Function (ALB only).

You cannot use public IP addresses as targets.

You cannot use instance IDs and IP address targets within the same target group.

A target group can only be associated with one load balancer.

The following diagram illustrates the basic components. Notice that each listener contains a default rule, and one listener contains another rule that routes requests to a different target group. One target is registered with two target groups.

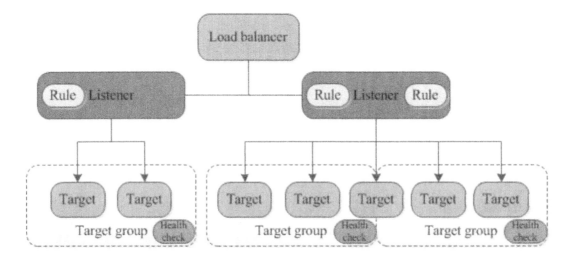

Target groups are used for registering instances against an ALB or NLB.

Target groups are a regional construct.

The following diagram shows how target groups can be used with host-based and target-based routing to route traffic to multiple websites, running on multiple ports, on a single EC2 instance:

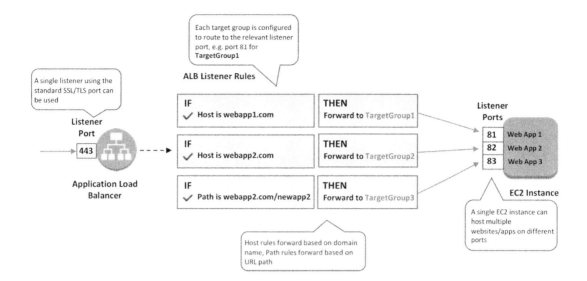

The following attributes can be defined:

- Deregistration delay – the amount of time for Elastic Load Balancing to wait before deregistering a target.

- Slow start duration – the time period, in seconds, during which the load balancer sends a newly registered target a linearly increasing share of the traffic to the target group.

- Stickiness – indicates whether sticky sessions are enabled.

The default settings for attributes are shown below:

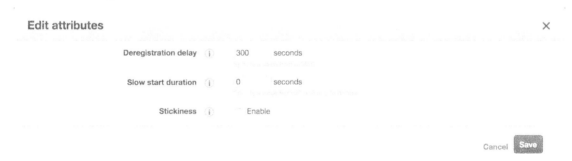

Auto Scaling groups can scale each target group individually.

You can only use Auto Scaling with the load balancer if using instance IDs in your target group.

Health checks are defined per target group.

ALB can route to multiple target groups.

You can register the same EC2 instance or IP address with the same target group multiple times using different ports (used for routing requests to micro-services).

If you register by instance ID the traffic is routed using the primary private IP address of the primary network interface.

If you register by IP address you can route traffic to an instance using any private address from one or more network interfaces.

You cannot mix different types within a target group (EC2, ECS, IP).

An EC2 instance can be registered with the same target group multiple times using multiple ports.

IP addresses can be used to register:

- Instances in a peered VPC.
- AWS resources that are addressable by IP address and port.
- On-premises resources linked to AWS through Direct Connect or a VPN connection.

Listeners and Rules

Listeners:

- Each ALB needs at least one listener and can have up to 10.
- Listeners define the port and protocol to listen on.
- Can add one or more listeners.
- Cannot have the same port in multiple listeners.

Listener rules:

- Rules determine how the load balancer routes requests to the targets in one or more target groups.
- Each rule consists of a priority, one or more actions, an optional host condition, and an optional path condition.
- Only one action can be configured per rule.
- One or more rules are required.
- Each listener has a default rule and you can optionally define additional rules.
- Up to 100 rules per ALB.
- Rules determine what action is taken when the rule matches the client request.
- Rules are defined on listeners.
- You can add rules that specify different target groups based on the content of the request (content-based routing).
- If no rules are found the default rule will be followed which directs traffic to the default target groups.

The image below shows a ruleset with a host-based and path-based entry and a default rule at the end:

Default rules:

- When you create a listener, you define an action for the default rule.
- Default rules cannot have conditions.
- You can delete the non-default rules for a listener at any time.
- You cannot delete the default rule for a listener.
- When you delete a listener all of its rules are deleted.
- If no conditions for any of a listener's rules are met, the action for the default rule is taken.

Rule priority:

- Each rule has a priority and they are evaluated in order of lowest to highest.
- The default rule is evaluated last.
- You can change the value of a non-default rule at any time.
- You cannot change the value of the default rule.

Rule action:

- Only one target group per action.
- Each rule has a type and a target group.
- The only supported action type is forward, which forwards requests to the target group.
- You can change the target group for a rule at any time.

Rule conditions:

- There are two types of rule condition: host and path.
- When the conditions for a rule are met the action is taken.
- Each rule can have up to 2 conditions, 1 path condition and 1 host condition.
- Optional condition is the path pattern you want the ALB to evaluate in order for it to route requests.

Request routing:

- After the load balancer receives a request it evaluates the listener rules in priority order to determine which rule to apply, and then selects a target from the target group for the rule action using the round robin routing algorithm.
- Routing is performed independently for each target group even when a target is registered with multiple target groups.
- You can configure listener rules to route requests to different target groups based on the content of the application traffic.

Content-based routing:

- ALB can route requests based on the content of the request in the host field: host-based or path-based.
- Host-based is domain name-based routing e.g. example.com or app1.example.com.
- The host field contains the domain name and optionally the port number.
- Path-based is URL based routing e.g. example.com/images, example.com/app1.
- You can also create rules that combine host-based and path-based routing.

- Anything that doesn't match content routing rules will be sent to a default target group.

ALB and ECS

ECS service maintains the "desired count" of instances.

Optionally a load balancer can distribute traffic across tasks.

All containers in a single task definition are placed on a single EC2 container instance.

You can put multiple containers in the same task definition behind a CLB.

- Define multiple host ports in the service definition.
- Define these listener ports as listeners on the CLB.

ECS service can only use a single load balancer.

If your task definition requires multiple ports per container you must use a CLB with multiple listeners.

ALB cannot do multiple listeners on a single task definition.

AWS does not recommend connecting multiple services to the same CLB.

ALB allows containers to use dynamic host port mapping so that multiple tasks from the same service are allowed on the same container host.

ALB supports path-based routing and priority rules.

ALB integrates with EC2 container service using service load balancing.

If a service uses multiple ports then multiple task definitions will need to be created with multiple target groups.

Federated authentication:

- ALB now supports authentication from OIDC compliant identity providers such as Google, Facebook and Amazon.
- Implemented through an authentication action on a listener rule that integrates with Amazon Cognito to create user pools.
- AWS SAM can also be used with Amazon Cognito.

NETWORK LOAD BALANCER

Network Load Balancer operates at the connection level (Layer 4), routing connections to targets – Amazon EC2 instances, containers and IP addresses based on IP protocol data.

It is architected to handle millions of requests/sec, sudden volatile traffic patterns and provides extremely low latencies.

Network Load Balancer supports features including:

- WebSockets
- TLS termination
- Preserves the source IP of the clients
- Provides stable IP support and Zonal isolation
- Long-running connections that are very useful for WebSocket type applications

High throughput – designed to handle traffic as it grows and can load balance millions of requests/second.

Extremely low latencies for latency-sensitive applications.

Uses static IP addresses – each NLB provides a single IP address for each AZ.

Can also assign an Elastic IP to the load balancer per AZ.

The IP-per-AZ feature reduces latency with improved performance, improves availability through isolation and fault tolerance and makes the use of NLBs transparent to your client applications.

Preserves the source IP of clients and provides stable IP support and Zonal isolation.

Can load balance any application hosted in AWS or on-premises using IP addresses of the application back-ends as targets.

NLB supports connections from clients to IP-based targets in peered VPCs across different AWS Regions.

Supports both network and application target health checks.

Supports long-running/lived connections (ideal for WebSocket applications).

Supports failover between IP addresses within and across regions (uses Route 53 health checks).

Integration with Route 53 enables the removal of a failed load balancer IP address from service and subsequent redirection of traffic to an alternate Network Load Balancer in another region.

Supports cross-zone load balancing (not enabled by default when created through the console, unlike ALB and CLB).

Uses the same API as the Application Load Balancer.

Also uses Target Groups (see section above).

Target groups for Network Load Balancers support the following protocols and ports:

- **Protocols:** TCP, TLS, UDP, TCP_UDP.
- **Ports:** 1-65535.

The following table summarizes the supported combinations of listener protocol and target group settings:

Listener Protocol	Target Group Protocol	Target Group Type	Health Check Protocol
TCP	TCP | TCP_UDP	instance | ip	HTTP | HTTPS | TCP
TLS	TCP | TLS	instance | ip	HTTP | HTTPS | TCP
UDP	UDP | TCP_UDP	instance	HTTP | HTTPS | TCP
TCP_UDP	TCP_UDP	instance	HTTP | HTTPS | TCP

CloudWatch reports Network Load Balancer metrics.

Enhanced logging – can use the Flow Logs feature to record all requests sent to your load balancer.

AWS AUTO SCALING

AMAZON EC2 AUTO SCALING

AWS Auto Scaling monitors your applications and automatically adjusts capacity to maintain steady, predictable performance at the lowest possible cost.

AWS Auto Scaling refers to a collection of Auto Scaling capabilities across several AWS services.

The services within the AWS Auto Scaling family include:

- Amazon EC2 (known as Amazon EC2 Auto Scaling)
- Amazon ECS
- Amazon DynamoDB
- Amazon Aurora

GENERAL AUTO SCALING CONCEPTS

Amazon EC2 Auto Scaling helps you ensure that you have the correct number of Amazon EC2 instances available to handle the load for your application.

You create collections of EC2 instances, called Auto Scaling groups.

Automatically provides horizontal scaling (scale-out) for your instances.

Triggered by an event of scaling action to either launch or terminate instances.

Availability, cost, and system metrics can all factor into scaling.

Auto Scaling is a region-specific service.

Auto Scaling can span multiple AZs within the same AWS region.

Auto Scaling can be configured from the Console, CLI, SDKs and APIs.

There is no additional cost for Auto Scaling, you just pay for the resources (EC2 instances) provisioned.

Auto Scaling works with ELB, CloudWatch and CloudTrail.

You can determine which subnets Auto Scaling will launch new instances into.

Auto Scaling will try to distribute EC2 instances evenly across AZs.

Launch configuration is the template used to create new EC2 instances and includes parameters such as instance family, instance type, AMI, key pair and security groups.

You cannot edit a launch configuration once defined.

A launch configuration:

- Can be created from the AWS console or CLI.
- You can create a new launch configuration, or.
- You can use an existing running EC2 instance to create the launch configuration.
    - The AMI must exist on EC2.
    - EC2 instance tags and any additional block store volumes created after the instance launch will not be taken into account.

- If you want to change your launch configurations you have to create a new one, make the required changes, and use that with your auto scaling groups.

You can use a launch configuration with multiple Auto Scaling Groups (ASG).

An ASG is a logical grouping of EC2 instances managed by an Auto Scaling Policy.

An ASG can be edited once defined.

You can attach one or more classic ELBs to your existing ASG.

You can attach one or more Target Groups to your ASG to include instances behind an ALB.

The ELBs must be in the same region.

Once you do this any EC2 instance existing or added by the ASG will be automatically registered with the ASG defined ELBs.

If adding an instance to an ASG would result in exceeding the maximum capacity of the ASG the request will fail.

You can add a running instance to an ASG if the following conditions are met:

- The instance is in a running state.

- The AMI used to launch the instance still exists.

- The instance is not part of another ASG.

- The instance is in the same AZs for the ASG.

SCALING

The scaling options define the triggers and when instances should be provisioned/de-provisioned.

There are four scaling options:

- Maintain – keep a specific or minimum number of instances running.

- Manual – use maximum, minimum, or a specific number of instances.

- Scheduled – increase or decrease the number of instances based on a schedule.

- Dynamic – scale based on real-time system metrics (e.g. CloudWatch metrics).

The following table describes the scaling options available and when to use them:

Scaling Type	What it is	When to use
Maintain	Ensures the required number of instances are running	Use when you always need a known number of instances running at all times
Manual	Manually change desired capacity via the console or CLI	Use when your needs change rarely enough that you're OK to make manual changes
Scheduled	Adjust min/max instances on specific dates/times or recurring time periods	Use when you know when your busy and quiet times are. Useful for ensuring enough instances are available *before* very busy times
Dynamic	Scale in response to system load or other triggers using metrics	Useful for changing capacity based on system utilization, e.g. CPU hits 80%

The scaling options are configured through Scaling Policies which determine when, if, and how the ASG scales and shrinks.

The following table describes the scaling policy types available for dynamic scaling policies and when to use them (more detail further down the page):

Scaling	What it is	When to use
Target Tracking Policy	The scaling policy adds or removes capacity as required to keep the metric at, or close to, the specified target value	A use case is that you want to keep the aggregate CPU usage of your ASG at 70%
Simple Scaling Policy	Waits until health check and cool down period expires before re-evaluating	This is a more conservative way to add/remove instances. Useful when load is erratic. AWS recommend step scaling instead of simple in most cases
Step Scaling Policy	Increase or decrease the current capacity of your Auto Scaling group based on a set of scaling adjustments, known as step adjustments	Useful when you want to vary adjustments based on the size of the alarm breach

The diagram below depicts an Auto Scaling group with a Scaling policy set to a minimum size of 1 instance, a desired capacity of 2 instances, and a maximum size of 4 instances:

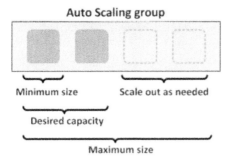

SCALING BASED ON AMAZON SQS

Can also scale based on an Amazon Simple Queue Service (SQS) queue.

This comes up as an exam question for SAA-C02.

Uses a custom metric that's sent to Amazon CloudWatch that measures the number of messages in the queue per EC2 instance in the Auto Scaling group.

Then use a target tracking policy that configures your Auto Scaling group to scale based on the custom metric and a set target value. CloudWatch alarms invoke the scaling policy.

Use a custom "backlog per instance" metric to track not just the number of messages in the queue but the number available for retrieval.

Can base off the SQS Metric "ApproximateNumberOfMessages".

ASG BEHAVIOR AND CONFIGURATION

EC2 Auto Scaling – Termination Policy:

- Termination policies control which instances are terminated first when a scale-in event occurs.
- There is a default termination policy and options for configuring your own customized termination policies.
- The default termination policy is designed to help ensure that your instances span Availability Zones evenly for high availability.
- The default policy is kept generic and flexible to cover a range of scenarios.

You can define Instance Protection which stops Auto Scaling from scaling in and terminating the instances.

If Auto Scaling fails to launch instances in an AZ it will try other AZs until successful.

The default health check grace period is 300 seconds.

Scale-out is the process in which EC2 instances are launched by the scaling policy.

Scale-in is the process in which EC2 instances are terminated by the scaling policy.

It is recommended to create a scale-in event for each scale-out event created.

Auto Scaling can perform rebalancing when it finds that the number of instances across AZs is not balanced.

Auto Scaling rebalances by launching new EC2 instances in the AZs that have fewer instances first, only then will it start terminating instances in AZs that had more instances.

Auto Scaling may go over the maximum number of instances by 10% temporarily for the purposes of rebalancing.

An imbalance may occur due to:

- Manually removing AZs/subnets from the configuration.
- Manually terminating EC2 instances.
- EC2 capacity issues.
- Spot price is reached.

Health checks:

- By default uses EC2 status checks.
- Can also use ELB health checks and custom health checks.
- ELB health checks are in addition to the EC2 status checks.
- If any health check returns an unhealthy status the instance will be terminated.
- With ELB an instance is marked as unhealthy if ELB reports it as OutOfService.
- A healthy instance enters the InService state.
- If an instance is marked as unhealthy it will be scheduled for replacement.
- If connection draining is enabled, Auto Scaling waits for in-flight requests to complete or timeout before terminating instances.
- The health check grace period allows a period of time for a new instance to warm up before performing a health check (300 seconds by default).

If using an ELB it is best to enable ELB health checks as otherwise EC2 status checks may show an instance as being healthy that the ELB has determined is unhealthy. In this case the instance will be removed from service by the ELB but will not be terminated by Auto Scaling.

Elastic IPs and EBS volumes are detached from terminated instances and will need to be manually reattached.

Using custom health checks a CLI command can be issued to set the instance's status to unhealthy, e.g.:

aws autoscaling set–instance-health –instance-id i-123abc45d –health-status Unhealthy

Once in a terminating state an EC2 instance cannot be put back into service again.

However, there is a short time period in which a CLI command can be run to change an instance to healthy.

Unlike AZ rebalancing, termination of unhealthy instances happens first, then Auto Scaling attempts to launch new instances to replace terminated instances.

You can manually remove (detach) instances from an ASG using the AWS Console or CLI.

When detaching an instance, you can optionally decrement the ASG's desired capacity (so it doesn't launch another instance).

An instance can be attached to one ASG at a time.

You can suspend and then resume one or more of the scaling processes for your Auto Scaling group.

Suspending scaling processes can be useful when you want to investigate a configuration problem or other issue with your web application and then make changes to your application, without invoking the scaling processes.

You can manually move an instance from an ASG and put it in the standby state.

Instances in standby state are still managed by Auto Scaling, are charged as normal, and do not count towards available EC2 instance for workload/application use.

Auto scaling does not perform health checks on instances in the standby state.

Standby state can be used for performing updates/changes/troubleshooting etc. without health checks being performed or replacement instances being launched.

When you delete an ASG the instances will be terminated.

You can choose to use Spot instances in launch configurations and specify a bid price.

Auto Scaling treats spot instances the same as on-demand instances.

You cannot mix Spot instances with on-demand.

If you want to change the bid price you need to create a new launch configuration.

Auto Scaling can be configured to send an SNS email when:

- An instance is launched.
- An instance is terminated.
- An instance fails to launch.
- An instance fails to terminate.

Merging ASGs

- You can merge multiple single AZ Auto Scaling Groups into a single multi-AZ ASG.
- Merging can only be performed by using the CLI.
- Process is to rezone one of the groups to cover/span the other AZs for the other ASGs.
- Then delete the other ASGs.
- Can be performed on ASGs with or without ELBs attached to them.
- The resulting ASG must be one of the pre-existing ASGs.

Cooldown Period

- The cooldown period is a configurable setting for your Auto Scaling group that helps to ensure that it doesn't launch or terminate additional instances before the previous scaling activity takes effect.
- The default cooldown period is applied when you create your Auto Scaling group.
- The default value is 300 seconds.
- You can configure the default cooldown period when you create the Auto Scaling group, using the AWS Management Console, the create-auto-scaling-group command (AWS CLI), or the CreateAutoScalingGroup API operation.
- Automatically applies to dynamic scaling and optionally to manual scaling but not supported for scheduled scaling.
- Can override the default cooldown via scaling-specific cooldown.

Scheduled:

- You cannot configure two scheduled activities at the same date/time.
- Scheduled actions can be edited from the AWS Console or CLI.

- Cooldown timer is not supported for scheduled or step on-demand scaling.

Dynamic:

- An alarm is an object that watches over a single metric, e.g. CPU/memory/network utilization.

- You need to have a scale-out and a scale-in policy configured.

Step scaling:

- Configure multiple steps/adjustments.

- Does not support cool down timers.

- Can respond to multiple alarms and initiate multiple scaling activities.

- Supports a warm-up timer which is the time it will take a newly launched instance to be ready.

The warm-up period is the period of time in which a newly created EC2 instance launched by ASG using step scaling is not considered toward the ASG metrics.

MONITORING

Basic monitoring sends EC2 metrics to CloudWatch about ASG instances every 5 minutes.

Detailed can be enabled and sends metrics every 1 minute (chargeable).

When the launch configuration is created from the console basic monitoring of EC2 instances is enabled by default.

When the launch configuration is created from the CLI detailed monitoring of EC2 instances is enabled by default.

When you enable Auto Scaling group metrics, Auto Scaling sends sampled data to CloudWatch every minute.

Configure ASG and EC2 monitoring options so they use the same time period, e.g. detailed monitoring (EC2) and 60 seconds (ASG), or basic monitoring (EC2) and 300 seconds (ASG).

LIMITS

Name	Default Limit
Auto Scaling Groups	200
Launch Configurations	200

AMAZON ECS

GENERAL ECS CONCEPTS

Amazon Elastic Container Service (ECS) is a highly scalable, high-performance container management service that supports Docker containers and allows you to easily run applications on a managed cluster of Amazon EC2 instances.

Amazon ECS eliminates the need for you to install, operate, and scale your own cluster management infrastructure.

Using API calls you can launch and stop container-enabled applications, query the complete state of clusters, and access many familiar features like security groups, Elastic Load Balancing, EBS volumes, and IAM roles.

Amazon ECS can be used to schedule the placement of containers across clusters based on resource needs and availability requirements.

There is no additional charge for Amazon ECS. You pay for:

- Resources created with the EC2 Launch Type (e.g. EC2 instances and EBS volumes).
- The number and configuration of tasks you run for the Fargate Launch Type.

Possible to use Elastic Beanstalk to handle the provisioning of an Amazon ECS cluster, balancing load, auto-scaling, monitoring, and placing your containers across your cluster.

Alternatively, use ECS directly for more fine-grained control for customer application architectures.

LAUNCH TYPES

An Amazon ECS launch type determines the type of infrastructure on which your tasks and services are hosted.

There are two launch types and the table below describes some of the differences between the two launch types:

Amazon EC2	Amazon Fargate
You explicitly provision EC2 instances	The control plane asks for resources and Fargate automatically provisions
You're responsible for upgrading, patching, care of EC2 pool	Fargate provisions compute as needed
You must handle cluster optimization	Fargate handles cluster optimization
More granular control over infrastructure	Limited control, as infrastructure is automated

Fargate Launch Type

- The Fargate launch type allows you to run your containerized applications without the need to provision and manage the backend infrastructure. Just register your task definition and Fargate launches the container for you.
- Fargate Launch Type is a serverless infrastructure managed by AWS.
- Fargate only supports container images hosted on Elastic Container Registry (ECR) or Docker Hub.

EC2 Launch Type

- The EC2 launch type allows you to run your containerized applications on a cluster of Amazon EC2 instances that you manage.
- Private repositories are only supported by the EC2 Launch Type.

The following diagram shows the two launch types and summarises some key differences:

Registry:
ECR, Docker Hub, Self-hosted

Registry:
ECR, Docker Hub

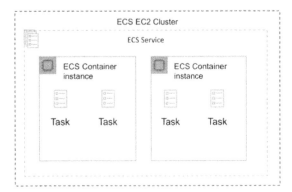

EC2 Launch Type
- You explicitly provision EC2 instances
- You're responsible for managing EC2 instances
- Charged per running EC2 instance
- EFS and EBS integration
- You handle cluster optimization
- More granular control over infrastructure

Fargate Launch Type
- Fargate automatically provisions resources
- Fargate provisions and manages compute
- Charged for running tasks
- No EFS and EBS integration
- Fargate handles cluster optimization
- Limited control, infrastructure is automated

ECS TERMINOLOGY

The following table provides an overview of some of the terminology used with Amazon ECS:

Elastic Container Service (ECS) Term	Description
Cluster	Logical grouping of EC2 instances
Container instance	EC2 instance running the ECS agent
Task Definition	Blueprint that describes how a docker container should launch
Task	A running container using settings in a Task Definition
Service	Defines long running tasks – can control task count with Auto Scaling and attach an ELB

These high-level concepts are all depicted in the image below:

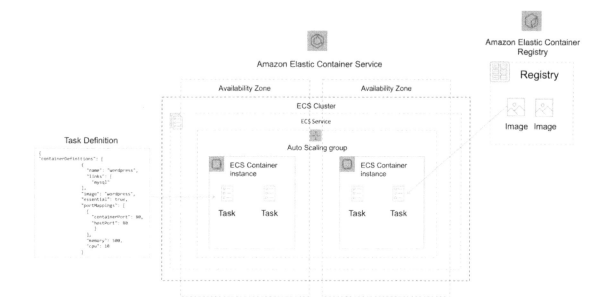

CLUSTERS

ECS Clusters are a logical grouping of container instances that you can place tasks on.

A default cluster is created but you can then create multiple clusters to separate resources.

ECS allows the definition of a specified number (desired count) of tasks to run in the cluster.

Clusters can contain tasks using the Fargate and EC2 launch type.

For clusters with the EC2 launch type clusters can contain different container instance types.

Each container instance may only be part of one cluster at a time.

"Services" provide auto-scaling functions for ECS.

Clusters are region-specific.

You can create IAM policies for your clusters to allow or restrict users' access to specific clusters.

ECS CONTAINER INSTANCES & CONTAINER AGENT

You can use any AMI that meets the Amazon ECS AMI specification.

The EC2 instances used as container hosts must run an ECS agent.

The ECS container agent allows container instances to connect to the cluster.

The container agent runs on each infrastructure resource on an ECS cluster.

The ECS container agent is included in the Amazon ECS optimized AMI and can also be installed on any EC2 instance that supports the ECS specification (only supported on EC2 instances).

Linux and Windows-based.

For non-AWS Linux instances to be used on AWS you must manually install the ECS container agent.

The agent is configured in /etc/ecs/ecs.config.

IMAGES

Containers are created from a read-only template called an image which has the instructions for creating a Docker container.

Images are built from a Dockerfile.

Only Docker containers are currently supported on ECS.

Images are stored in a registry such as DockerHub or AWS Elastic Container Registry (ECR).

ECR is a managed AWS Docker registry service that is secure, scalable and reliable.

ECR supports private Docker repositories with resource-based permissions using AWS IAM in order to access repositories and images.

Can use the Docker CLI to push, pull and manage images.

TASKS AND TASK DEFINITIONS

A task definition is required to run Docker containers in Amazon ECS.

A task definition is a text file in JSON format that describes one or more containers, up to a maximum of 10.

Task definitions use Docker images to launch containers.

You specify the number of tasks to run (i.e. the number of containers).

Some of the parameters you can specify in a task definition include:

- Which Docker images to use with the containers in your task.

- How much CPU and memory to use with each container.

- Whether containers are linked together in a task.

- The Docker networking mode to use for the containers in your task.

- What (if any) ports from the container are mapped to the host container instances.

- Whether the task should continue if the container finished or fails.

- The commands the container should run when it is started.

- Environment variables that should be passed to the container when it starts.

- Data volumes that should be used with the containers in the task.

- IAM role the task should use for permissions.

You can use Amazon ECS "Run task" to run one or more tasks once.

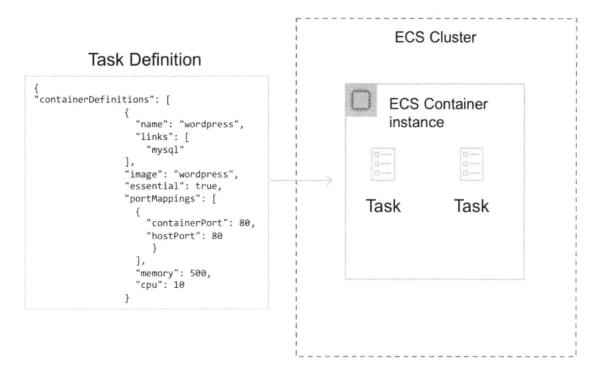

TASK PLACEMENT STRATEGY

A task placement strategy is an algorithm for selecting instances for task placement or tasks for termination. Task placement strategies can be specified when either running a task or creating a new service.

This is relevant only to the EC2 launch type.

Amazon ECS supports the following task placement strategies:

binpack – place tasks based on the least available amount of CPU or memory. This minimizes the number of instances in use.

random – place tasks randomly.

spread – place tasks evenly based on the specified value. Accepted values are instanceId (or host, which has the same effect), or any platform or custom attribute that is applied to a container instance, such as attribute:ecs.availability-zone. Service tasks are spread based on the tasks from that service. Standalone tasks are spread based on the tasks from the same task group.

A task placement constraint is a rule that is considered during task placement.

Amazon ECS supports the following types of task placement constraints:

- distinctInstance – Place each task on a different container instance.

- memberOf – Place tasks on container instances that satisfy an expression.

CLUSTER QUERY LANGUAGE

Cluster queries are expressions that enable you to group objects.

For example, you can group container instances by attributes such as Availability Zone, instance type, or custom metadata.

Expressions have the following syntax: subject operator [argument]

Example 1: The following expression selects instances with the specified instance type.

attribute:ecs.instance-type == t2.small

Example 2: The following expression selects instances in the us-east-1a or us-east-1b Availability Zone.

attribute:ecs.availability-zone in [us-east-1a, us-east-1b]

Example 3: The following expression selects instances that are hosting tasks in the service:production group.

task:group == service:production

SERVICE SCHEDULER

You can schedule ECS using Service Scheduler and Custom Scheduler.

Ensures that the specified number of tasks is constantly running and reschedules tasks when a task fails.

It can ensure tasks are registered against an ELB.

CUSTOM SCHEDULER

You can create your own schedulers to meet business needs.

Leverage third-party schedulers such as Blox.

The Amazon ECS schedulers leverage the same cluster state information provided by the Amazon ECS API to make appropriate placement decisions.

AUTO SCALING

Service Auto Scaling

Amazon ECS service can optionally be configured to use Service Auto Scaling to adjust the desired task count up or down automatically.

Service Auto Scaling leverages the Application Auto Scaling service to provide this functionality.

Amazon ECS Service Auto Scaling supports the following types of scaling policies:

- Target Tracking Scaling Policies—Increase or decrease the number of tasks that your service runs based on a target value for a specific CloudWatch metric.
- Step Scaling Policies—Increase or decrease the number of tasks that your service runs in response to CloudWatch alarms. Step scaling is based on a set of scaling adjustments, known as step adjustments, which vary based on the size of the alarm breach.
- Scheduled Scaling—Increase or decrease the number of tasks that your service runs based on the date and time.

- ➤ 1. Metric reports CPU > 80%
- ➤ 2. CloudWatch notifies ASG
- ➤ 3. AWS launches additional task

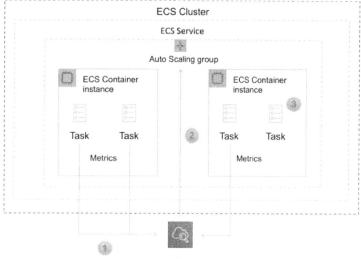

CLUSTER AUTO SCALING

This is a new feature released in December 2019.

Uses a new ECS resource type called a Capacity Provider.

A Capacity Provider can be associated with an EC2 Auto Scaling Group (ASG).

When you associate an ECS Capacity Provider with an ASG and add the Capacity Provider to an ECS cluster, the cluster can now scale your ASG automatically by using two new features of ECS:

1. **Managed scaling**, with an automatically-created scaling policy on your ASG, and a new scaling metric (Capacity Provider Reservation) that the scaling policy uses; and

2. **Managed instance termination protection**, which enables container-aware termination of instances in the ASG when scale-in happens.

- ➤ 1. Metric reports target capacity > 80%
- ➤ 2. CloudWatch notifies ASG
- ➤ 3. AWS launches additional container instance

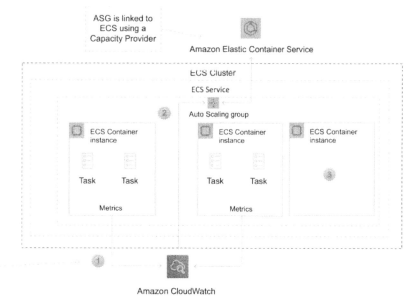

SECURITY/SLA

EC2 instances use an IAM role to access ECS.

ECS tasks can have IAM Roles attached (including Fargate tasks).

ECS tasks use the IAM role to access services and resources.

The container agent makes calls to the ECS API on your behalf through the applied IAM roles and policies.

You need to apply IAM roles to container instances before they are launched (EC2 launch type).

Best practices:

- AWS recommends limiting the permissions that are assigned to the container instance's IAM roles.

- Assign extra permissions to tasks through separate IAM roles (IAM Roles for Tasks).

Security groups attach at the instance or container level.

You have root-level access to the operating system of the EC2 instances.

The Compute SLA guarantees a Monthly Uptime Percentage of at least 99.99% for Amazon ECS.

ECS WITH X-RAY

There are two ways to run X-Ray:

As a daemon: X-Ray agent runs in a daemon container.

As a "sidecar": X-Ray runs alongside each container.

For Fargate the X-Ray daemon only runs as a sidecar.

Daemon Container	Local Daemon in Container	Local Daemon in Container

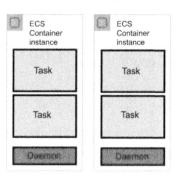 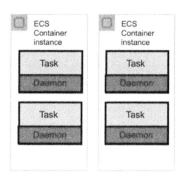 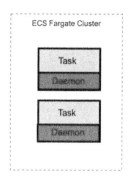

Task definition:

- X-Ray runs on port 2000 UDP.

- Must specify the daemon address.

- Must link the containers together.

X-Ray provides a Docker container image that you can deploy alongside your application:

-

    - Command: *docker pull amazon/aws-xray-daemon*

ECS WITH ELASTIC BEANSTALK

There are two options: Single and Multi- Docker container mode.

Single Container Docker

The single container platform can be used to deploy a Docker image (described in a Dockerfile or Dockerrun.aws.json definition) and source code to EC2 instances running in an Elastic Beanstalk environment.

Use the single container platform when you only need to run one container per instance.

Multicontainer Docker

The other basic platform, Multicontainer Docker, uses the Amazon Elastic Container Service to coordinate the deployment of multiple Docker containers to an Amazon ECS cluster in an Elastic Beanstalk environment.

The instances in the environment each run the same set of containers, which are defined in a Dockerrun.aws.json file.

Use the multicontainer platform when you need to deploy multiple Docker containers to each instance.

ElasticBeanstalk creates the following resources:

- ECS cluster.

- EC2 container instances.

- Load balancers (for high availability mode).

- Task definitions and execution.

Requires a config file Dockerrun.aws.json at the root of the source code.

Your Docker images must be pre-built (can be stored in ECR).

AMAZON ELASTIC CONTAINER REGISTRY (ECR)

Amazon Elastic Container Registry (ECR) is a fully-managed Docker container registry that makes it easy for developers to store, manage, and deploy Docker container images.

Amazon ECR is integrated with Amazon Elastic Container Service (ECS).

Amazon ECR hosts your images in a highly available and scalable architecture, allowing you to reliably deploy containers for your applications.

Integration with AWS Identity and Access Management (IAM) provides resource-level control of each repository.

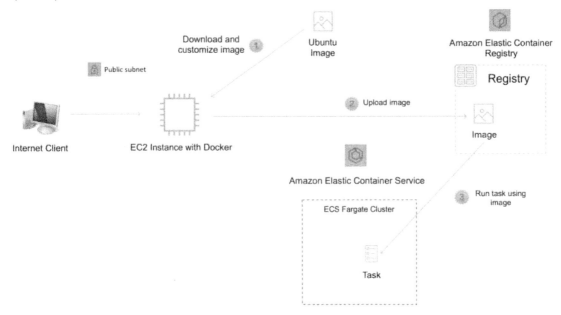

PUSHING AND PULLING IMAGES TO ECR

You must first authenticate.

To authenticate Docker to an Amazon ECR registry with get-login-password, run the **aws ecr get-login-password** command:

aws ecr get-login-password --region us-east-1 | docker login --username AWS --password-stdin aws_account_id.dkr.ecr.us-east-1.amazonaws.com

Note: In the AWS CLI version 1 the command is aws ecr get-login (without the -password). This is still appearing in the exam.

Tag your image:

docker tag e9ae3c220b23 aws_account_id.dkr.ecr.region.amazonaws.com/my-web-app

Push the image using the **docker push** command:

docker push aws_account_id.dkr.ecr.region.amazonaws.com/my-web-app

Pull the image using the **docker pull** command. The image name format should be registry/repository[:tag] to pull by tag, or registry/repository[@digest] to pull by digest.

docker pull aws_account_id.dkr.ecr.region.amazonaws.com/my-web-app:e9ae3c220b23

USING AN AMAZON ELASTIC LOAD BALANCER WITH ECS

Amazon ECS with Elastic Load Balancing

It is possible to associate a service on Amazon ECS to an Amazon Elastic Load Balancer (ELB).

The ALB supports a target group that contains a set of instance ports.

You can specify a dynamic port in the ECS task definition which gives the container an unused port when it is scheduled on the EC2 instance (this is specific to ALB only).

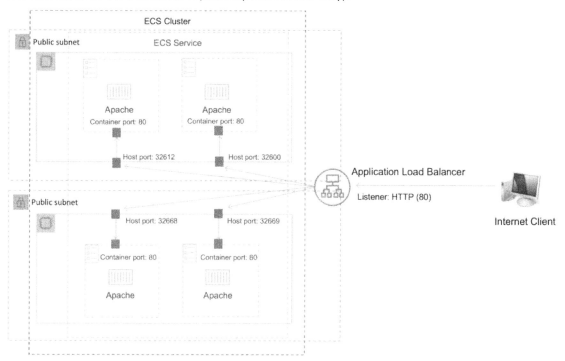

AWS LAMBDA

GENERAL AWS LAMBDA CONCEPTS

AWS Lambda is a serverless compute service that runs your code in response to events and automatically manages the underlying compute resources for you.

You can use AWS Lambda to extend other AWS services with custom logic, or create your own back-end services that operate at AWS scale, performance, and security.

AWS Lambda can automatically run code in response to multiple events, such as HTTP requests via Amazon API Gateway, modifications to objects in Amazon S3 buckets, table updates in Amazon DynamoDB, and state transitions in AWS Step Functions.

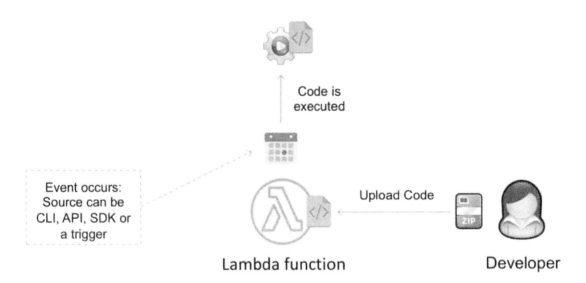

Lambda runs your code on high-availability compute infrastructure and performs all the administration of the compute resources, including server and operating system maintenance, capacity provisioning and automatic scaling, code and security patch deployment, and code monitoring and logging.

All you need to do is supply the code.

You are charged based on the number of requests for your functions and the duration, the time it takes for your code to execute.

The AWS Lambda free usage tier includes 1M free requests per month and 400,000 GB-seconds of compute time per month.

The price depends on the amount of memory you allocate to your function.

In the AWS Lambda resource model, you choose the amount of memory you want for your function, and are allocated proportional CPU power and other resources.

An increase in memory size triggers an equivalent increase in CPU available to your function.

Lambda scales continuously.

Lambda Functions can trigger other functions.

When using API Gateway in front of Lambda, traffic can go back through API Gateway.

Lambda scales out – not up.

Lambda functions are independent 1 event = 1 function.

1 event can = x functions when functions trigger other functions.

Lambda can work globally. E.g. backing up S3 buckets to other S3 buckets.

COMPARING AWS COMPUTE SERVICE

The following table compares the different AWS compute services covered in the AWS Certified Developer Associate certification:

EC2	ECS (EC2 Launch Type)	ECS (Fargate Launch Type)	Lambda
You manage the operating system	You manage container instance (EC2) and the containers (tasks)	You manage the containers (tasks)	You manage the code
Scale vertically – more CPU/Mem/HDD or scale horizontally (automatic) with Auto Scaling	Manually add container instances or use ECS Services and EC2 Auto Scaling	AWS scales the cluster automatically	Lambda automatically scales concurrent executions up to default limit (1000)
Use for traditional applications and long running tasks	Use for microservices and batch use cases where you need containers and need to retain management of underlying platform	Use for microservices and batch use cases	Use for ETL, infrastructure automation, data validation, mobile backends
No timeout issues	No timeout issues	No timeout issues	Limited to 900 seconds execution time for single execution (3 second default)
Pay for instance run time based on family/type	Pay for instance run time based on family/type	Pay for container run time based on allocated resources	Pay only for execution time based on memory allocation

INVOKING LAMBDA FUNCTIONS

You can invoke Lambda functions directly with the Lambda console, the Lambda API, the AWS SDK, the AWS CLI, and AWS toolkits.

You can also configure other AWS services to invoke your function, or you can configure Lambda to read from a stream or queue and invoke your function.

When you invoke a function, you can choose to invoke it synchronously or asynchronously.

Other AWS services and resources invoke your function directly.

For example, you can configure CloudWatch Events to invoke your function on a timer, or you can configure Amazon S3 to invoke your function when an object is created.

Each service varies in the method it uses to invoke your function, the structure of the event, and how you configure it.

SYNCHRONOUS INVOCATION

You wait for the function to process the event and return a response.

When you invoke a function synchronously, Lambda runs the function and waits for a response.

When the function execution ends, Lambda returns the response from the function's code with additional data, such as the version of the function that was executed. To invoke a function synchronously with the AWS CLI, use the invoke command.

```
$ aws lambda invoke --function-name my-function --payload '{ "key": "value" }' response.json {
"ExecutedVersion": "$LATEST", "StatusCode": 200 }
```

ASYNCHRONOUS INVOCATION

When you invoke a function asynchronously, you don't wait for a response from the function code.

For asynchronous invocation, Lambda handles retries and can send invocation records to a destination.

For asynchronous invocation, Lambda places the event in a queue and returns a success response without additional information. A separate process reads events from the queue and sends them to your function. To invoke a function asynchronously, set the invocation type parameter to Event.

```
$ aws lambda invoke --function-name my-function --invocation-type Event --payload '{ "key": "value" }'
response.json

{

"StatusCode": 202

}
```

The output file (response.json) doesn't contain any information, but is still created when you run this command. If Lambda isn't able to add the event to the queue, the error message appears in the command output.

EVENT SOURCE MAPPINGS

An event source mapping is an AWS Lambda resource that reads from an event source and invokes a Lambda function. You can use event source mappings to process items from a stream or queue in services that don't invoke Lambda functions directly. Lambda provides event source mappings for the following services.

Services that Lambda reads events From:

- Amazon Kinesis

- Amazon DynamoDB

- Amazon Simple Queue Service

An event source mapping uses permissions in the function's execution role to read and manage items in the event source. Permissions, event structure, settings, and polling behavior vary by event source.

To process items from a stream or queue, you can create an event source mapping.

Each event that your function processes can contain hundreds or thousands of items.

The configuration of the event source mapping for stream-based services (DynamoDB, Kinesis), and Amazon SQS, is made on the Lambda side.

The image below depicts an event source mapping where AWS Lambda reads messages from an Amazon SQS queue:

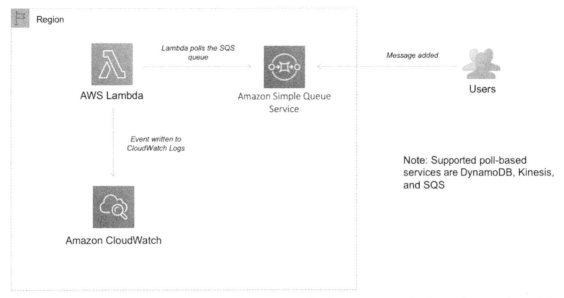

Note: for other services such as Amazon S3 and SNS, the function is invoked asynchronously and the configuration is made on the source (S3/SNS) rather than Lambda.

LAMBDA VERSIONS

Versioning means you can have multiple versions of your function.

You can use versions to manage the deployment of your AWS Lambda functions. For example, you can publish a new version of a function for beta testing without affecting users of the stable production version.

The function version includes the following information:

- The function code and all associated dependencies.
- The Lambda runtime that executes the function.
- All of the function settings, including the environment variables.
- A unique Amazon Resource Name (ARN) to identify this version of the function.

You work on $LATEST which is the latest version of the code – this is mutable (changeable).

When you're ready to publish a Lambda function you create a version (these are numbered).

Numbered versions are assigned a number starting with 1 and subsequent versions are incremented by 1.

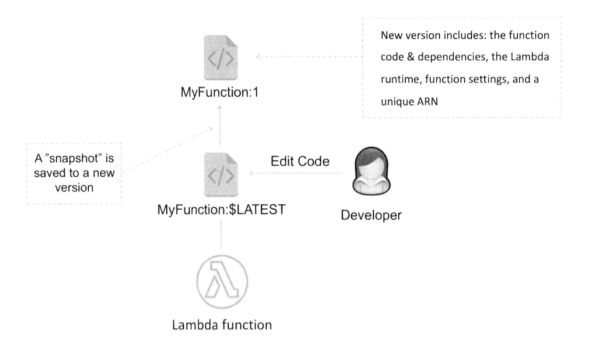

Versions are immutable (code cannot be edited).

Each version has it's own ARN.

Because different versions have unique ARNs this allows you to effectively manage them for different environments like Production, Staging or Development.

A qualified ARN has a version suffix.

An unqualified ARN does not have a version suffix.

You cannot create an alias from an unqualified ARN.

LAMBDA ALIASES

Lambda aliases are pointers to a specific Lambda version.

Using an alias you can invoke a function without having to know which version of the function is being referenced.

Aliases are mutable.

Aliases enable stable configuration of event triggers / destinations.

Aliases also have static ARNs but can point to any version of the same function.

Aliases can also be used to split traffic between Lambda versions (blue/green).

Aliases enable blue / green deployment by assigning weights to Lambda version (doesn't work for $LATEST, you need to create an alias for $LATEST).

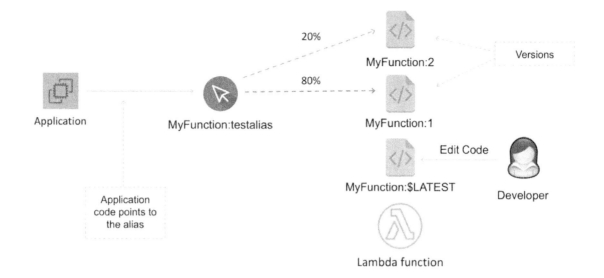

LAMBDA HANDLER

A handler is a function which Lambda will invoke to execute your code – it is an entry point.

When you create a Lambda function, you specify a handler that AWS Lambda can invoke when the service executes the function on your behalf.

You define a Lambda function handler as an instance or static method in a class.

FUNCTION DEPENDENCIES

If your Lambda function depends on external libraries such as AWS X-Ray SDK, database clients etc. you need to install the packages with the code and zip it all up.

- For Node.js use npm & "node modules" directory.
- For Python use pip — target options.
- For Java include the relevant .jar files.

Upload the zip file straight to Lambda if it's less than 50MB, otherwise upload to S3.

Native libraries work: they need to be compiled on Amazon Linux.

AWS SDK comes with every Lambda function by default.

THE /TMP SPACE

Can use the /tmp directory if the function needs to download a large file or disk space for operations.

Max size is 512 MB.

Content is frozen within the execution context so multiple invocations can use the data.

Not persistent (use S3 instead).

AWS LAMBDA LAYERS

You can configure your Lambda function to pull in additional code and content in the form of layers.

A layer is a ZIP archive that contains libraries, a custom runtime, or other dependencies.

With layers, you can use libraries in your function without needing to include them in your deployment package.

A function can use up to 5 layers at a time.

Layers are extracted to the /opt directory in the function execution environment.

Each runtime looks for libraries in a different location under /opt, depending on the language.

CONCURRENT EXECUTIONS

Managing Concurrency

The first time you invoke your function, AWS Lambda creates an instance of the function and runs its handler method to process the event. When the function returns a response, it stays active and waits to process additional events. If you invoke the function again while the first event is being processed, Lambda initializes another instance, and the function processes the two events concurrently.

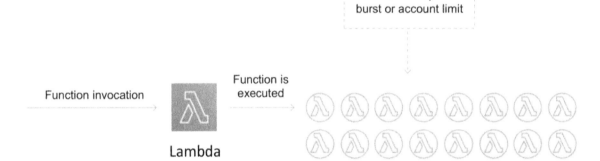

Your functions' concurrency is the number of instances that serve requests at a given time. For an initial burst of traffic, your functions' cumulative concurrency in a Region can reach an initial level of between 500 and 3000, which varies per Region.

Burst Concurrency Limits:

- 3000 – US West (Oregon), US East (N. Virginia), Europe (Ireland).

- 1000 – Asia Pacific (Tokyo), Europe (Frankfurt).

- 500 – Other Regions.

After the initial burst, your functions' concurrency can scale by an additional 500 instances each minute. This continues until there are enough instances to serve all requests, or until a concurrency limit is reached.

The default account limit is up to 1000 executions per second, per region (can be increased).

This is a safety feature to limit the number of concurrent executions across all functions in a given region per account.

Each invocation over the concurrency limit will trigger a throttle.

TooManyRequestsExeception may be experienced if the concurrent execution limit is exceeded.

You may receive a HTTP status code: 429 and the message is "Request throughput limit exceeded".

Throttle behavior:

- For synchronous invocations returns throttle error 429.
- For asynchronous invocations retries automatically (twice) then goes to a Dead Letter Queue (DLQ).

A DLQ can be an SNS topic or SQS queue.

The original event payload is sent to the DLQ.

The Lambda function needs an IAM role with permissions to SNS / SQS.

Lambda also integrates with X-Ray for debugging.

- Can trace Lambda with X-Ray.
- Need to enable in the Lambda configuration and it will run the X-Ray daemon.
- Use AWS SDK in your code.

Reserved Concurrency

You can set a reserved concurrency at the function level to guarantee a set number of concurrent executions will be available for a critical function.

You can reserve up to the **Unreserved account concurrency** value that is shown in the console, minus 100 for functions that don't have reserved concurrency.

To throttle a function, set the reserved concurrency to zero. This stops any events from being processed until you remove the limit.

To reserve concurrency for a function

1. Open the Lambda console Functions page.
2. Choose a function.
3. Under **Concurrency**, choose **Reserve concurrency**.
4. Enter the amount of concurrency to reserve for the function.
5. Choose **Save**.

Configure provisioned concurrency

Provisioned concurrency

Version: 3

Aliases: -

Provisioned concurrency

To maintain capacity for your function to serve a large number of concurrent requests, without waiting for it to scale up, use provisioned concurrency. Provisioned concurrency runs continually and is billed in addition to standard invocation costs. **Learn more** Estimate your cost [↗]

```
100
```

900 available

Cancel   Save

Provisioned Concurrency

When provisioned concurrency is allocated, the function scales with the same burst behavior as standard concurrency.

After it's allocated, provisioned concurrency serves incoming requests with very low latency.

When all provisioned concurrency is in use, the function scales up normally to handle any additional requests.

Application Auto Scaling takes this a step further by providing autoscaling for provisioned concurrency.

With Application Auto Scaling, you can create a target tracking scaling policy that adjusts provisioned concurrency levels automatically, based on the utilization metric that Lambda emits.

Use the Application Auto Scaling API to register an alias as a scalable target and create a scaling policy.

Provisioned concurrency runs continually and is billed in addition to standard invocation costs.

SUCCESS AND FAILURE DESTINATIONS

Lambda asynchronous invocations can put an event or message on Amazon Simple Notification Service (SNS), Amazon Simple Queue Service (SQS), or Amazon EventBridge for further processing.

With Destinations, you can route asynchronous function results as an execution record to a destination resource without writing additional code.

An execution record contains details about the request and response in JSON format including version, timestamp, request context, request payload, response context, and response payload.

For each execution status such as Success or Failure you can choose one of four destinations: another Lambda function, SNS, SQS, or EventBridge. Lambda can also be configured to route different execution results to different destinations.

On-Success:

- When a function is invoked successfully, Lambda routes the record to the destination resource for every successful invocation.

- You can use this to monitor the health of your serverless applications via execution status or build workflows based on the invocation result.

On-Failure:

- Destinations gives you the ability to handle the Failure of function invocations along with their Success.

- When a function invocation fails, such as when retries are exhausted or the event age has been exceeded (hitting its TTL),

- Destinations routes the record to the destination resource for every failed invocation for further investigation or processing.

- Destinations provide more useful capabilities than Dead Letter Queues (DLQs) by passing additional function execution information, including code exception stack traces, to more destination services.

- Destinations and DLQs can be used together and at the same time although Destinations should be considered a more preferred solution.

DEAD LETTER QUEUE (DLQ)

You can configure a dead letter queue (DLQ) on AWS Lambda to give you more control over message handling for all asynchronous invocations, including those delivered via AWS events (S3, SNS, IoT, etc).

A dead-letter queue saves discarded events for further processing. A dead-letter queue acts the same as an on-failure destination in that it is used when an event fails all processing attempts or expires without being processed.

However, a dead-letter queue is part of a function's version-specific configuration, so it is locked in when you publish a version. On-failure destinations also support additional targets and include details about the function's response in the invocation record.

You can setup a DLQ by configuring the 'DeadLetterConfig' property when creating or updating your Lambda function.

You can provide an SQS queue or an SNS topic as the 'TargetArn' for your DLQ, and AWS Lambda will write the event object invoking the Lambda function to this endpoint after the standard retry policy (2 additional retries on failure) is exhausted.

TRACING WITH AWS X-RAY

You can use AWS X-Ray to visualize the components of your application, identify performance bottlenecks, and troubleshoot requests that resulted in an error.

Your Lambda functions send trace data to X-Ray, and X-Ray processes the data to generate a service map and searchable trace summaries.

The AWS X-Ray Daemon is a software application that gathers raw segment data and relays it to the AWS X-Ray service.

The daemon works in conjunction with the AWS X-Ray SDKs so that data sent by the SDKs can reach the X-Ray service.

When you trace your Lambda function, the X-Ray daemon automatically runs in the Lambda environment to gather trace data and send it to X-Ray.

Must have permissions to write to X-Ray in the execution role.

CONNECTING A LAMBDA FUNCTION TO A VPC

You can configure a function to connect to private subnets in a virtual private cloud (VPC) in your account.

Connect your function to the VPC to access private resources during execution.

To enable this, you need to allow the function to connect to a private subnet.

Lambda needs the following VPC configuration information so that it can connect to the VPC:

- Private subnet ID.
- Security Group ID (with required access).

Lambda uses this information to setup an Elastic Network Interface (ENI) using an available IP address from your private subnet.

You must connect to a private subnet with a NAT Gateway for Internet access (no public IP).

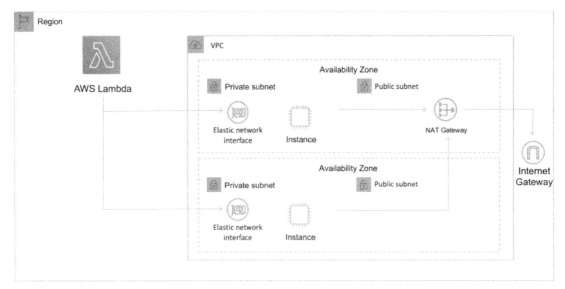

Careful with DNS resolution of public hostnames as it could add to function running time (cost).

Cannot connect to a dedicated tenancy VPC.

Exam tip: If a Lambda function needs to connect to a VPC and needs Internet access, make sure you connect to a private subnet that has a route to a NAT Gateway (the NAT Gateway will be in a public subnet).

Lambda uses your function's permissions to create and manage network interfaces. To connect to a VPC, your function's execution role must have the following permissions:

- ec2:CreateNetworkInterface
- ec2:DescribeNetworkInterfaces
- ec2:DeleteNetworkInterface

These permissions are included in the AWSLambdaVPCAccessExecutionRole managed policy.

Only connect to a VPC if you need to, can slow down function execution.

ELASTIC LOAD BALANCING

Application Load Balancers (ALBs) support AWS Lambda functions as targets.

You can register your Lambda functions as targets and configure a listener rule to forward requests to the target group for your Lambda function.

Exam tip: Functions can be registered to target groups using the API, AWS Management Console or the CLI.

When the load balancer forwards the request to a target group with a Lambda function as a target, it invokes your Lambda function and passes the content of the request to the Lambda function, in JSON format.

Limits:

- The Lambda function and target group must be in the same account and in the same Region.
- The maximum size of the request body that you can send to a Lambda function is 1 MB.
- The maximum size of the response JSON that the Lambda function can send is 1 MB.

- WebSockets are not supported. Upgrade requests are rejected with an HTTP 400 code.

By default, health checks are disabled for target groups of type lambda.

You can enable health checks in order to implement DNS failover with Amazon Route 53. The Lambda function can check the health of a downstream service before responding to the health check request.

If you create the target group and register the Lambda function using the AWS Management Console, the console adds the required permissions to your Lambda function policy on your behalf.

Otherwise, after you create the target group and register the function using the AWS CLI, you must use the add-permission command to grant Elastic Load Balancing permission to invoke your Lambda function.

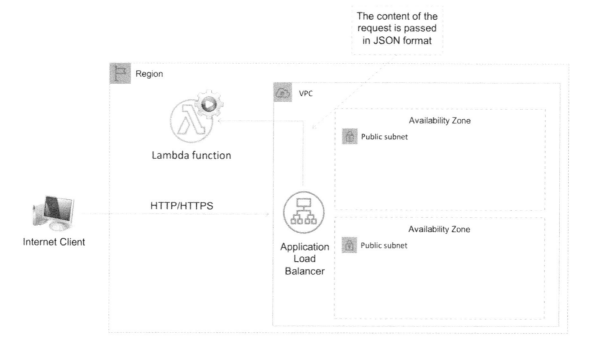

LIMITS

Memory allocation 128MB – 3008MB in 64MB increments.

Maximum execution time is 15 minutes (900 seconds).

Size of environment variables maximum 4KB.

Disk capacity in the "function container" (/tmp) is 512 MB.

Concurrency limits: 1000 concurrent executions.

Function burst concurrency 500 -3000 (region dependent).

Invocation payload:

- Synchronous 6 MB.

- Asynchronous 256 KB

Lambda function deployment size is 50 MB (zipped), 250 MB unzipped.

BEST PRACTICES

Perform one-off time-consuming tasks outside of the function handler, e.g.:

- Connect to databases.

- Initialize the AWS SDK.

- Pull in dependencies or datasets.

Use environment variables for:

- Connection strings, S3 bucket etc.

- Passwords and other sensitive data (can be encrypted with KMS).

Minimize deployment packages size to runtime necessities.

- Break down the function if required.

- Remember the Lambda limits.

Avoid using recursive code, never have a Lambda function call itself.

Don't put you Lambda function in a VPC unless you need to (can take longer to initialize).

ELASTIC BEANSTALK

GENERAL AWS ELASTIC BEANSTALK CONCEPTS

AWS Elastic Beanstalk can be used to quickly deploy and manage applications in the AWS Cloud.

Developers upload applications and Elastic Beanstalk handles the deployment details of capacity provisioning, load balancing, auto-scaling, and application health monitoring.

AWS Elastic Beanstalk leverages Elastic Load Balancing and Auto Scaling to automatically scale your application in and out based on your application's specific needs.

In addition, multiple availability zones give you an option to improve application reliability and availability by running in more than one zone.

Considered a Platform as a Service (PaaS) solution.

Supports Java, .NET, PHP, Node.js, Python, Ruby, Go, and Docker web applications.

Supports the following languages and development stacks:

- Apache Tomcat for Java applications

- Apache HTTP Server for PHP applications

- Apache HTTP Server for Python applications

- Nginx or Apache HTTP Server for Node.js applications

- Passenger or Puma for Ruby applications

- Microsoft IIS 7.5, 8.0, and 8.5 for .NET applications

- Java SE

- Docker

- Go

Deploys to server platforms such as Apache Tomcat, Nginx, Passenger, Puma, and IIS.

Developers can focus on writing code and don't need to worry about deploying infrastructure.

You maintain full control of the underlying resources.

You pay only for the resources provisioned, not for Elastic Beanstalk itself.

Elastic Beanstalk automatically scales your application up and down.

You can select the EC2 instance type that is optimal for your application.

Can retain full administrative control or have Elastic Beanstalk do it for you.

The Managed Platform Updates feature automatically applies updates for your operating system, Java, PHP, Node.js etc.

Elastic Beanstalk monitors and manages application health and information is viewable via a dashboard.

AWS CloudFormation is used by Elastic Beanstalk to deploy the resources.

Integrated with CloudWatch and X-Ray for performance data and metrics.

ELASTIC BEANSTALK LAYERS

There are several layers that make up Elastic Beanstalk and each layer is described below:

Application:

- Within Elastic Beanstalk, an application is a collection of different elements, such as environments, environment configurations, and application versions.
- You can have multiple application versions held within an application.

Application version:

- An application version is a very specific reference to a section of deployable code.
- The application version will point typically to an Amazon s3 bucket containing the code.

Environment:

- An environment refers to an application version that has been deployed on AWS resources.
- The resources are configured and provisioned by AWS Elastic Beanstalk.
- The environment is comprised of all the resources created by Elastic Beanstalk and not just an EC2 instance with your uploaded code.

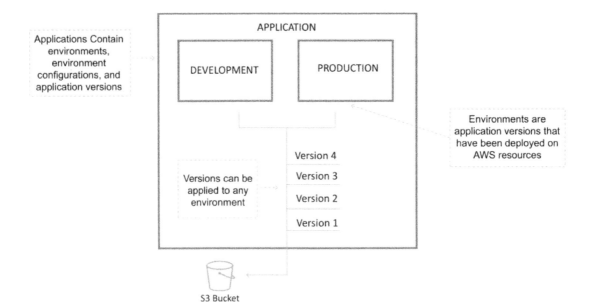

Environment tier:

- Determines how Elastic Beanstalk provisions resources based on what the application is designed to do.

- **Web servers** are standard applications that listen for and then process HTTP requests, typically over port 80.

- **Workers** are specialized applications that have a background processing task that listens for messages on an Amazon SQS queue.

Environment configurations:

- An environment configuration is a collection of parameters and settings that dictate how an environment will have its resources provisioned by Elastic Beanstalk and how these resources will behave.

Configuration template:

- This is a template that provides the baseline for creating a new, unique environment configuration.

DEPLOYMENT OPTIONS

AWS Elastic Beanstalk provides several options for how deployments are processed, including deployment policies and options that let you configure batch size and health check behavior during deployments.

Deployment options

Single instance: great for development.

High availability with load balancer: great for production.

Deployment policies

The deployment policies are: All at once, Rolling, Rolling with additional batch, and Immutable.

All at once:

- Deploys the new version to all instances simultaneously.
- All of your instances are out of service while the deployment takes place.
- Fastest deployment.
- Good for quick iterations in the development environment.
- You will experience an outage while the deployment is taking place – not ideal for mission-critical systems.
- If the update fails, you need to roll back the changes by re-deploying the original version to all of your instances.
- No additional cost.

Rolling:

- Update a few instances at a time (batch), and then move onto the next batch once the first batch is healthy (downtime for 1 batch at a time).
- The application is running both versions simultaneously.
- Each batch of instances is taken out of service while the deployment takes place.
- Your environment capacity will be reduced by the number of instances in a batch while the deployment takes place.
- Not ideal for performance-sensitive systems.
- If the update fails, you need to perform an additional rolling update to roll back the changes.
- No additional cost.
- Long deployment time.

Rolling with additional batch:

- Like Rolling but launches new instances in a batch ensuring that there is full availability.
- The application is running at capacity.
- You can set the bucket size.
- The application is running both versions simultaneously.
- Small additional cost.
- Additional batch is removed at the end of the deployment.
- Longer deployment.
- Good for production environments.

Immutable:

- Launches new instances in a new ASG and deploys the version update to these instances before swapping traffic to these instances once healthy.
- Zero downtime.
- New code is deployed to new instances using an ASG.
- High cost as double the number of instances running during updates.
- Longest deployment.
- Quick rollback in case of failures.

- Great for production environments.

Additionally, Elastic Beanstalk supports blue/green deployment.

Blue / Green deployment:

- This is not a feature within Elastic Beanstalk

- You create a new "staging" environment and deploy updates there.

- The new environment (green) can be validated independently and you can roll back if there are issues.

- Route 53 can be set up using weighted policies to redirect a percentage of traffic to the staging environment.

- Using Elastic Beanstalk, you can "swap URLs" when done with the environment test.

- Zero downtime.

The following tables summarizes the different deployment policies:

Deployment Policy	Deploy Time	Zero Downtime	Rollback	Extra Cost	Reduction in capacity
All at once	🕐	NO	Manual redeploy	NONE	YES (total)
Rolling	🕐🕐	YES	Manual redeploy	NONE	YES (batch size)
Rolling with additional batch	🕐🕐🕐	YES	Manual redeploy	YES (batch size)	NO
Immutable	🕐🕐🕐🕐	YES	Terminate new instances	YES (total)	NO
Blue/green	🕐🕐🕐🕐	YES	Swap URL	YES (varies)	NO

ELASTIC BEANSTALK CLI

There is an additional CLI called "eb cli".

The EB CLI is a command-line interface for AWS Elastic Beanstalk that provides interactive commands that simplify creating, updating and monitoring environments from a local repository.

You can use the EB CLI as part of your everyday development and testing cycle as an alternative to the Elastic Beanstalk console.

SECURITY

Elastic Beanstalk works with HTTPS:

- Load the SSL certificate onto the load balancer.

- Can be performed from the console or in code (.ebextensions/securelistener-alb.config).

- SSL certificate can be provisioned using ACM or CLI.

For redirecting HTTP to HTTPS:

- Configure in the application.

- Configure the ALB with a rule.
- Ensure health checks are not redirected.

LIFECYCLE POLICIES

Elastic Beanstalk can store at most 1000 application versions.

To phase out old versions use a lifecycle policy:

- Time-based – specify max age.
- Count based – specify max number to retain.

Versions that are in use will not be deleted.

Option to not delete the source bundle in S3 to prevent data loss.

WORKER ENVIRONMENTS

If an application performs tasks that take a long time to complete (long-running tasks), offload to a worker environment.

It allows you to decouple your application tiers.

Can define periodic tasks in the cron.yaml file.

ELASTIC BEANSTALK EXTENSIONS

You can add AWS Elastic Beanstalk configuration files (.ebextensions) to your web application's source code to configure your environment and customize the AWS resources that it contains.

Customization includes defining packages to install, create Linux users and groups, running shell commands, specifying services to enable, configuring a load balancer, etc.

Configuration files are YAML- or JSON-formatted documents with a .config file extension that you place in a folder named .ebextensions and deploy in your application source bundle.

The .ebextensions folder must be included in the top-level directory of your application source code bundle.

All the parameters set in the UI can be configured in the code.

Requirements:

- Must be located in the .ebextensions/ directory of the source code.
- YAML or JSON format.
- .config extensions can be included (e.g. logging.config).
- You can modify some default settings using "option_settings".
- You can add resources such as RDS, ElastiCache, and DynamoDB.

Resources managed by .ebextensions get deleted if the environment is terminated.

ELASTIC BEANSTALK WITH AMAZON RELATIONAL DATABASE SERVICE (RDS)

You can deploy Amazon RDS within an Elastic Beanstalk environment as in the diagram below:

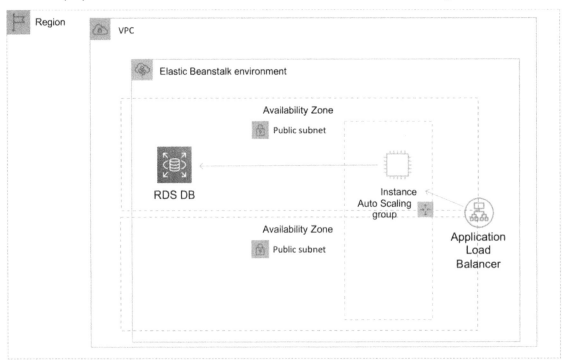

However, if you terminate your Elastic Beanstalk environment you also lose the database.

The use case is only for development environments, typically not suitable for production.

For production, it is preferable to create the Amazon RDS database outside of Elastic Beanstalk as in the diagram below:

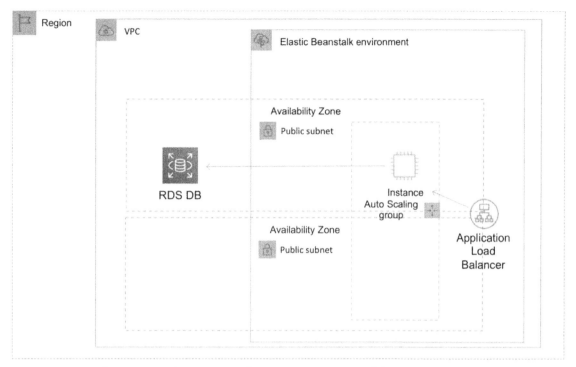

Steps to migrate from RDS within a Beanstalk environment to standalone RDS:

- Take a snapshot of the RDS DB.

- Enable deletion protection on the RDS DB.

- Create a new environment without an RDS DB and point applications to the existing RDS DB.

- Perform a blue/green deployment and swap the new and old environments.

- Terminate the old environment (RDS will not be deleted due to termination protection).

- Delete the CloudFormation stack (will be in the DELETE_FAILED state).

CONNECTING TO AN AMAZON RDS DATABASE

When the environment update is complete, the DB instance's hostname and other connection information are available to your application through the following environment properties:

- RDS_HOSTNAME – The hostname of the DB instance.

- RDS_PORT – The port on which the DB instance accepts connections. The default value varies among DB engines.

- RDS_DB_NAME – The database name, ebdb.

- RDS_USERNAME – The user name that you configured for your database.

- RDS_PASSWORD – The password that you configured for your database.

AWS SERVERLESS APPLICATION MODEL (SAM)

GENERAL AWS SERVERLESS APPLICATION MODEL (SAM) CONCEPTS

The AWS Serverless Application Model (SAM) is an open-source framework for building serverless applications.

It provides shorthand syntax to express functions, APIs, databases, and event source mappings.

With just a few lines per resource, you can define the application you want and model it using YAML.

During deployment, SAM transforms and expands the SAM syntax into AWS CloudFormation syntax, enabling you to build serverless applications faster.

Supports all CloudFormation template items such as Outputs, Mappings, Parameters, etc.

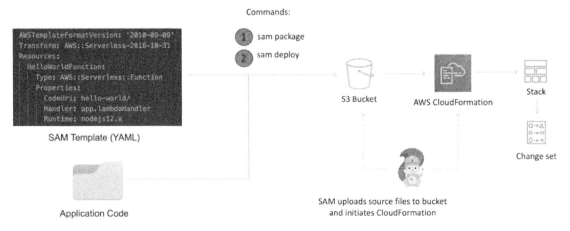

To get started with building SAM-based applications, use the AWS SAM CLI. SAM CLI provides a Lambda-like execution environment that lets you locally build, test, and debug applications defined by SAM templates.

You can also use the SAM CLI to deploy your applications to AWS.

KEY BENEFITS OF SAM

Single deployment configuration:

- You can use SAM to organize related components, share configuration such as memory and timeouts between resources, and deploy all related resources together as a single, versioned entity.

Integration with development tools:

- SAM integrates with a suite of AWS serverless tools.
- You can find new applications in the AWS Serverless Application Repository
- The AWS Cloud9 IDE can be used to author, test, and debug SAM-based serverless applications,
- AWS CodeBuild, AWS CodeDeploy, and AWS CodePipeline can be used to build a deployment pipeline.

Local testing and debugging:

- You can use SAM CLI to step-through and debug your code.

- SAM CLI provides a Lambda-like execution environment locally and helps you catch issues upfront.

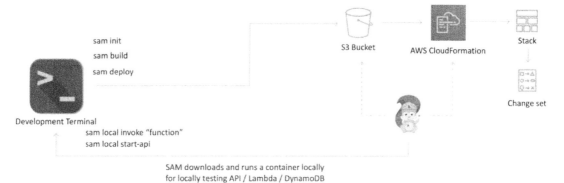

sam init
sam build
sam deploy

Development Terminal

sam local invoke "function"
sam local start-api

S3 Bucket

AWS CloudFormation

Stack

Change set

SAM downloads and runs a container locally
for locally testing API / Lambda / DynamoDB

Built on AWS CloudFormation:

- AWS SAM is an extension of AWS CloudFormation, so you get the reliable deployment capabilities of CloudFormation.

- You can also define resources using CloudFormation in your SAM template and use the full suite of resources, intrinsic functions, and other template features that are available in AWS CloudFormation.

Built-in best practices:

- You can deploy your infrastructure as config to leverage best practices such as code reviews.

- You can enable gradual deployments through AWS CodeDeploy and tracing using AWS X-Ray with just a few lines of SAM config.

DEPLOYMENT DETAILS

A SAM template file is a YAML configuration that represents the architecture of a serverless application.

You use the template to declare all of the AWS resources that comprise your serverless application in one place.

AWS SAM templates are an extension of AWS CloudFormation templates, so any resource that you can declare in an AWS CloudFormation template can also be declared in an AWS SAM template.

All configuration code is in YAML.

The "Transform" header indicates it's a SAM template: Transform: 'AWS::Serverless-2016-10-31'

There are several resources types:

- AWS::Serverless::Function (AWS Lambda)

- AWS::Serverless::Api (API Gateway)

- AWS::Serverless::SimpleTable (DynamoDB)

- AWS::Serverless::Application (AWS Serverless Application Repository)

- AWS::Serverless::HttpApi (API Gateway HTTP API)

- AWS::Serverless::LayerVersion (Lambda layers)

Only two commands are required to package and deploy to AWS. Use either:

sam package

sam deploy

Or use:

aws cloudformation package

aws cloudformation deploy

SAM Policy Templates are a list of templates to apply permissions to your Lambda functions.

Examples:

- S3ReadPolicy.
- SQSPollerPolicy.
- DynamoDBCrudPolicy.

SERVERLESS APPLICATION REPOSITORY

The AWS Serverless Application Repository is a managed repository for serverless applications.

It enables teams, organizations, and individual developers to store and share reusable applications, and easily assemble and deploy serverless architectures in powerful new ways.

Using the Serverless Application Repository, you don't need to clone, build, package, or publish source code to AWS before deploying it.

Instead, you can use pre-built applications from the Serverless Application Repository in your serverless architectures, helping you and your teams reduce duplicated work, ensure organizational best practices, and get to market faster.

Integration with AWS Identity and Access Management (IAM) provides resource-level control of each application, enabling you to publicly share applications with everyone or privately share them with specific AWS accounts.

You can browse all applications in the serverless application repository here:

https://serverlessrepo.aws.amazon.com/applications

COMPUTE QUIZ QUESTIONS

Answers and explanations are provided below after the last question in this section.

Questions 1: What do you need to securely connect using SSH to an EC2 instance launched from the Amazon Linux 2 AMI?

1. A signed cookie

2. An access key ID and secret access key

3. A key pair

4. A password

Question 2: What can you use to run a script at startup on an Amazon EC2 Linux instance?

1. User data

2. Metadata

3. AWS Batch

4. AWS Config

Question 3: Which EC2 pricing model would you use for a short term requirement that needs to complete over a weekend?

1. Reserved Instance

2. Spot Instance

3. Dedicated Instance

4. On-Demand Instance

Question 4: An organization uses an application that uses per-socket licensing and they need full control over the placement of their EC2 instances on underlying hardware. What should they use?

1. Dedicated instances

2. Dedicated hosts

3. Spot instances

4. Reserved instances

Question 5: What type of storage is suitable for a use case that requires extremely high-performance local disks that do not need to be persistent?

1. Elastic Block Store (EBS)

2. Snapshots

3. Instance Store

4. Amazon S3

Question 6: An Amazon EC2 instance requires a static public IP address. What would you choose?

1. Public IP address

2. Private IP address

3. Elastic IP address

Question 7: An organization has launched EC2 instances in private subnets. They need to enable Internet connectivity for the subnets. The service should be highly available and scale automatically. What do they need to configure?

1. Launch a NAT instance in a public subnet and add a route in the private subnet route table

2. Attach an Internet gateway to the private subnet and update the route table

3. Attach an Internet gateway to the public subnet and add a route in the private subnet route table

4. Launch a NAT gateway in a public subnet and add a route in the private subnet route table

Question 8: A Developer would like to use an Elastic Load Balancer to forward traffic to different back-end applications for https://dctlabs.com/orders and https://dctlabs.com/account. Which type of ELB should be used?

1. Application Load Balancer with path-based routing

2. Application Load Balancer with host-based routing

3. Network Load Balancer with TCP port-based routing

4. Classic Load Balancer with Layer 7 routing

Question 9: Which type of ELB is best suited for use cases that require ultra-low latency TCP connections?

1. Application Load Balancer

2. Network Load Balancer

3. Classic Load Balancer

Question 10: Which of the following listener / protocol combinations is INCORRECT?

1. Application Load Balancer TCP and HTTP/HTTPS

2. Classic Load Balancer TCP and HTTP/HTTPS

3. Network Load Balancer and TCP

Question 11: Which type of scaling is provided by Amazon EC2 Auto Scaling?

1. Vertical

2. Horizontal

Question 12: When using Auto Scaling with Elastic Load Balancing which type of health checks do AWS recommend you configure?

1. EC2 Status Checks

2. ELB Health Checks

3. EC2 Status Checks and ELB Health Checks

Question 13: Which type of scaling policy should be used to keep the aggregate CPU usage in an ASG at 60%?

1. Target Tracking Policy

2. Simple Scaling Policy

3. Step Scaling Policy

Question 14: A Developer needs to deploy an update to an Elastic Beanstalk application. That update should be completed quickly and an outage is acceptable. What's the fastest way to deploy the update?

1. Use an All at once deployment policy

2. Use an Immutable deployment policy

3. Use Rolling deployment policy

Question 15: What type of Elastic Beanstalk environment should be used for long-running tasks?

1. Web server environment

2. Worker environment

Question 16: How can a Developer deploy updated code to an Elastic Beanstalk environment?

1. Create a new Application

2. Create a new Environment Tier

3. Create a new Application Version

4. Add a .ebextensions file to the source code

Question 17: A Developer needs to deploy updated code to an Elastic Beanstalk environment with 12 instances. The update should not reduce capacity and should be rolled out gradually and be cost-effective. Which deployment policy should the Developer choose?

1. Blue/green

2. Rolling

3. Rolling with additional batch

4. Immutable

Question 18: A Developer needs to be able to repeatably provision AWS infrastructure resources such as VPCs, Internet Gateways, and Security Groups in several regions. Which AWS service can make implementing this infrastructure easier and more consistent?

1. AWS Elastic Beanstalk

2. AWS CloudFormation

3. AWS Systems Manager

4. AWS OpsWorks

Question 19: A Developer has defined some extensions for an Elastic Beanstalk environment in a .config file. Where must the file be placed?

1. In the option_settings directory

2. In the root of the package.json file

3. In the .ebextensions folder

Question 20: How can a Developer increase the amount of CPU assigned to an AWS Lambda function?

1. Increase the CPU allocation

2. Increase the memory allocation

3. Increase the concurrency

Question 21: Where should a Developer put code to connect to a database?

1. Inside the function handler

2. Outside the function handler

Question 22: An AWS Lambda function is invoked asynchronously and there have been some events that have failed to process successfully. How can a Developer save the discarded events for root cause analysis?

1. Configure a FIFO queue

2. Configure AWS CloudTrail

3. Configure AWS X-Ray

4. Configure a Dead Letter Queue (DLQ)

Question 23: A Developer has written code that processes information from a file in an Amazon S3 bucket. How can the Developer make the file available so multiple invocations can use the data with reduced latency?

1. Keep the file on Amazon S3 and reference it in the code.

2. Use the /tmp space

3. Add the file in the code outside the function handler

Question 24: An application is being written that will reference an AWS Lambda function. The Lambda function will have new versions published regularly. A Developer wishes to avoid needing to update the application code when a new Lambda version is published. How can this be achieved?

1. Use a Lambda Alias
2. Use a Lambda Handler
3. Use an Event Source Mapping

Question 25: A Developer is attempting to update the code for an AWS Lambda function version. The version appears to be locked and the code cannot be changed. How can the Developer edit the function code?

1. Edit the $LATEST version
2. Create an Alias and edit the function code using the Alias
3. Use a version with a qualified ARN

Question 26: A team of Developers is migrating Docker containers from an on-premises environment to the AWS cloud. They do not want to manage the underlying compute layer. Which AWS service should they use?

1. Amazon Elastic Container Service (ECS)
2. AWS OpsWorks
3. AWS Fargate

Question 27: A Developer has launched several Amazon EC2 instances using the ECS Optimized AMI. How can the Developer configure the instances to connect to an Amazon ECS Cluster using the EC2 Launch Type?

1. Change the launch type to AWS Fargate
2. Install the ECS Agent
3. Configure the cluster name in the /etc/ecs/ecs.config file

Question 28: Where can a Developer configure the container ports and how they map to the host container instances?

1. In the task definition
2. In the container image
3. On the ECS container instance

Question 29: Which task placement strategy can be used to assign tasks evenly to container instances based on availability zone?

1. binpack
2. random
3. spread

Question 30: A new application will be deployed on Amazon ECS that will consist of several tasks in a microservices architecture. To optimize usage of existing resources how can the tasks be placed to reduce the number of instances used?

1. Use a spread task placement strategy

2. Use a random task placement strategy

3. Use a binpack task placement strategy

Question 31: An Amazon ECS cluster runs several services each with a large number of containers. The tasks in each service require different access levels to AWS services. What is the BEST method of providing this access?

1. Split the services onto different ECS clusters and use IAM roles applied to the container instances

2. Specify a different IAM role in the task definition for the tasks in each service.

3. Embed access keys in the application code of the ECS tasks in each service that provide the necessary access levels

Question 32: Which commands should be run the package and deploy using AWS SAM?

1. sam package and sam deploy

2. sam build and sam deploy

3. aws sam package and aws sam deploy

Question 33: Which resource type should be used to deploy a DynamoDB table using AWS SAM?

1. AWS::Serverless::Function

2. AWS::Serverless::Api

3. AWS::Serverless::SimpleTable

Question 34: Which of the following commands will successfully package an application for deployment using AWS SAM?

1. aws cloudformation package --template-file template.yaml --s3-bucket dctlabs --output-template-file packaged-template.yaml

2. sam package -t template.json --s3-bucket dctlabs --output-template-file packaged-template.json

Question 35: Which of the following is NOT a serverless resource type in an AWS SAM template?

1. AWS::Serverless::Api

2. AWS::Serverless::HttpApi

3. AWS::Serverless::LayerVersion

4. AWS::EC2::Instance

COMPUTE - QUIZ QUESTIONS & ANSWERS

Questions 1: What do you need to securely connect using SSH to an EC2 instance launched from the Amazon Linux 2 AMI?

1. A signed cookie

2. An access key ID and secret access key

3. A key pair

4. A password

Question 1 - Answer 3

Explanation:

1 is incorrect. Signed cookies are not an authentication method for EC2.

2 is incorrect. An access key ID and secret access key are used for programmatic access to AWS.

3 is correct. Key pairs are used to securely connect to EC2 instances. A key pair consists of a public key that AWS stores, and a private key file that you store. For Linux AMIs, the private key file allows you to securely SSH (secure shell) into your instance.

4 is incorrect. You do not need a password to connect to instances launched from the Amazon Linux 2 AMI.

Question 2: What can you use to run a script at startup on an Amazon EC2 Linux instance?

1. User data

2. Metadata

3. AWS Batch

4. AWS Config

Question 2 - Answer 1

Explanation:

1 is correct. User data is data that is supplied by the user at instance launch in the form of a script.

2 is incorrect. Instance metadata is data about your instance that you can use to configure or manage the running instance.

3 is incorrect. AWS Batch is used for running batch computing jobs across many instances.

4 is incorrect. AWS Config is a service that enables you to assess, audit, and evaluate the configurations of your AWS resources.

Question 3: Which EC2 pricing model would you use for a short term requirement that needs to complete over a weekend?

1. Reserved Instance

2. Spot Instance

3. Dedicated Instance

4. On-Demand Instance

Question 3, Answer 4

Explanation:

1 is incorrect. Reserved instances require a commitment over 1 or 3 years.

2 is incorrect. Spot instances are good for cost-sensitive workloads that can afford to be interrupted. This workload must complete so Spot instances would not be ideal.

3 is incorrect. Dedicated Instances are Amazon EC2 instances that run in a VPC on hardware that's dedicated to a single customer. This would be more expensive and there is no need for dedicated hardware in this case.

4 is correct. On-demand instances are ideal for short-term or unpredictable workloads. You don't get a discount but you do have more flexibility with no commitments.

Question 4: An organization uses an application that uses per-socket licensing and they need full control over the placement of their EC2 instances on underlying hardware. What should they use?

1. Dedicated instances

2. Dedicated hosts

3. Spot instances

4. Reserved instances

Questions 4, Answer 2

Explanation:

1 is incorrect. Dedicated instances provide dedicated hardware but you don't get visibility of sockets, cores, or targeted instance placement.

2 is correct. Dedicated hosts provide dedicated hardware and they give you full visibility of sockets and cores and targeted instance placement.

3 is incorrect. With Spot instances you do not have control of instance placement on underlying hardware.

4 is incorrect. With Reserved instances you do not have control of instance placement on underlying hardware.

Question 5: What type of storage is suitable for a use case that requires extremely high-performance local disks that do not need to be persistent?

1. Elastic Block Store (EBS)

2. Snapshots

3. Instance Store

4. Amazon S3

Question 5, Answer 3

Explanation:

1 is incorrect. EBS volumes are persistent. You can get high performance but they are network attached disks, not local disks.

2 is incorrect. Snapshots are used for taking a backup of EBS volumes.

3 is correct. Instance store volumes are ephemeral (non-persistent) local disks that offer very high performance.

4 is incorrect. Amazon S3 is an object storage system. It is not a local disk nor is it non-persistent.

Question 6: An Amazon EC2 instance requires a static public IP address. What would you choose?

1. Public IP address

2. Private IP address

3. Elastic IP address

Question 6, Answer 3

Explanation:

1 is incorrect. Public IP addresses are public but not static, you lose them when you stop the instance.

2 is incorrect. Private IP addresses are neither public or static.

3 is correct. Elastic IP addresses are public addresses and are static.

Question 7: An organization has launched EC2 instances in private subnets. They need to enable Internet connectivity for the subnets. The service should be highly available and scale automatically. What do they need to configure?

1. Launch a NAT instance in a public subnet and add a route in the private subnet route table

2. Attach an Internet gateway to the private subnet and update the route table

3. Attach an Internet gateway to the public subnet and add a route in the private subnet route table

4. Launch a NAT gateway in a public subnet and add a route in the private subnet route table

Question 7, Answer 4

Explanation:

1 is incorrect. A NAT instance does not provide high availability or scale automatically.

2 is incorrect. You cannot attach an Internet gateway to a private subnet. Internet Gateways are attached to VPCs and entries are added to route table in public subnets.

3 is incorrect. You cannot add a route to an Internet gateway to a route table in a private subnet. You must use a NAT gateway or NAT instance.

4 is correct. A NAT Gateway provides high availability and automatic scaling. You attach a NAT Gateway to a public subnet and then add a route to it in the private subnet.

Question 8: A Developer would like to use an Elastic Load Balancer to forward traffic to different back-end applications for https://dctlabs.com/orders and https://dctlabs.com/account. Which type of ELB should be used?

1. Application Load Balancer with path-based routing

2. Application Load Balancer with host-based routing

3. Network Load Balancer with TCP port-based routing

4. Classic Load Balancer with Layer 7 routing

Question 8, Answer 1

Explanation:

1 is correct. To forward based on the path (e.g. /orders or /account) you can use the ALB with path-based routing.

2 is incorrect. Host-based routing uses the host name (e.g. dctlabs.com or amazon.com) rather than the path (e.g. /orders or /account).

3 is incorrect. The NLB can forward based on different ports/listeners. However all of this traffic will be coming on the single port for HTTPS (443).

4 is incorrect. The CLB is a layer 7 router but there is not concepts of path-based routing.

Question 9: Which type of ELB is best suited for use cases that require ultra-low latency TCP connections?

1. Application Load Balancer

2. Network Load Balancer

3. Classic Load Balancer

Question 9, Answer 2

Explanation:

1 is incorrect. ALB is a layer 7 ELB and is not the best choice when you need ultra-low latency.

2 is correct. NLB routes connections based on IP protocol data (layer 4) and offers ultra-high performance, low latency and TLS offloading at scale.

3 is incorrect. CLB is a layer 4 and 7 ELB. It is not the best choice here and is being deprecated and is not recommended by AWS for new deployments.

Question 10: Which of the following listener / protocol combinations is INCORRECT?

1. Application Load Balancer TCP and HTTP/HTTPS

2. Classic Load Balancer TCP and HTTP/HTTPS

3. Network Load Balancer and TCP

Question 10, Answer 1

Explanation:

1 is correct. The ALB only support layer 7 which is HTTP and HTTPS – not TCP.

2 is incorrect. This is a correct combination of listener / protocol.

3 is incorrect. This is a correct combination of listener / protocol.

Question 11: Which type of scaling is provided by Amazon EC2 Auto Scaling?

1. Vertical

2. Horizontal

Question 11, Answer 2

Explanation:

1 is incorrect. EC2 Auto Scaling is not an example of vertical scaling.

2 is correct. EC2 Auto Scaling scales horizontally by launching or terminating EC2 instances.

Question 12: When using Auto Scaling with Elastic Load Balancing which type of health checks do AWS recommend you configure?

1. EC2 Status Checks

2. ELB Health Checks

3. EC2 Status Checks and ELB Health Checks

Question 12, Answer 3

Explanation:

1 is incorrect. You should not use EC2 status checks only.

2 is incorrect. You actually cannot configure this. If you select ELB health checks both are used automatically.

3 is correct. You should use both EC2 status checks and ELB health checks. If you select ELB health checks both are used automatically. This configuration ensures that the ELB does not forward traffic to instances determined by EC2 status checks to be unhealthy.

Question 13: Which type of scaling policy should be used to keep the aggregate CPU usage in an ASG at 60%?

1. Target Tracking Policy

2. Simple Scaling Policy

3. Step Scaling Policy

Question 13, Answer 1

Explanation:

1 is correct. This scaling policy adds or removes capacity as required to keep the metric at, or close to, the specified target value.

2 is incorrect. The simple scaling policy makes scaling adjustments when metrics are reached but it's not used for maintaining a specific target value.

3 is incorrect. The step scaling policy makes scaling adjustments when metrics are reached but it's not used for maintaining a specific target value.

Question 14: A Developer needs to deploy an update to an Elastic Beanstalk application. That update should be completed quickly and an outage is acceptable. What's the fastest way to deploy the update?

1. Use an All at once deployment policy

2. Use an Immutable deployment policy

3. Use Rolling deployment policy

Question 14, Answer 1

Explanation:

1 is correct. This deployment policy deploys the new version to all instances simultaneously. This is the fastest option but does cause a total outage.

2 is incorrect. This deployment policy launches new instances in a new ASG and deploys the version update to these instances before swapping traffic to these instances once healthy. This is better for when you need to have no outage and no reduction in capacity (it's more costly though)

3 is incorrect. This deployment policy updates a few instances at a time (batch), and then move onto the next batch once the first batch is healthy (downtime for 1 batch at a time). This is not the fastest option.

Question 15: What type of Elastic Beanstalk environment should be used for long-running tasks?

1. Web server environment

2. Worker environment

Question 15, Answer 2

Explanation:

1 is incorrect. Use this to run a website, web application, or web API that serves HTTP requests.

2 is correct. If your AWS Elastic Beanstalk application performs operations or workflows that take a long time to complete, you can offload those tasks to a dedicated worker environment.

Question 16: How can a Developer deploy updated code to an Elastic Beanstalk environment?

1. Create a new Application

2. Create a new Environment Tier

3. Create a new Application Version

4. Add a .ebextensions file to the source code

Question 16, Answer 3

Explanation:

1 is incorrect. Within Elastic Beanstalk, an application is a collection of different elements, such as environments, environment configurations, and application versions.

2 is incorrect. The environment tier determines how Elastic Beanstalk provisions resources based on what the application is designed to do.

3 is correct. An application version is a very specific reference to a section of deployable code.

4 is incorrect. The .ebextensions file is used to add configuration files to the source code. Extensions are a zip file containing code that must be deployed to Elastic Beanstalk.

Question 17: A Developer needs to deploy updated code to an Elastic Beanstalk environment with 12 instances. The update should not reduce capacity and should be rolled out gradually and be cost-effective. Which deployment policy should the Developer choose?

1. Blue/green

2. Rolling

3. Rolling with additional batch

4. Immutable

Question 17, Answer 3

Explanation:

1 is incorrect. The blue/green deployment type is not actually an Elastic Beanstalk deployment policy. It does not roll out gradually it is used to deploy new instances to a separate environment and you then swap URLs to cutover (can use weighted routing to direct percentages of traffic)

2 is incorrect. This deployment policy would reduce the capacity of the environment by the size of the batch.

3 is correct. This is the best choice here as it will roll out the changes gradually to batches and uses an additional batch to ensure capacity is not reduced.

4 is incorrect. This is a deployment policy that launches new instances in a new ASG and deploys the version update to these instances before swapping traffic to these instances once healthy. This is the most expensive option.

Question 18: A Developer needs to be able to repeatably provision AWS infrastructure resources such as VPCs, Internet Gateways, and Security Groups in several regions. Which AWS service can make implementing this infrastructure easier and more consistent?

1. AWS Elastic Beanstalk

2. AWS CloudFormation

3. AWS Systems Manager

Question 18, Answer 2

Explanation:

1 is incorrect. Elastic Beanstalk deploys web apps, it does not deploy the infrastructure the Developer requires.

2 is correct. This is an ideal use case for AWS CloudFormation.

3 is incorrect. Systems Manager provides a unified user interface so you can view operational data from multiple AWS services and allows you to automate operational tasks across your AWS resources.

4 is incorrect. Search Results Web result with site links AWS OpsWorks – Configuration Management - Amazon Web ...aws.amazon.com › opsworks AWS OpsWorks is a configuration management service that provides managed instances of Chef and Puppet

Question 19: A Developer has defined some extensions for an Elastic Beanstalk environment in a .config file. Where must the file be placed?

1. In the option_settings directory

2. In the root of the package.json file

3. In the .ebextensions folder

Question 19, Answer 3

Explanation:

1 is incorrect. This is not a directory. You can use the option_settings key to modify the Elastic Beanstalk configuration and define variables that can be retrieved from your application using environment variables. This is part of the code that is included in a .config file that must be saved in the .ebextensions folder.

2 is incorrect. The package.json file is used to define parameters including dependencies. It is used with the Node.js platform.

3 is correct. You can add AWS Elastic Beanstalk configuration files (.ebextensions) to your web application's source code to configure your environment and customize the AWS resources that it contains. Configuration files are YAML- or JSON-formatted documents with a .config file extension that you place in a folder named .ebextensions and deploy in your application source bundle.

Question 20: How can a Developer increase the amount of CPU assigned to an AWS Lambda function?

1. Increase the CPU allocation

2. Increase the memory allocation

3. Increase the concurrency

Question 20, Answer 2

Explanation:

1 is incorrect. You cannot increase CPU allocation directly.

2 is correct. Lambda allocates CPU power linearly in proportion to the amount of memory configured. At 1,792 MB, a function has the equivalent of one full vCPU (one vCPU-second of credits per second).

3 is incorrect. Your functions' concurrency is the number of instances that serve requests at a given time.

Question 21: Where should a Developer put code to connect to a database?

1. Inside the function handler

2. Outside the function handler

Question 21, Answer 2

Explanation:

1 is incorrect. This is not the best practice as it can slow down function execution.

2 is correct. You should perform one-off time-consuming tasks outside of the function handler, e.g.: Connect to databases, initialize the AWS SDK, or pull in dependencies or datasets.

Question 22: An AWS Lambda function is invoked asynchronously and there have been some events that have failed to process successfully. How can a Developer save the discarded events for root cause analysis?

1. Configure a FIFO queue

2. Configure AWS CloudTrail

3. Configure AWS X-Ray

4. Configure a Dead Letter Queue (DLQ)

Question 22, Answer 4

Explanation:

1 is incorrect. This is a type of Amazon SQS queue but it needs to be specified as a DLQ in Lambda for this scenario.

2 is incorrect. AWS CloudTrail logs information about API activity it will not save the information required.

3 is incorrect. AWS X-Ray is used for tracing but would not save the event data for root cause analysis.

4 is correct. A dead-letter queue saves discarded events for further processing. A dead-letter queue acts the same as an on-failure destination in that it is used when an event fails all processing attempts or expires without being processed.

Question 23: A Developer has written code that processes information from a file in an Amazon S3 bucket. How can the Developer make the file available so multiple invocations can use the data with reduced latency?

1. Keep the file on Amazon S3 and reference it in the code.

2. Use the /tmp space

3. Add the file in the code outside the function handler

Question 23, Answer 2

Explanation:

1 is incorrect. Amazon S3 will not be the best option as it will add latency.

2 is correct. The Developer can use the /tmp directory if the function needs to download a large file. Content is frozen within the execution context so multiple invocations can use the data and this will reduce latency.

3 is incorrect. The code to download the file should be outside the function handler, however the actual file cannot be added itself, it must be stored somewhere outside the code.

Question 24: An application is being written that will reference an AWS Lambda function. The Lambda function will have new versions published regularly. A Developer wishes to avoid needing to update the application code when a new Lambda version is published. How can this be achieved?

1. Use a Lambda Alias

2. Use a Lambda Handler

3. Use an Event Source Mapping

Question 24, Answer 1

Explanation:

1 is correct. Lambda aliases are pointers to a specific Lambda version. Using an alias you can invoke a function without having to know which version of the function is being referenced.

2 is incorrect. A handler is a function which Lambda will invoke to execute your code – it is an entry point.

3 is incorrect. An event source mapping is an AWS Lambda resource that reads from an event source and invokes a Lambda function.

Question 25: A Developer is attempting to update the code for an AWS Lambda function version. The version appears to be locked and the code cannot be changed. How can the Developer edit the function code?

1. Edit the $LATEST version

2. Create an Alias and edit the function code using the Alias

3. Use a version with a qualified ARN

Question 25, Answer 1

Explanation:

1 is correct. You work on $LATEST which is the latest version of the code – this is mutable (changeable).

2 is incorrect. Lambda aliases are pointers to a specific Lambda version. You cannot use an alias to edit the function code

3 is incorrect. A qualified ARN has a version suffix. This means it's a published version and is therefore immutable (cannot be changed).

Question 26: A team of Developers is migrating Docker containers from an on-premises environment to the AWS cloud. They do not want to manage the underlying compute layer. Which AWS service should they use?

1. Amazon Elastic Container Service (ECS)

2. AWS OpsWorks

3. AWS Fargate

Question 26, Answer 3

Explanation:

1 is incorrect. With Amazon ECS you do need to manage the container instances which run on Amazon EC2 instances.

2 is incorrect. AWS OpsWorks is a configuration management service that provides managed instances of Chef and Puppet.

3 is correct. Fargate removes the need to provision and manage servers, lets you specify and pay for resources per application, and improves security through application isolation by design.

Question 27: A Developer has launched several Amazon EC2 instances using the ECS Optimized AMI. How can the Developer configure the instances to connect to an Amazon ECS Cluster using the EC2 Launch Type?

1. Change the launch type to AWS Fargate

2. Install the ECS Agent

3. Configure the cluster name in the /etc/ecs/ecs.config file

Question 27, Answer 3

Explanation:

1 is incorrect. AWS Fargate is serverless, you cannot add EC2 instances to the AWS Fargate launch type.

2 is incorrect. This is unnecessary as the Developer has used the ECS Optimized AMI which already has the agent installed.

3 is correct. The ECS agent must be configured with the details of the ECS cluster. The ecs.config file should be edited.

Question 28: Where can a Developer configure the container ports and how they map to the host container instances?

1. In the task definition

2. In the container image

3. On the ECS container instance

Question 28, Answer 1

Explanation:

1 is correct. A task definition is a text file in JSON format that describes one or more containers, up to a maximum of 10. You can configure what (if any) ports from the container are mapped to the host container instances using the task definition.

2 is incorrect. Containers are created from a read-only template called an image which has the instructions for creating a Docker container. You cannot add this information to a container image.

3 is incorrect. You cannot add this information to the container instance.

Question 29: Which task placement strategy can be used to assign tasks evenly to container instances based on availability zone?

1. binpack

2. random

3. spread

Question 29, Answer 3

Explanation:

1 is incorrect. This task placement strategy places tasks based on the least available amount of CPU or memory. This minimizes the number of instances in use.

2 is incorrect. This task placement strategy places tasks randomly.

3 is correct. This task placement strategy places tasks evenly based on the specified value. Accepted values are instanceId (or host, which has the same effect), or any platform or custom attribute that is applied to a container instance, such as attribute:ecs.availability-zone.

Question 30: A new application will be deployed on Amazon ECS that will consist of several tasks in a microservices architecture. To optimize usage of existing resources how can the tasks be placed to reduce the number of instances used?

1. Use a spread task placement strategy

2. Use a random task placement strategy

3. Use a binpack task placement strategy

Question 30, Answer 3

Explanation:

1 is incorrect. This would spread the tasks across more container instances

2 is incorrect. This would assign the tasks randomly and would not optimize placement to reduce the number of instances used.

3 is correct. This would reduce the number of instances used by placing tasks based on the least available amount of CPU or memory.

Question 31: An Amazon ECS cluster runs several services each with a large number of containers. The tasks in each service require different access levels to AWS services. What is the BEST method of providing this access?

1. Split the services onto different ECS clusters and use IAM roles applied to the container instances

2. Specify a different IAM role in the task definition for the tasks in each service.

3. Embed access keys in the application code of the ECS tasks in each service that provide the necessary access levels

Question 31, Answer 2

Explanation:

1 is incorrect. You should not use the IAM role applied at the container level for assigning permissions to tasks. This complicates the architecture and may require additional resources (cost).

2 is correct. This is the correct way to provide access levels to containers. ECS tasks can have IAM Roles attached (including Fargate tasks). ECS tasks use the IAM role to access services and resources.

3 is incorrect. This is NOT a good practice. You should always try and avoid using access keys in code as it is a security risk.

Question 32: Which commands should be run the package and deploy using AWS SAM?

1. sam package and sam deploy

2. sam build and sam deploy

3. aws sam package and aws sam deploy

Question 32, Answer 1

Explanation:

1 is correct. These are the only two commands required to package and deploy to AWS using AWS SAM.

2 is incorrect. sam build is not used for packaging, it is used for building

3 is incorrect. The commands should not have "aws" at the beginning. The SAM CLI is different to the AWS CLI.

Question 33: Which resource type should be used to deploy a DynamoDB table using AWS SAM?

1. AWS::Serverless::Function

2. AWS::Serverless::Api

3. AWS::Serverless::SimpleTable

Question 33, Answer 3

Explanation:

1 is incorrect. This would deploy a Lambda function.

2 is incorrect. This would deploy an API using Amazon API Gateway.

3 is correct. This deploys an Amazon DynamoDB table.

Question 34: Which of the following commands will successfully package an application for deployment using AWS SAM?

1. aws cloudformation package --template-file template.yaml --s3-bucket dctlabs --output-template-file packaged-template.yaml

2. sam package -t template.json --s3-bucket dctlabs --output-template-file packaged-template.json

Question 34, Answer 1

Explanation:

1 is correct. This command will successfully package the application using the template file provided. The template must be a YAML formatted document even with the aws cloudformation CLI commands.

2 is incorrect. The template files must always be YAML formatted documents so this will not work.

Question 35: Which of the following is NOT a serverless resource type in an AWS SAM template?

1. AWS::Serverless::Api

2. AWS::Serverless::HttpApi

3. AWS::Serverless::LayerVersion

4. AWS::EC2::Instance

Question 35, Answer 4

Explanation:

1 is incorrect. This is a serverless resource type for an Amazon API Gateway API.

2 is incorrect. This is a serverless resource type for an Amazon API Gateway HTTP API.

3 is incorrect. This is a serverless resource type for creating an AWS Lambda LayerVersion that contains library or runtime code needed by a Lambda Function.

4 is correct. This is not a serverless resource as it is an Amazon EC2 instance resource.

AWS STORAGE

S3

GENERAL AMAZON S3 CONCEPTS

Amazon S3 is object storage built to store and retrieve any amount of data from anywhere on the Internet.

It's a simple storage service that offers an extremely durable, highly available, and infinitely scalable data storage infrastructure at very low costs.

Amazon S3 is a distributed architecture and objects are redundantly stored on multiple devices across multiple facilities (AZs) in an Amazon S3 region.

Amazon S3 is a simple key-based object store.

Keys can be any string, and they can be constructed to mimic hierarchical attributes.

Alternatively, you can use S3 Object Tagging to organize your data across all of your S3 buckets and/or prefixes.

Amazon S3 provides a simple, standards-based REST web services interface that is designed to work with any Internet-development toolkit.

Files can be from 0 bytes to 5TB.

The largest object that can be uploaded in a single PUT is 5 gigabytes.

For objects larger than 100 megabytes use the Multipart Upload capability.

Updates to an object are atomic – when reading an updated object you will either get the new object or the old one, you will never get partial or corrupt data.

There is unlimited storage available.

It is recommended to access S3 through SDKs and APIs (the console uses APIs).

Event notifications for specific actions, can send alerts or trigger actions.

Notifications can be sent to:

- SNS Topics.
- SQS Queue.
- Lambda functions.
- Need to configure SNS/SQS/Lambda before S3.
- No extra charges from S3 but you pay for SNS, SQS and Lambda.

Requester pays function causes the requester to pay (removes anonymous access).

Can provide time-limited access to objects.

Provides read after write consistency for PUTS of new objects.

Provides eventual consistency for overwrite PUTS and DELETES (takes time to propagate).

You can only store files (objects) on S3.

HTTP 200 code indicates a successful write to S3.

S3 data is made up of:

- Key (name).
- Value (data).
- Version ID.
- Metadata.
- Access Control Lists.

Amazon S3 automatically scales to high request rates.

For example, your application can achieve at least 3,500 PUT/POST/DELETE and 5,500 GET requests per second per prefix in a bucket.

There are no limits to the number of prefixes in a bucket.

For read intensive requests you can also use CloudFront edge locations to offload from S3.

ADDITIONAL CAPABILITIES

Additional capabilities offered by Amazon S3 include:

Additional S3 Capability	How it Works
Transfer Acceleration	Speed up data uploads using CloudFront in reverse
Requester Pays	The requester rather than the bucket owner pays for requests and data transfer
Tags	Assign tags to objects to use in costing, billing, security etc.
Events	Trigger notifications to SNS, SQS, or Lambda when certain events happen in your bucket
Static Web Hosting	Simple and massively scalable static website hosting
BitTorrent	Use the BitTorrent protocol to retrieve any publicly available object by automatically generating a .torrent file

USE CASES

Typical use cases include:

- **Backup and Storage** – Provide data backup and storage services for others.
- **Application Hosting** – Provide services that deploy, install, and manage web applications.
- **Media Hosting** – Build a redundant, scalable, and highly available infrastructure that hosts video, photo, or music uploads and downloads.
- **Software Delivery** – Host your software applications that customers can download.
- **Static Website** – you can configure a static website to run from an S3 bucket.

S3 is a persistent, highly durable data store.

Persistent data stores are non-volatile storage systems that retain data when powered off.

This is in contrast to transient data stores and ephemeral data stores which lose the data when powered off.

The following table provides a description of persistent, transient and ephemeral data stores and which AWS service to use:

Storage Type	Description	Examples
Persistent Data Store	Data is durable and sticks around after reboots, restarts, or power cycles	S3, Glacier, EBS, EFS
Transient Data Store	Data is just temporarily stored and passed along to another process or persistent store	SQS, SNS
Ephemeral Data Store	Data is lost when the system is stopped	EC2 Instance Store, Memcached

BUCKETS

Files are stored in buckets:

- A bucket can be viewed as a container for objects.
- A bucket is a flat container of objects.
- It does not provide a hierarchy of objects.
- You can use an object key name (prefix) to mimic folders.

100 buckets per account by default.

You can store unlimited objects in your buckets.

You can create folders in your buckets (only available through the Console).

You cannot create nested buckets.

Bucket ownership is not transferrable.

Bucket names cannot be changed after they have been created.

If a bucket is deleted its name becomes available again.

Bucket names are part of the URL used to access the bucket.

An S3 bucket is region specific.

S3 is a universal namespace so names must be unique globally.

URL is in this format: https://s3-**eu-west-1**.amazonaws.com/**<bucketname>.**

Can backup a bucket to another bucket in another account.

Can enable logging to a bucket.

Bucket naming:

- Bucket names must be at least 3 and no more than 63 character in length.
- Bucket names must start and end with a lowercase character or a number.
- Bucket names must be a series of one or more labels which are separated by a period.
- Bucket names can contain lowercase letters, numbers and hyphens.
- Bucket names cannot be formatted as an IP address.

For better performance, lower latency, and lower cost, create the bucket closer to your clients.

OBJECTS

Each object is stored and retrieved by a unique key (ID or name).

An object in S3 is uniquely identified and addressed through:

- Service end-point.
- Bucket name.
- Object key (name).
- Optionally, an object version.

Objects stored in a bucket will never leave the region in which they are stored unless you move them to another region or enable cross-region replication.

You can define permissions on objects when uploading and at any time afterwards using the AWS Management Console.

SUBRESOURCES

Sub-resources are subordinate to objects, they do not exist independently but are always associated with another entity such as an object or bucket.

Sub-resources (configuration containers) associated with buckets include:

- Lifecycle – define an object's lifecycle.
- Website – configuration for hosting static websites.
- Versioning – retain multiple versions of objects as they are changed.
- Access Control Lists (ACLs) – control permissions access to the bucket.
- Bucket Policies – control access to the bucket.
- Cross Origin Resource Sharing (CORS).
- Logging.

Sub-resources associated with objects include:

- ACLs – define permissions to access the object.
- Restore – restoring an archive.

STORAGE CLASSES

There are six S3 storage classes.

- S3 Standard (durable, immediately available, frequently accessed).

- S3 Intelligent-Tiering (automatically moves data to the most cost-effective tier).

- S3 Standard-IA (durable, immediately available, infrequently accessed).

- S3 One Zone-IA (lower cost for infrequently accessed data with less resilience).

- S3 Glacier (archived data, retrieval times in minutes or hours).

- S3 Glacier Deep Archive (lowest cost storage class for long term retention).

The table below provides the details of each Amazon S3 storage class:

	S3 Standard	S3 Intelligent-Tiering*	S3 Standard-IA	S3 One Zone-IA†	S3 Glacier	S3 Glacier Deep Archive
Designed for durability	99.999999999% (11 9's)	99.999999999% (11 9's)	99.999999999% (11 9's)	99.999999999% (11 9's)	99.999999999% (11 9's)	99.999999999% (11 9's)
Designed for availability	99.99%	99.9%	99.9%	99.5%	99.99%	99.99%
Availability SLA	99.9%	99%	99%	99%	99.9%	99.9%
Availability Zones	≥3	≥3	≥3	1	≥3	≥3
Minimum capacity charge per object	N/A	N/A	128KB	128KB	40KB	40KB
Minimum storage duration charge	N/A	30 days	30 days	30 days	90 days	180 days
Retrieval fee	N/A	N/A	per GB retrieved	per GB retrieved	per GB retrieved	per GB retrieved
First byte latency	milliseconds	millseconds	milliseconds	milliseconds	select minutes or hours	select hours
Storage type	Object	Object	Object	Object	Object	Object
Lifecycle transitions	Yes	Yes	Yes	Yes	Yes	Yes

Objects stored in the S3 One Zone-IA storage class are stored redundantly within a single Availability Zone in the AWS Region you select.

ACCESS AND ACCESS POLICIES

There are four mechanisms for controlling access to Amazon S3 resources:

- IAM policies.

- Bucket policies.

- Access Control Lists (ACLs).

- Query string authentication (URL to an Amazon S3 object which is only valid for a limited time).

Access auditing can be configured by configuring an Amazon S3 bucket to create access log records for all requests made against it.

For capturing IAM/user identity information in logs configure AWS CloudTrail Data Events.

By default a bucket, its objects, and related sub-resources are all private.

By default only a resource owner can access a bucket.

The resource owner refers to the AWS account that creates the resource.

With IAM the account owner rather than the IAM user is the owner.

Within an IAM policy you can grant either programmatic access or AWS Management Console access to Amazon S3 resources.

Amazon Resource Names (ARN) are used for specifying resources in a policy.

The format for any resource on AWS is:

arn:partition:service:region:namespace:relative-id.

For S3 resources:

- aws is a common partition name.

- s3 is the service.

- You don't specify Region and namespace.

- For Amazon S3, it can be a bucket-name or a bucket-name/object-key. You can use wild card.

The format for S3 resources is:

arn:aws:s3:::bucket_name.

arn:aws:s3:::bucket_name/key_name.

A bucket owner can grant cross-account permissions to another AWS account (or users in an account) to upload objects.

- The AWS account that uploads the objects owns them.

- The bucket owner does not have permissions on objects that other accounts own, however:

    - The bucket owner pays the charges.

    - The bucket owner can deny access to any objects regardless of ownership.

    - The bucket owner can archive any objects or restore archived objects regardless of ownership.

Access to buckets and objects can be granted to:

- Individual users.

- AWS accounts.

- Everyone (public/anonymous).

- All authenticated users (AWS users).

Access policies define access to resources and can be associated with resources (buckets and objects) and users.

You can use the AWS Policy Generator to create a bucket policy for your Amazon S3 bucket.

The categories of policy are resource-based policies and user policies.

Resource-based policies:

- Attached to buckets and objects.

- ACL-based policies define permissions.

- ACLs can be used to grant read/write permissions to other accounts.

- Bucket policies can be used to grant other AWS accounts or IAM users permission to the bucket and objects.

User policies:

- Can use IAM to manage access to S3 resources.

- Using IAM you can create users, groups and roles and attach access policies to them granting them access to resources.

- You cannot grant anonymous permissions in an IAM user policy as the policy is attached to a user.

- User policies can grant permissions to a bucket and the objects in it.

ACLs:

- S3 ACLs enable you to manage access to buckets and objects.

- Each bucket and object has an ACL attached to it as a subresource.

- Bucket and object permissions are independent of each other.

- The ACL defines which AWS accounts (grantees) or pre-defined S3 groups are granted access and the type of access.

- A grantee can be an AWS account or one of the predefined Amazon S3 groups.

- When you create a bucket or an object, S3 creates a default ACL that grants the resource owner full control over the resource.

Cross account access:

- You grant permission to another AWS account using the email address or the canonical user ID.

- However, if you provide an email address in your grant request, Amazon S3 finds the canonical user ID for that account and adds it to the ACL.

- Grantee accounts can then then delegate the access provided by other accounts to their individual users.

PRE-DEFINED GROUPS

Authenticated Users group:

- This group represents all AWS accounts.

- Access permission to this group allows any AWS account access to the resource.

- All requests must be signed (authenticated).

- Any authenticated user can access the resource.

All Users group:

- Access permission to this group allows anyone in the world access to the resource.

- The requests can be signed (authenticated) or unsigned (anonymous).

- Unsigned requests omit the authentication header in the request.

- AWS recommends that you never grant the All Users group WRITE, WRITE_ACP, or FULL_CONTROL permissions.

Log Delivery group:

- Providing WRITE permission to this group on a bucket enables S3 to write server access logs.
- Not applicable to objects.

The following table lists the set of permissions that Amazon S3 supports in an ACL.

- The set of ACL permissions is the same for an object ACL and a bucket ACL.
- Depending on the context (bucket ACL or object ACL), these ACL permissions grant permissions for specific buckets or object operations.
- The table lists the permissions and describes what they mean in the context of objects and buckets.

Permission	When granted on a bucket	When granted on an object
READ	Allows grantee to list the objects in the bucket	Allows grantee to read the object data and its metadata
WRITE	Allows grantee to create, overwrite, and delete any object in the bucket	Not applicable
READ_ACP	Allows grantee to read the bucket ACL	Allows grantee to read the object ACL
WRITE_ACP	Allows grantee to write the ACL for the applicable bucket	Allows grantee to write the ACL for the applicable object
FULL_CONTROL	Allows grantee the READ, WRITE, READ_ACP, and WRITE_ACP permissions on the bucket	Allows grantee the READ, READ_ACP, and WRITE_ACP permissions on the object

Note the following:

- Permissions are assigned at the account level for authenticated users.
- You cannot assign permissions to individual IAM users.
- When Read is granted on a bucket it only provides the ability to list the objects in the bucket.
- When Read is granted on an object the data can be read.
- ACP means access control permissions and READ_ACP/WRITE_ACP control who can read/write the ACLs themselves.
- WRITE is only applicable to the bucket level (except for ACP).

Bucket policies are limited to 20 KB in size.

Object ACLs are limited to 100 granted permissions per ACL.

The only recommended use case for the bucket ACL is to grant write permissions to the S3 Log Delivery group.

There are limits to managing permissions using ACLs:

- You cannot grant permissions to individual users.

- You cannot grant conditional permissions.
- You cannot explicitly deny access.

When granting other AWS accounts the permissions to upload objects, permissions to these objects can only be managed by the object owner using object ACLs.

You can use bucket policies for:

- Granting users permissions to a bucket owned by your account.
- Managing object permissions (where the object owner is the same account as the bucket owner).
- Managing cross-account permissions for all Amazon S3 permissions.

You can use user policies for:

- Granting permissions for all Amazon S3 operations.
- Managing permissions for users in your account.
- Granting object permissions to users within the account.

For an IAM user to access resources in another account the following must be provided:

- Permission from the parent account through a user policy.
- Permission from the resource owner to the IAM user through a bucket policy, or the parent account through a bucket policy, bucket ACL or object ACL.

If an AWS account owns a resource it can grant permissions to another account, that account can then delegate those permissions or a subset of them to uses in the account (permissions delegation).

An account that receives permissions from another account cannot delegate permissions cross-account to a third AWS account.

MULTIPART UPLOAD

Can be used to speed up uploads to S3.

Multipart upload uploads objects in parts independently, in parallel and in any order.

Performed using the S3 Multipart upload API.

It is recommended for objects of 100MB or larger.

- Can be used for objects from 5MB up to 5TB.
- Must be used for objects larger than 5GB.

If transmission of any part fails it can be retransmitted.

Improves throughput.

Can pause and resume object uploads.

Can begin upload before you know the final object size.

S3 COPY

You can create a copy of objects up to 5GB in size in a single atomic operation.

For files larger than 5GB you must use the multipart upload API.

Can be performed using the AWS SDKs or REST API.

The copy operation can be used to:

- Generate additional copies of objects.

- Renaming objects.

- Changing the copy's storage class or encryption at rest status.

- Move objects across AWS locations/regions.

- Change object metadata.

Once uploaded to S3 some object metadata cannot be changed, copying the object can allow you to modify this information.

TRANSFER ACCELERATION

Amazon S3 Transfer Acceleration enables fast, easy, and secure transfers of files over long distances between your client and your Amazon S3 bucket.

S3 Transfer Acceleration leverages Amazon CloudFront's globally distributed AWS Edge Locations.

Used to accelerate object uploads to S3 over long distances (latency).

Transfer acceleration is as secure as a direct upload to S3.

You are charged only if there was a benefit in transfer times.

Need to enable transfer acceleration on the S3 bucket.

Cannot be disabled, can only be suspended.

May take up to 30 minutes to implement.

URL is: <bucketname>.s3-accelerate.amazonaws.com.

Bucket names must be DNS compliance and cannot have periods between labels.

Now HIPAA compliant.

You can use multipart uploads with transfer acceleration.

Must use one of the following endpoints:

- .s3-accelerate.amazonaws.com.

- .s3-accelerate.dualstack.amazonaws.com (dual-stack option).

S3 Transfer Acceleration supports all bucket level features including multipart uploads.

PRE-SIGNED URLS

Pre-signed URLs can be used to provide temporary access to a specific object to those who do not have AWS credentials.

By default all objects are private and can only be accessed by the owner.

To share an object you can either make it public or generate a pre-signed URL.

Expiration date and time must be configured.

These can be generated using SDKs for Java and .Net and AWS explorer for Visual Studio.

Can be used for downloading and uploading S3 objects.

VERSIONING

Versioning stores all versions of an object (including all writes and even if an object is deleted).

Versioning protects against accidental object/data deletion or overwrites.

Enables "roll-back" and "un-delete" capabilities.

Versioning can also be used for data retention and archive.

Old versions count as billable size until they are permanently deleted.

Enabling versioning does not replicate existing objects.

Can be used for backup.

Once enabled versioning cannot be disabled only suspended.

Can be integrated with lifecycle rules.

Multi-factor authentication (MFA) delete can be enabled.

MFA delete can also be applied to changing versioning settings.

MFA delete applies to:

- Changing the bucket's versioning state.
- Permanently deleting an object.

Cross Region Replication requires versioning to be enabled on the source and destination buckets.

Reverting to previous versions isn't replicated.

By default a HTTP GET retrieves the most recent version.

Only the S3 bucket owner can permanently delete objects once versioning is enabled.

When you try to delete an object with versioning enabled a DELETE marker is placed on the object.

You can delete the DELETE marker and the object will be available again.

Deletion with versioning replicates the delete marker. But deleting the delete marker is not replicated.

Bucket versioning states:

- Enabled.
- Versioned.
- Un-versioned.

Objects that existed before enabling versioning will have a version ID of NULL.

Suspension:

- If you suspend versioning the existing objects remain as they are however new versions will not be created.
- While versioning is suspended new objects will have a version ID of NULL and uploaded objects of the same name will overwrite the existing object.

ENCRYPTION

Exam tip: The AWS Certified Developer Associate exam tests your understanding of S3 encryption heavily. Make sure you understand S3 encryption well before taking the exam.

You can securely upload/download your data to Amazon S3 via SSL endpoints using the HTTPS protocol (In Transit – SSL/TLS).

Encryption options:

Encryption Option	How it Works
SSE-S3	Use S3's existing encryption key for AES-256
SSE-C	Upload your own AES-256 encryption key which S3 uses when it writes objects
SSE-KMS	Use a key generated and managed by AWS KMS
Client-Side	Encrypt objects using your own local encryption process before uploading to S3

Server side encryption options

Server-side encryption protects data at rest.

Amazon S3 encrypts each object with a unique key.

As an additional safeguard, it encrypts the key itself with a master key that it rotates regularly.

Amazon S3 server-side encryption uses one of the strongest block ciphers available to encrypt your data, 256-bit Advanced Encryption Standard (AES-256).

If you need server-side encryption for all of the objects that are stored in a bucket, use a bucket policy.

To request server-side encryption using the object creation REST APIs, provide the x-amz-server-side-encryption request header.

Note: You need the kms:Decrypt permission when you upload or download an Amazon S3 object encrypted with an AWS Key Management Service (AWS KMS) customer master key (CMK), and that is in addition to kms:ReEncrypt, kms:GenerateDataKey, and kms:DescribeKey permissions.

There are three options for using server-side encryption: SSE-S3, SSE-KMS and SSE-C. These are detailed below,

SSE-S3 – Server Side Encryption with S3 managed keys

When you use Server-Side Encryption with Amazon S3-Managed Keys (SSE-S3), each object is encrypted with a unique key.

As an additional safeguard, it encrypts the key itself with a master key that it regularly rotates.

Amazon S3 server-side encryption uses one of the strongest block ciphers available, 256-bit Advanced Encryption Standard (AES-256), to encrypt your data.

- Each object is encrypted with a unique key.
- Encryption key is encrypted with a master key.
- AWS regularly rotate the master key.
- Uses AES 256.

SSE-KMS – Server Side Encryption with AWS KMS keys

Server-Side Encryption with Customer Master Keys (CMKs) Stored in AWS Key Management Service (SSE-KMS) is similar to SSE-S3, but with some additional benefits and charges for using this service.

There are separate permissions for the use of a CMK that provides added protection against unauthorized access of your objects in Amazon S3.

SSE-KMS also provides you with an audit trail that shows when your CMK was used and by whom.

Additionally, you can create and manage customer managed CMKs or use AWS managed CMKs that are unique to you, your service, and your Region.

- KMS uses Customer Master Keys (CMKs) to encrypt.
- Can use the automatically created CMK key.
- OR you can select your own key (gives you control for management of keys).
- An envelope key protects your keys.
- Chargeable.

SSE-C – Server Side Encryption with client provided keys

With Server-Side Encryption with Customer-Provided Keys (SSE-C), you manage the encryption keys and Amazon S3 manages the encryption, as it writes to disks, and decryption, when you access your objects.

- Client manages the keys, S3 manages encryption.
- AWS does not store the encryption keys.
- If keys are lost data cannot be decrypted.

When using server-side encryption with customer-provided encryption keys (SSE-C), you must provide encryption key information using the following request headers:

x-amz-server-side-encryption-customer-algorithm – Use this header to specify the encryption algorithm. The header value must be "AES256".

x-amz-server-side-encryption-customer-key – Use this header to provide the 256-bit, base64-encoded encryption key for Amazon S3 to use to encrypt or decrypt your data.

x-amz-server-side-encryption-customer-key-MD5 – Use this header to provide the base64-encoded 128-bit MD5 digest of the encryption key according to RFC 1321. Amazon S3 uses this header for a message integrity check to ensure that the encryption key was transmitted without error.

Client-side encryption

This is the act of encrypting data before sending it to Amazon S3.

To enable client-side encryption, you have the following options:

1. Use a customer master key (CMK) stored in AWS Key Management Service (AWS KMS).
2. Use a master key you store within your application.

Option 1. Use a customer master key (CMK) stored in AWS Key Management Service (AWS KMS)

When uploading an object—Using the customer master key (CMK) ID, the client first sends a request to AWS KMS for a CMK that it can use to encrypt your object data. AWS KMS returns two versions of a randomly generated data key:

- A plaintext version of the data key that the client uses to encrypt the object data.
- A cipher blob of the same data key that the client uploads to Amazon S3 as object metadata.

When downloading an object—The client downloads the encrypted object from Amazon S3 along with the cipher blob version of the data key stored as object metadata. The client then sends the cipher blob to AWS KMS to get the plaintext version of the data key so that it can decrypt the object data.

Option 2. Use a master key you store within your application

When uploading an object—You provide a client-side master key to the Amazon S3 encryption client. The client uses the master key only to encrypt the data encryption key that it generates randomly. The process works like this:

1. The Amazon S3 encryption client generates a one-time-use symmetric key (also known as a data encryption key or data key) locally. It uses the data key to encrypt the data of a single Amazon S3 object. The client generates a separate data key for each object.

2. The client encrypts the data encryption key using the master key that you provide. The client uploads the encrypted data key and its material description as part of the object metadata. The client uses the material description to determine which client-side master key to use for decryption.

3. The client uploads the encrypted data to Amazon S3 and saves the encrypted data key as object metadata (x-amz-meta-x-amz-key) in Amazon S3.

When downloading an object—The client downloads the encrypted object from Amazon S3. Using the material description from the object's metadata, the client determines which master key to use to decrypt the data key. The client uses that master key to decrypt the data key and then uses the data key to decrypt the object.

The following diagram depicts the options for enabling encryption and shows you where the encryption is applied and where the keys are managed:

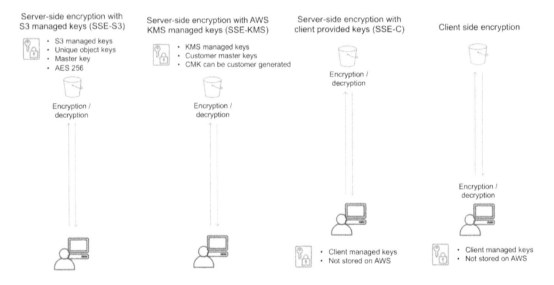

EVENT NOTIFICATIONS

Amazon S3 event notifications can be sent in response to actions in Amazon S3 like PUTs, POSTs, COPYs, or DELETEs.

Amazon S3 event notifications enable you to run workflows, send alerts, or perform other actions in response to changes in your objects stored in S3.

To enable notifications, you must first add a notification configuration that identifies the events you want Amazon S3 to publish and the destinations where you want Amazon S3 to send the notifications.

You can configure notifications to be filtered by the prefix and suffix of the key name of objects.

Amazon S3 can publish notifications for the following events:

- New object created events.
- Object removal events.
- Restore object events.
- Reduced Redundancy Storage (RRS) object lost events.
- Replication events.

Amazon S3 can send event notification messages to the following destinations:

- Publish event messages to an Amazon Simple Notification Service (Amazon SNS) topic.
- Publish event messages to an Amazon Simple Queue Service (Amazon SQS) queue.
- Publish event messages to AWS Lambda by invoking a Lambda function and providing the event message as an argument.

Need to grant Amazon S3 permissions to post messages to an Amazon SNS topic or an Amazon SQS queue.

Need to also grant Amazon S3 permission to invoke an AWS Lambda function on your behalf. For information about granting these permissions.

OBJECT TAGS

S3 object tags are key-value pairs applied to S3 objects which can be created, updated or deleted at any time during the lifetime of the object.

Allow you to create Identity and Access Management (IAM) policies, setup S3 Lifecycle policies, and customize storage metrics.

Up to ten tags can be added to each S3 object and you can use either the AWS Management Console, the REST API, the AWS CLI, or the AWS SDKs to add object tags.

AMAZON S3 CLOUDWATCH METRICS

You can use the AWS Management Console to enable the generation of 1-minute CloudWatch request metrics for your S3 bucket or configure filters for the metrics using a prefix or object tag.

Alternatively, you can call the S3 PUT Bucket Metrics API to enable and configure publication of S3 storage metrics.

CloudWatch Request Metrics will be available in CloudWatch within 15 minutes after they are enabled.

CloudWatch Storage Metrics are enabled by default for all buckets, and reported once per day.

The S3 metrics that can be monitored include:

- S3 requests.
- Bucket storage.
- Bucket size.
- All requests.
- HTTP 4XX/5XX errors.

CROSS REGION REPLICATION

CRR is an Amazon S3 feature that automatically replicates data across AWS Regions.

With CRR, every object uploaded to an S3 bucket is automatically replicated to a destination bucket in a different AWS Region that you choose.

Provides automatic, asynchronous copying of objects between buckets in different regions.

CRR is configured at the S3 bucket level.

You enable a CRR configuration on your source bucket by specifying a destination bucket in a different Region for replication.

You can use either the AWS Management Console, the REST API, the AWS CLI, or the AWS SDKs to enable CRR.

Versioning must be enabled for both the source and destination buckets .

Source and destination buckets must be in different regions.

With CRR you can only replication between regions, not within a region (see SRR below for single region replication).

Replication is 1:1 (one source bucket, to one destination bucket).

You can configure separate S3 Lifecycle rules on the source and destination buckets.

You can replicate KMS-encrypted objects by providing a destination KMS key in your replication configuration.

You can set up CRR across AWS accounts to store your replicated data in a different account in the target region.

Provides low latency access for data by copying objects to buckets that are closer to users.

To activate CRR you need to configure the replication on the source bucket:

- Define the bucket in the other region to replicate to.
- Specify to replicate all objects or a subset of objects with specific key name prefixes.

The replicas will be exact replicas and share the same key names and metadata.

You can specify a different storage class (by default the source storage class will be used).

AWS S3 will encrypt data in-transit with SSL.

AWS S3 must have permission to replicate objects.

Bucket owners must have permission to read the object and object ACL.

Can be used across accounts but the source bucket owner must have permission to replicate objects into the destination bucket.

Triggers for replication are:

- Uploading objects to the source bucket.
- DELETE of objects in the source bucket.
- Changes to the object, its metadata, or ACL.

What is replicated:

- New objects created after enabling replication.

- Changes to objects.
- Objects created using SSE-S3 using the AWS managed key.
- Object ACL updates.

What isn't replicated:

- Objects that existed before enabling replication (can use the copy API).
- Objects created with SSE-C and SSE-KMS.
- Objects to which the bucket owner does not have permissions.
- Updates to bucket-level subresources.
- Actions from lifecycle rules are not replicated.
- Objects in the source bucket that are replicated from another region are not replicated.

Deletion behaviour:

- If a DELETE request is made without specifying an object version ID a delete marker will be added and replicated.
- If a DELETE request is made specifying an object version ID the object is deleted but the delete marker is not replicated.

Charges:

- Requests for upload.
- Inter-region transfer.
- S3 storage in both regions.

SAME REGION REPLICATION (SRR)

As the name implies you can use SRR to replication objects to a destination bucket within the same region as the source bucket.

This feature was released in September 2018.

Replication is automatic and asynchronous.

New objects uploaded to an Amazon S3 bucket are configured for replication at the bucket, prefix, or object tag levels.

Replicated objects can be owned by the same AWS account as the original copy or by different accounts, to protect from accidental deletion.

Replication can be to any Amazon S3 storage class, including S3 Glacier and S3 Glacier Deep Archive to create backups and long-term archives.

When an S3 object is replicated using SRR, the metadata, Access Control Lists (ACL), and object tags associated with the object are also part of the replication.

Once SRR is configured on a source bucket, any changes to the object, metadata, ACLs, or object tags trigger a new replication to the destination bucket.

S3 ANALYTICS

Can run analytics on data stored on Amazon S3.

This includes data lakes, IoT streaming data, machine learning, and artificial intelligence.

The following strategies can be used:

S3 Analytics Strategies	Service Used
Data Lake Concept	Athena, RedShift Spectrum, QuickSight
IoT Streaming Data Repository	Kinesis Firehose
Machine Learning and AI Storage	Rekognition, Lex, MXNet
Storage Class Analysis	S3 Management Analytics

S3 PERFORMANCE GUIDELINES

AWS provide some performance guidelines for Amazon S3. These are summarized here:

Measure Performance – When optimizing performance, look at network throughput, CPU, and DRAM requirements. Depending on the mix of demands for these different resources, it might be worth evaluating different Amazon EC2 instance types.

Scale Storage Connections Horizontally – You can achieve the best performance by issuing multiple concurrent requests to Amazon S3. Spread these requests over separate connections to maximize the accessible bandwidth from Amazon S3.

Use Byte-Range Fetches – Using the Range HTTP header in a GET Object request, you can fetch a byte-range from an object, transferring only the specified portion. You can use concurrent connections to Amazon S3 to fetch different byte ranges from within the same object. This helps you achieve higher aggregate throughput versus a single whole-object request. Fetching smaller ranges of a large object also allows your application to improve retry times when requests are interrupted.

Retry Requests for Latency-Sensitive Applications – Aggressive timeouts and retries help drive consistent latency. Given the large scale of Amazon S3, if the first request is slow, a retried request is likely to take a different path and quickly succeed. The AWS SDKs have configurable timeout and retry values that you can tune to the tolerances of your specific application.

Combine Amazon S3 (Storage) and Amazon EC2 (Compute) in the Same AWS Region – Although S3 bucket names are globally unique, each bucket is stored in a Region that you select when you create the bucket. To optimize performance, we recommend that you access the bucket from Amazon EC2 instances in the same AWS Region when possible. This helps reduce network latency and data transfer costs.

Use Amazon S3 Transfer Acceleration to Minimize Latency Caused by Distance – Amazon S3 Transfer Acceleration manages fast, easy, and secure transfers of files over long geographic distances between the client and an S3 bucket. Transfer Acceleration takes advantage of the globally distributed edge locations in Amazon CloudFront. As the data arrives at an edge location, it is routed to Amazon S3 over an optimized network path. Transfer Acceleration is ideal for transferring gigabytes to terabytes of data regularly across continents. It's also useful for clients that upload to a centralized bucket from all over the world.

PRICING

No charge for data transferred between EC2 and S3 in the same region.

Data transfer into S3 is free of charge.

Data transferred to other regions is charged.

Data Retrieval (applies to S3 Standard-IA and S3 One Zone-IA, S3 Glacier and S3 Glacier Deep Archive).

Charges are:

- Per GB/month storage fee.
- Data transfer out of S3.
- Upload requests (PUT and GET).
- Retrieval requests (S3-IA or Glacier).

Requester pays:

- The bucket owner will only pay for object storage fees.
- The requester will pay for requests (uploads/downloads) and data transfers.
- Can only be enabled at the bucket level.

AWS STORAGE QUIZ QUESTIONS

Question 1: Which type Amazon storage service uses standards-based REST web interfaces to manage objects?

1. Amazon Elastic File System (EFS)

2. Amazon Elastic Block Store (EBS)

3. Amazon Simple Storage Service (S3)

4. Amazon FSx for Windows File Server

Question 2: What is the maximum file size allowed in Amazon S3?

1. 5 terabytes

2. 0 bytes

3. 5 gigabytes

4. Unlimited

Question 3: What type of consistency model is provided in Amazon S3 when you upload a new version of an object?

1. Read after write consistency

2. Eventual consistency

Question 4: Which Amazon S3 capability uses Amazon CloudFront and enables fast uploads for objects?

1. Multipart upload

2. Cross region replication (CRR)

3. BitTorrent

4. Transfer acceleration

Question 5: How can you create a hierarchy that mimics a filesystem in Amazon S3?

1. Create buckets within other buckets

2. Use folders in your buckets

3. Upload objects within other objects

4. Use lifecycle rules to tier your data

Question 6: A US based organization is concerned about uploading data to Amazon S3 as data sovereignty rules mean they cannot move their data outside of the US. What would you tell them?

1. Data never leaves a region unless specifically configured to do so.

2. Data will be replicated globally so they cannot use Amazon S3.

Question 7: An organization offers free content for premium subscribers from an Amazon S3 bucket shared using Amazon CloudFront. Access is restricted to the CloudFront content using signed URLs. The organization needs to ensure that it is not possible to circumvent CloudFront and access the objects directly from the Amazon S3 bucket using the S3 URL.

How can this be achieved?

1. Use an Origin Access Identity (OAI)

2. Use CloudFront signed cookies

3. Use Field-Level encryption

4. Configure the origin policy to use HTTPS only

Question 8: Which service is best suited to improving content download performance for globally distributed users?

1. Amazon S3 Transfer Acceleration

2. Amazon S3 Static Website with ElastiCache

3. Amazon CloudFront with a custom origin

4. Amazon CloudFront with an Amazon ECS origin

AWS STORAGE - QUIZ QUESTIONS & ANSWERS

Question 1: Which type Amazon storage service uses standards-based REST web interfaces to manage objects?

1. Amazon Elastic File System (EFS)

2. Amazon Elastic Block Store (EBS)

3. Amazon Simple Storage Service (S3)

4. Amazon FSx for Windows File Server

Question 1, Answer 3

Explanation:

1 is incorrect. EFS is a file-based storage system that is accessed using the NFS protocol.

2 is incorrect. EBS is a block-based storage system for mounting volumes.

3 is correct. Amazon S3 is an object-based storage system that uses standards-based REST web interfaces to work with objects.

4 is incorrect. Amazon FSx for Windows File Server provides a fully managed Microsoft filesystem that is mounted using SMB.

Question 2: What is the maximum file size allowed in Amazon S3?

1. 5 terabytes

2. 0 bytes

3. 5 gigabytes

4. Unlimited

Question 2, Answer 1

Explanation:

1 is correct. The maximum file size for Amazon S3 objects is 5 terabytes.

2 is incorrect. This is the minimum file size possible in Amazon S3.

3 is incorrect. 5GB is not the maximum file size possible in Amazon S3.

4 is incorrect. There is a limit on the maximum file size for objects in Amazon S3.

Question 3: What type of consistency model is provided in Amazon S3 when you upload a new version of an object?

1. Read after write consistency

2. Eventual consistency

Question 3, Answer 2

Explanation:

1 is incorrect. You do not get read after write consistency for overwrite PUT and DELETES.

2 is correct. In Amazon S3 you get eventual consistency for overwrite PUTS and DELETES.

Question 4: Which Amazon S3 capability uses Amazon CloudFront and enables fast uploads for objects?

1. Multipart upload

2. Cross region replication (CRR)

3. BitTorrent

4. Transfer acceleration

Question 4, Answer 4

Explanation:

1 is incorrect. Multipart upload is recommended for uploading objects larger than 100MB but it does not use CloudFront.

2 is incorrect. CRR is used for replicating objects between buckets in different regions.

3 is incorrect. BitTorrent can be used for retrieving objects from Amazon S3. It is not used for uploading and doesn't use CloudFront.

4 is correct. Transfer Acceleration speeds up data uploads by using the CloudFront network.

Question 5: How can you create a hierarchy that mimics a filesystem in Amazon S3?

1. Create buckets within other buckets

2. Use folders in your buckets

3. Upload objects within other objects

4. Use lifecycle rules to tier your data

Question 5, Answer 2

Explanation:

1 is incorrect. You cannot nest buckets (create buckets inside other buckets).

2 is correct. You can mimic the hierarchy of a filesystem by creating folder in your buckets.

3 is incorrect. You cannot upload objects within other objects.

4 is incorrect. Tiering your data is done for performance not to mimic a filesystem.

Question 6: A US based organization is concerned about uploading data to Amazon S3 as data sovereignty rules mean they cannot move their data outside of the US. What would you tell them?

1. Data never leaves a region unless specifically configured to do so.

2. Data will be replicated globally so they cannot use Amazon S3.

Question 6, Answer 1

Explanation:

1 is correct. S3 is a global service but buckets are created within a region. Data is never replicated outside of that region unless you configure it (e.g. through CRR).

2 is incorrect. Data is not replicated globally with Amazon S3.

Question 7: An organization offers free content for premium subscribers from an Amazon S3 bucket shared using Amazon CloudFront. Access is restricted to the CloudFront content using signed URLs. The organization needs to ensure that it is not possible to circumvent CloudFront and access the objects directly from the Amazon S3 bucket using the S3 URL.

How can this be achieved?

1. Use an Origin Access Identity (OAI)

2. Use CloudFront signed cookies

3. Use Field-Level encryption

4. Configure the origin policy to use HTTPS only

Question 7, Answer 1

Explanation:

1 is correct. A special type of user called an Origin Access Identity (OAI) can be used to restrict access to content in an Amazon S3 bucket. By using an OAI you can restrict users so they cannot access the content directly using the S3 URL, they must connect via CloudFront.

2 is incorrect. Signed cookies are similar in function to signed URLs. They restrict access to the content in CloudFront, but won't stop people from accessing the S3 bucket directly.

3 is incorrect. Field-level encryption adds an additional layer of security on top of HTTPS that lets you protect specific data so that it is only visible to specific applications. This will not prevent users from accessing S3 directly.

4 is incorrect. This just means that the connection to the origin from CloudFront will be HTTPS.

Question 8: Which service is best suited to improving content download performance for globally distributed users?

1. Amazon S3 Transfer Acceleration

2. Amazon S3 Static Website with ElastiCache

3. Amazon CloudFront with a custom origin

4. Amazon CloudFront with an Amazon ECS origin

Question 8, Answer 3

Explanation:

1 is incorrect. S3 Transfer acceleration is used for improving upload speeds, not downloads.

2 is incorrect. You cannot put Amazon ElastiCache in front of an S3 static website, it is a database cache that you put in front of services such as RDS.

3 is correct. This is a good solution for improving content download performance for global users. Note that the origin is irrelevant and just serves as a distraction. All origins support content download from CloudFront.

4 is incorrect. You cannot use Amazon ECS as a CloudFront origin.

AWS DATABASE

RDS

GENERAL AMAZON RDS CONCEPTS

Amazon Relational Database Service (Amazon RDS) is a managed service that makes it easy to set up, operate, and scale a relational database in the cloud.

RDS is an Online Transaction Processing (OLTP) type of database.

The primary use case is a transactional database (rather than analytical).

Best for structured, relational data store requirements.

Aims to be a drop-in replacement for existing on-premise instances of the same databases.

Automated backups and patching applied in customer-defined maintenance windows.

Push-button scaling, replication, and redundancy.

A DB instance is a database environment in the cloud with the compute and storage resources you specify.

Database instances are accessed via endpoints.

Endpoints can be retrieved via the DB instance description in the AWS Management Console, DescribeDBInstances API or describe–db–instances command.

Amazon RDS supports the following database engines:

- Amazon Aurora.
- MySQL.
- MariaDB.
- Oracle.
- SQL Server.
- PostgreSQL.

RDS is a managed service and you do not have access to the underlying EC2 instance (no root access).

ENCRYPTION

You can encrypt your Amazon RDS instances and snapshots at rest by enabling the encryption option for your Amazon RDS DB instances.

Encryption at rest is supported for all DB types and uses AWS KMS.

When using encryption at rest the following elements are also encrypted:

- All DB snapshots.
- Backups.
- DB instance storage.
- Read Replicas.

You cannot encrypt an existing DB, you need to create a snapshot, copy it, encrypt the copy, then build an encrypted DB from the snapshot.

You don't need to modify your database client applications to use encryption.

Encryption/decryption is handled transparently.

RDS supports SSL encryption between applications and RDS DB instances.

RDS generates a certificate for the instance.

Manging encryption keys using Key Management Service (KMS):

- To manage the keys used for encrypting and decrypting your RDS resources, you use KMS.

- Using KMS, you can create encryption keys and define the policies that control how these keys can be used.

- A two-tiered hierarchy is used with envelope encryption:

    - A unique data key encrypts customer data.

    - KMS master keys encrypt the data keys.

Read replica encryption:

- A Read Replica of an Amazon RDS encrypted instance is also encrypted using the same key as the master instance when both are in the same region.

- If the master and Read Replica are in different regions, you encrypt using the encryption key for that region.

- You can't have an encrypted Read Replica of an unencrypted DB instance or an unencrypted Read Replica of an encrypted DB instance.

MULTI-AZ AND READ REPLICAS

Used for high availability, fault tolerance and performance scaling.

The table below compares multi-AZ deployments to Read Replicas:

Multi-AZ Deployments	Read Replicas
Synchronous replication – highly durable	Asynchronous replication – highly scalable
Only database engine on primary instance is active	All read replicas are accessible and can be used for read scaling
Automated backups are taken from standby	No backups configured by default
Always span two Availability Zones within a single Region	Can be within an Availability Zone, Cross-AZ, or Cross-Region
Database engine version upgrades happen on primary	Database engine version upgrade is independent from source instance
Automatic failover to standby when a problem is detected	Can be manually promoted to a standalone database instance

MULTI-AZ

Multi-AZ RDS creates a replica in another AZ and synchronously replicates to it (DR only).

There is an option to choose multi-AZ during the launch wizard.

AWS recommends the use of provisioned IOPS storage for multi-AZ RDS DB instances.

Each AZ runs on its own physically distinct, independent infrastructure, and is engineered to be highly reliable.

You cannot choose which AZ in the region will be chosen to create the standby DB instance.

You can view which AZ the standby DB instance is created in.

During failover RDS automatically updates configuration (including DNS endpoint) to use the second node.

Depending on the instance class it can take 1 to a few minutes to failover to a standby DB instance.

It is recommended to implement DB connection retries in your application.

Recommended to use the endpoint rather than the IP address to point applications to the RDS DB.

The method to initiate a manual RDS DB instance failover is to reboot selecting the option to failover.

A DB instance reboot is required for changes to take effect when you change the DB parameter group or when you change a static DB parameter.

The secondary DB in a multi-AZ configuration cannot be used as an independent read node (read or write).

There is no charge for data transfer between primary and secondary RDS instances.

Multi-AZ deployments for the MySQL, MariaDB, Oracle and PostgreSQL engines use Amazon's failover technology.

Multi-AZ deployments for the SQL Server engine use SQL Server Database Mirroring (DBM).

System upgrades like OS patching, DB Instance scaling and system upgrades, are applied first on the standby, before failing over and modifying the other DB Instance.

In multi-AZ configurations snapshots and automated backups are performed on the standby to avoid I/O suspension on the primary instance.

READ REPLICA SUPPORT FOR MULTI-AZ

- Amazon RDS Read Replicas for MySQL and MariaDB support Multi-AZ deployments.
- Combining Read Replicas with Multi-AZ enables you to build a resilient disaster recovery strategy and simplify your database engine upgrade process.
- A Read Replica in a different region than the source database can be used as a standby database and promoted to become the new production database in case of a regional disruption.
- This allows you to scale reads whilst also having multi-AZ for DR.
- Note that RDS for PostgreSQL does not yet support this feature.

The process for implementing maintenance activities is as follows:

- Perform operations on standby.
- Promote standby to primary.
- Perform operations on new standby (demoted primary).

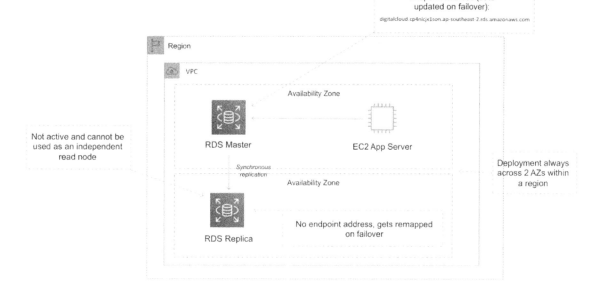

READ REPLICAS

Read replicas are used for read heavy DBs and replication is asynchronous.

Read replicas are for workload sharing and offloading.

Read replicas provide read-only DR.

Read replicas are created from a snapshot of the master instance.

Must have automated backups enabled on the primary (retention period > 0).

Only supported for transactional database storage engines (InnoDB not MyISAM).

Read replicas are available for MySQL, PostgreSQL, MariaDB, Oracle and Aurora (not SQL Server).

For the MySQL, MariaDB, PostgreSQL, and Oracle database engines, Amazon RDS creates a second DB instance using a snapshot of the source DB instance.

It then uses the engines' native asynchronous replication to update the read replica whenever there is a change to the source DB instance.

Amazon Aurora employs an SSD-backed virtualized storage layer purpose-built for database workloads.

You can take snapshots of PostgreSQL read replicas but cannot enable automated backups.

You can enable automatic backups on MySQL and MariaDB read replicas.

You can enable writes to the MySQL and MariaDB Read Replicas.

You can have 5 read replicas of a production DB.

You cannot have more than four instances involved in a replication chain.

You can have read replicas of read replicas for MySQL and MariaDB but not for PostgreSQL.

Read replicas can be configured from the AWS Console or the API.

You can specify the AZ the read replica is deployed in.

The read replicas storage type and instance class can be different from the source but the compute should be at least the performance of the source.

You cannot change the DB engine.

In a multi-AZ failover the read replicas are switched to the new primary.

Read replicas must be explicitly deleted.

If a source DB instance is deleted without deleting the replicas each replica becomes a standalone single-AZ DB instance.

You can promote a read replica to primary.

Promotion of read replicas takes several minutes.

Promoted read replicas retain:

- Backup retention window.

- Backup window.

- DB parameter group.

Existing read replicas continue to function as normal.

Each read replica has its own DNS endpoint.

Read replicas can have multi-AZ enabled and you can create read replicas of multi-AZ source DBs.

Read replicas can be in another region (uses asynchronous replication).

This configuration can be used for centralizing data from across different regions for analytics.

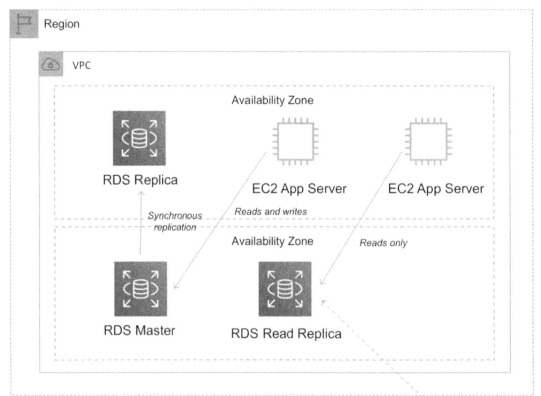

SCALING AMAZON RDS

You can only scale RDS up (compute and storage).

You cannot decrease the allocated storage for an RDS instance.

You can scale storage and change the storage type for all DB engines except MS SQL.

For MS SQL the workaround is to create a new instance from a snapshot with the new configuration.

Scaling storage can happen while the RDS instance is running without outage however there may be performance degradation.

Scaling compute will cause downtime.

You can choose to have changes take effect immediately, however the default is within the maintenance window.

Scaling requests are applied during the the specified maintenance window unless "apply immediately" is used.

All RDS DB types support a maximum DB size of 64 TiB except for Microsoft SQL Server (16 TiB).

Billing and Provisioning:

AWS Charge for:

- DB instance hours (partial hours are charged as full hours).
- Storage GB/month.
- I/O requests/month – for magnetic storage.
- Provisioned IOPS/month – for RDS provisioned IOPS SSD.
- Egress data transfer.
- Backup storage (DB backups and manual snapshots).
- Backup storage for the automated RDS backup is free of charge up to the provisioned EBS volume size.

However, AWS replicate data across multiple AZs and so you are charged for the extra storage space on S3.

For multi-AZ you are charged for:

- Multi-AZ DB hours.
- Provisioned storage.
- Double write I/Os.
- For multi-AZ you are not charged for DB data transfer during replication from primary to standby.

Oracle and Microsoft SQL licences are included or you can bring your own (BYO).

On-demand and reserved instance pricing available.

Reserved instances are defined based on the following attributes which must not be changed:

- DB engine.
- DB instance class.
- Deployment type (standalone, multi-AZ_.

- License model.
- Region.

Reserved instances:

- Can be moved between AZs in the same region.
- Are available for multi-AZ deployments.
- Can be applied to Read Replicas if DB instance class and region are the same.
- Scaling is achieved through changing the instance class for compute, and modifying storage capacity for additional storage allocation.

AMAZON DYNAMODB

GENERAL AMAZON DYNAMODB CONCEPTS

Amazon DynamoDB is a fully managed NoSQL database service that provides fast and predictable performance with seamless scalability.

It is a non-relational, key-value type of database.

DynamoDB is a serverless service – there are no instances to provision or manage.

Push button scaling means that you can scale the DB at any time without incurring downtime.

Provides very low latency.

Data is stored on SSD storage.

Multi-AZ redundancy and Cross-Region Replication option.

The underlying hardware storing data is spread across 3 geographically distinct data centres.

DynamoDB is made up of:

- Tables.
- Items.
- Attributes.

Supports key value and document structures.

A key-value database stores data as a collection of key-value pairs in which a key serves as a unique identifier.

Key = the name of the data; Value = the data itself.

Documents can be written in JSON, HTML, or XML.

Some of the features and benefits of Amazon DynamoDB are summarized in the following table:

DynamoDB Feature	Benefit
Serverless	Fully managed, fault tolerant, service
Highly available	99.99% availability SLA - 99.999% for Global Tables!
NoSQL type of database with Name / Value structure	Flexible schema, good for when data is not well structured or unpredictable
Horizontal scaling	Seamless scalability to any scale with push button scaling or Auto Scaling
DynamoDB Streams	Captures a time-ordered sequence of item-level modifications in a DynamoDB table and durably stores the information for up to 24 hours. Often used with Lambda and the Kinesis Client Library (KCL)
DynamoDB Accelerator (DAX)	Fully managed in-memory cache for DynamoDB that increases performance (microsecond latency)
Transaction options	Strongly consistent or eventually consistent reads, support for ACID transactions
Backup	Point-in-time recovery down to the second in last 35 days; On-demand backup and restore
Global Tables	Fully managed multi-region, multi-master solution

ACCESS CONTROL

All authentication and access control is managed using IAM.

DynamoDB supports identity-based policies:

- Attach a permissions policy to a user or a group in your account.
- Attach a permissions policy to a role (grant cross-account permissions).

DynamoDB doesn't support resource-based policies.

You can use a special IAM condition to restrict user access to only their own records.

In DynamoDB, the primary resources are tables.

DynamoDB also supports additional resource types, indexes, and streams.

You can create indexes and streams only in the context of an existing DynamoDB table (subresources).

These resources and subresources have unique Amazon Resource Names (ARNs) associated with them, as shown in the following table.

Resource Type	ARN Format
Table	arn:aws:dynamodb:region:account-id:table/table-name
Index	arn:aws:dynamodb:region:account-id:table/table-name/index/index-name
Stream	arn:aws:dynamodb:region:account-id:table/table-name/stream/stream-label

In addition to DynamoDB permissions, the console requires permissions from the following services:

- Amazon CloudWatch permissions to display metrics and graphs.

- AWS Data Pipeline permissions to export and import DynamoDB data.

- AWS Identity and Access Management permissions to access roles necessary for exports and imports.

- Amazon Simple Notification Service permissions to notify you whenever a CloudWatch alarm is triggered.

- AWS Lambda permissions to process DynamoDB Streams records.

PARTITIONS

Amazon DynamoDB stores data in partitions.

A partition is an allocation of storage for a table that is automatically replicated across multiple AZs within an AWS Region.

Partition management is handled entirely by DynamoDB—you never have to manage partitions yourself.

DynamoDB allocates sufficient partitions to your table so that it can handle your provisioned throughput requirements.

DynamoDB allocates additional partitions to a table in the following situations:

- If you increase the table's provisioned throughput settings beyond what the existing partitions can support.

- If an existing partition fills to capacity and more storage space is required.

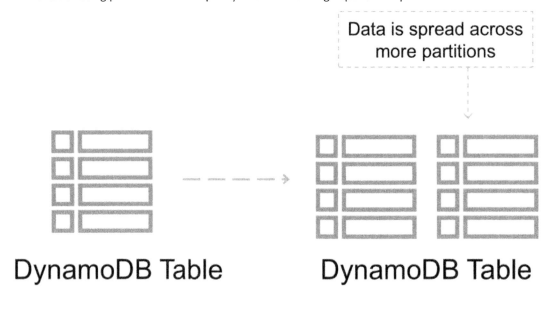

PRIMARY KEYS

DynamoDB stores and retrieves data based on a Primary key.

There are two types of Primary key:

Partition key – unique attribute (e.g. user ID).

- Value of the Partition key is input to an internal hash function which determines the partition or physical location on which the data is stored.

- If you are using the Partition key as your Primary key, then no two items can have the same partition key.

The image below depicts a table with a partition key:

Composite key – Partition key + Sort key in combination.

- Example is user posting to a forum. Partition key would be the user ID, Sort key would be the timestamp of the post.

- 2 items may have the same Partition key, but they must have a different Sort key.

- All items with the same Partition key are stored together, then sorted according to the Sort key value.

- Allows you to store multiple items with the same partition key.

The image below depicts a table with a composite key:

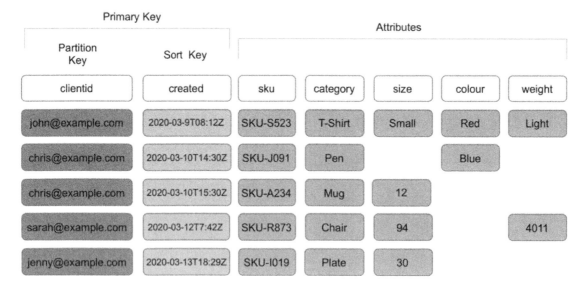

Primary Key		Attributes				
Partition Key	Sort Key					
clientid	created	sku	category	size	colour	weight
john@example.com	2020-03-9T08:12Z	SKU-S523	T-Shirt	Small	Red	Light
chris@example.com	2020-03-10T14:30Z	SKU-J091	Pen		Blue	
chris@example.com	2020-03-10T15:30Z	SKU-A234	Mug	12		
sarah@example.com	2020-03-12T7:42Z	SKU-R873	Chair	94		4011
jenny@example.com	2020-03-13T18:29Z	SKU-I019	Plate	30		

PARTITIONS AND PERFORMANCE

DynamoDB evenly distributes provisioned throughput—read capacity units (RCUs) and write capacity units (WCUs) among partitions

If your access pattern exceeds 3000 RCU or 1000 WCU for a single partition key value, your requests might be throttled.

Reading or writing above the limit can be caused by these issues:

- Uneven distribution of data due to the wrong choice of partition key.
- Frequent access of the same key in a partition (the most popular item, also known as a hot key).
- A request rate greater than the provisioned throughput.

Best practices for partition keys:

- Use high-cardinality attributes – e.g. e-mailid, employee_no, customerid, sessionid, orderid, and so on.
- Use composite attributes – e.g. customerid+productid+countrycode as the partition key and order_date as the sort key.
- Cache popular items – use DynamoDB accelerator (DAX) for caching reads.
- Add random numbers or digits from a predetermined range for write-heavy use cases – e.g. add a random suffix to an invoice number such as INV00023-04593

CONSISTENCY MODELS

DynamoDB supports eventually consistent and strongly consistent reads.

Eventually consistent reads:

- When you read data from a DynamoDB table, the response might not reflect the results of a recently completed write operation.
- The response might include some stale data.
- If you repeat your read request after a short time, the response should return the latest data.

Strongly consistent read:

- When you request a strongly consistent read, DynamoDB returns a response with the most up-to-date data, reflecting the updates from all prior write operations that were successful.

- A strongly consistent read might not be available if there is a network delay or outage. In this case, DynamoDB may return a server error (HTTP 500).

- Strongly consistent reads may have higher latency than eventually consistent reads.

- Strongly consistent reads are not supported on global secondary indexes.

- Strongly consistent reads use more throughput capacity than eventually consistent reads.

DynamoDB uses eventually consistent reads by default.

You can configure strongly consistent reads with the GetItem, Query and Scan APIs by setting the – consistent-read (or ConsistentRead) parameter to "true".

DYNAMODB TRANSACTIONS

Amazon DynamoDB transactions simplify the developer experience of making coordinated, all-or-nothing changes to multiple items both within and across tables.

Transactions provide atomicity, consistency, isolation, and durability (ACID) in DynamoDB.

Enables reading and writing of multiple items across multiple tables as an all or nothing operation.

Checks for a pre-requisite condition before writing to a table.

With the transaction write API, you can group multiple Put, Update, Delete, and ConditionCheck actions.

You can then submit the actions as a single TransactWriteItems operation that either succeeds or fails as a unit.

The same is true for multiple Get actions, which you can group and submit as a single TransactGetItems operation.

There is no additional cost to enable transactions for DynamoDB tables.

You pay only for the reads or writes that are part of your transaction.

DynamoDB performs two underlying reads or writes of every item in the transaction: one to prepare the transaction and one to commit the transaction.

These two underlying read/write operations are visible in your Amazon CloudWatch metrics.

The following diagram depicts a failed write using DynamoDB Transactions:

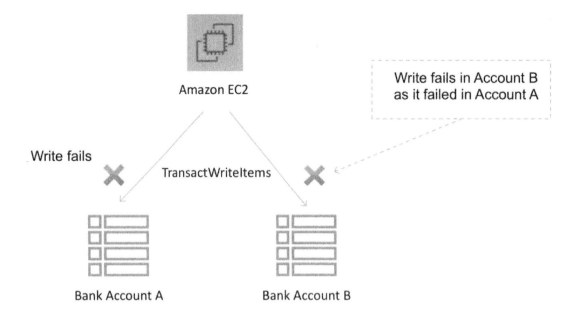

The following diagram depicts a successful write using DynamoDB Transactions:

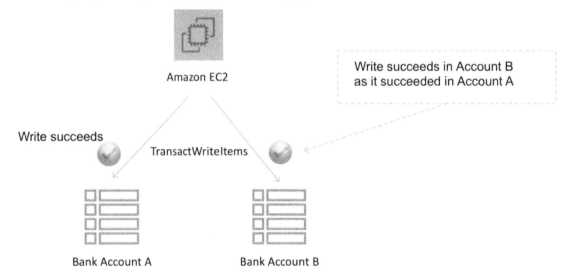

SCAN AND QUERY API CALLS

Scan

The Scan operation returns one or more items and item attributes by accessing every item in a table or a secondary index.

A single Scan operation reads up to the maximum number of items set (if using the Limit parameter) or a maximum of 1 MB.

Scan API calls can use a lot of RCUs as they access every item in the table.

You can use the ProjectionExpression parameter so that Scan only returns some of the attributes, rather than all of them.

If you need to further refine the Scan results, you can optionally provide a filter expression.

A filter expression is applied after a Scan finishes but before the results are returned.

Scan operations proceed sequentially.

For faster performance on a large table or secondary index, applications can request a parallel Scan operation by providing the Segment and TotalSegments parameters.

Scan uses eventually consistent reads when accessing the data in a table.

If you need a consistent copy of the data, as of the time that the Scan begins, you can set the ConsistentRead parameter to true.

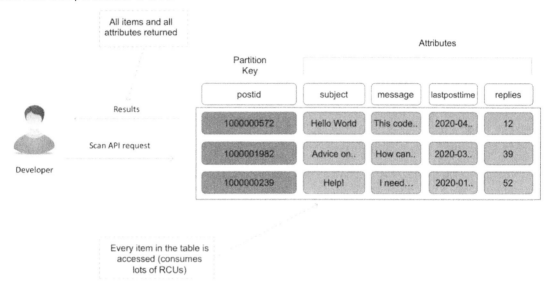

Query

A query operation finds items in your table based on the primary key attribute and a distinct value to search for.

For example, you might search for a user ID value and all attributes related to that item would be returned.

You can use an optional sort key name and value to refine the results.

For example, if your sort key is a timestamp, you can refine the query to only select items with a timestamp of the last 7 days.

By default, a query returns all the attributes for the items, but you can use the ProjectionExpression parameter if you want the query to only return the attributes you want to see.

Results are always sorted by the sort key.

Numeric order is used – by default in ascending order (e.g. 1,2,3,4).

ASCII character code values are used.

You can reverse the order by setting the ScanIndexForward (yes, it's a query, not a scan) parameter to false.

By default, queries are eventually consistent.

To use strongly consistent you need to explicitly set this in the query.

The following diagram shows a query API call with a projection expression limiting the attributes that are returned:

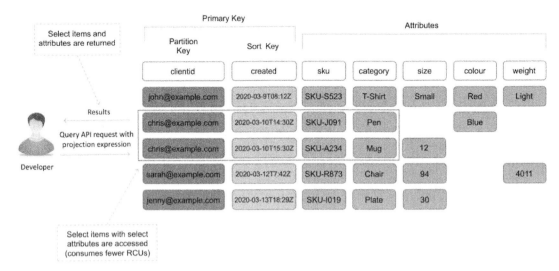

Scan vs Query

Query is more efficient than Scan.

Scan dumps the entire table, then filters out the values that provide the desired result (removing unwanted data).

This adds an extra step of removing the data you don't want.

As the table grows, the scan operation takes longer.

A Scan operation on a large table can use up the provisioned throughput for a large table in just a single operation.

PERFORMANCE OPTIMIZATION

You can reduce the impact of a query or scan by setting a smaller page size which uses fewer read operations.

A larger number of smaller operations will allow other requests to succeed without throttling.

Avoid using scan operations if you can: design tables in a way that you can use the Query, Get, or BatchGetItem APIs.

Scan performance optimization:

- By default, a scan operation processes data sequentially and returns data in 1MB increments before moving on to retrieve the next 1MB of data. It can only scan 1 partition at a time.

- You can configure DynamoDB to use Parallel scans instead by logically dividing a table or index into segments and scanning each segment in parallel.

Note: best to avoid parallel scans if your table or index is already incurring heavy read / write activity from other applications.

INDEXES

An index is a data structure which allows you to perform fast queries on specific columns in a table.

You select columns that you want included in the index and run your searches on the index instead of the entire dataset.

There are 2 types of index supported for speeding up queries in DynamoDB:

- Local Secondary Index.
- Global Secondary Index.

LOCAL SECONDARY INDEX (LSI)

An LSI provides an alternative sort key to use for scans and queries.

It provides an alternative range key for your table, local to the hash key.

You can have up to five LSIs per table.

The sort key consists of exactly one scalar attribute.

The attribute that you choose must be a scalar String, Number, or Binary.

An LSI must be created at table creation time.

It can only be created when you are creating your table.

You cannot add, remove, or modify it later.

It has the same partition key as your original table (different sort key).

It gives you a different view of your data, organized by an alternative sort key.

Any queries based on this sort key are much faster using the index than the main table.

An example might be having a user ID as a partition key and account creation date as the sort key.

The key benefit of an LSI is that you can query on additional values in the table other than the partition key / sort key.

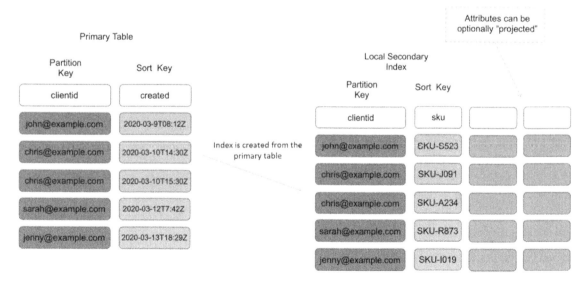

GLOBAL SECONDARY INDEX (GSI)

A GSI is used to speed up queries on non-key attributes use a GSI

You can create when you create your table or at any time later on.

A GSI has a different partition key as well as a different sort key.

It gives a completely different view of the data.

It speeds up any queries relating to this alternative partition and sort key.

An example might be an email address as the partition key, and last login date as the sort key.

With a GSI the index is a new "table" and you can project attributes on it.

- The partition key and sort key of the original table are always projected (KEYS_ONLY).

- Can specify extra attributes to project (INCLUDE).

- Can use all attributes from main table (ALL).

You must define RCU / WCU for the index

It is possible to add / modify GSI at any time.

If writes are throttled on the GSI, the main table will be throttled (even if there's enough WCUs on the main table). LSIs do not cause any special throttling considerations.

Exam tip: You typically need to ensure that you have at least the same, or more, RCU/WCU specified in your GSI as in your main table to avoid throttling on your main table.

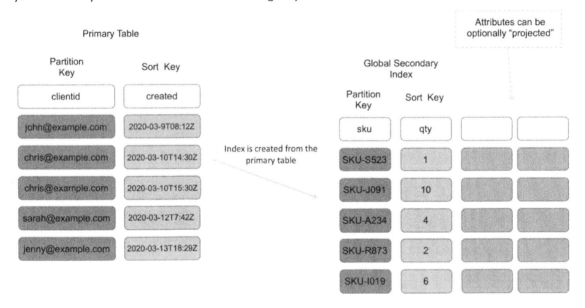

DYNAMODB PROVISIONED CAPACITY

With provisioned capacity mode (default), you specify the number of data reads and writes per second that you require for your application.

You can use auto scaling to automatically adjust your table's capacity based on the specified utilization rate to ensure application performance while reducing costs.

When you create your table you specify your requirements using Read Capacity Units (RCUs) and Write Capacity Units (WCUs).

Note: WCUs and RCUs are spread between partitions evenly.

You can also use Auto Scaling with provisioned capacity.

DynamoDB auto scaling uses the AWS Application Auto Scaling service to dynamically adjust provisioned throughput capacity on your behalf, in response to traffic patterns.

This enables a table or a global secondary index to increase its provisioned read and write capacity to handle sudden increases in traffic, without throttling.

Read capacity unit (RCU):

- Each API call to read data from your table is a read request.

- Read requests can be strongly consistent, eventually consistent, or transactional.

- For items up to 4 KB in size, one RCU can perform one *strongly consistent* read request per second.

- Items larger than 4 KB require additional RCUs.

- For items up to 4 KB in size, one RCU can perform two *eventually consistent* read requests per second.

- *Transactional* read requests require two RCUs to perform one read per second for items up to 4 KB.

- For example, a strongly consistent read of an 8 KB item would require two RCUs, an eventually consistent read of an 8 KB item would require one RCU, and a transactional read of an 8 KB item would require four RCUs.

Write capacity unit (WCU):

- Each API call to write data to your table is a write request.

- For items up to 1 KB in size, one WCU can perform one *standard* write request per second.

- Items larger than 1 KB require additional WCUs.

- *Transactional* write requests require two WCUs to perform one write per second for items up to 1 KB.

- For example, a standard write request of a 1 KB item would require one WCU, a standard write request of a 3 KB item would require three WCUs, and a transactional write request of a 3 KB item would require six WCUs.

Replicated write capacity unit (rWCU):

- When using DynamoDB global tables, your data is written automatically to multiple AWS Regions of your choice.

- Each write occurs in the local Region as well as the replicated Regions.

Streams read request unit:

- Each GetRecords API call to DynamoDB Streams is a streams read request unit.

- Each streams read request unit can return up to 1 MB of data.

Transactional read/write requests:

- In DynamoDB, a transactional read or write differs from a standard read or write because it guarantees that all operations contained in a single transaction set succeed or fail as a set.

DYNAMODB ON-DEMAND CAPACITY

With on-demand, you don't need to specify your requirements.

DynamoDB instantly scales up and down based on the activity of your application.

Great for unpredictable / spikey workloads or new workloads that aren't well understood.

You pay for what you use (pay per request).

You can switch between the provisioned capacity and on-demand pricing models once per day.

PERFORMANCE AND THROTTLING

Throttling occurs when the configured RCU or WCU are exceeded.

May receive the ProvisionedThroughputExceededException error.

This error indicates that your request rate is too high for the read / write capacity provisioned for the table.

The AWS SDKs for DynamoDB automatically retry requests that receive this exception.

Your request is eventually successful, unless your retry queue is too large to finish.

Possible causes of performance issues:

- Hot keys – one partition key is being read too often.

- Hot partitions – when data access is imbalanced, a "hot" partition can receive a higher volume of read and write traffic compared to other partitions.

- Large items – large items consume more RCUs and WCUs.

Resolution:

- Reduce the frequency of requests and use exponential backoff.

- Try to design your application for uniform activity across all logical partition keys in the table and its secondary indexes.

- Use burst capacity effectively – DynamoDB currently retains up to 5 minutes (300 seconds) of unused read and write capacity which can be consumed quickly.

DYNAMODB ACCELERATOR (DAX)

Amazon DynamoDB Accelerator (DAX) is a fully managed, highly available, in-memory cache for DynamoDB that delivers up to a 10x performance improvement.

Improves performance from milliseconds to microseconds, even at millions of requests per second.

DAX is a managed service that provides in-memory acceleration for DynamoDB tables.

Provides managed cache invalidation, data population, and cluster management.

DAX is used to improve READ performance (not writes).

You do not need to modify application logic, since DAX is compatible with existing DynamoDB API calls.

Ideal for read-heavy and bursty workloads such as auction applications, gaming, and retail sites when running special sales / promotions.

You can enable DAX with just a few clicks in the AWS Management Console or using the AWS SDK.

Just as with DynamoDB, you only pay for the capacity you provision.

Provisioned through clusters and charged by the node (runs on EC2 instances).

Pricing is per node-hour consumed and is dependent on the instance type you select.

How it works:

- DAX is a write-through caching service – this means the data is written to the cache as well as the back end store at the same time.

- Allows you to point your DynamoDB API calls at the DAX cluster and if the item is in the cache (cache hit), DAX returns the result to the application.

- If the item requested is not in the cache (cache miss) then DAX performs an Eventually Consistent GetItem operation against DynamoDB

- Retrieval of data from DAX reduces the read load on DynamoDB tables.

- This may result in being able to reduce the provisioned read capacity on the table.

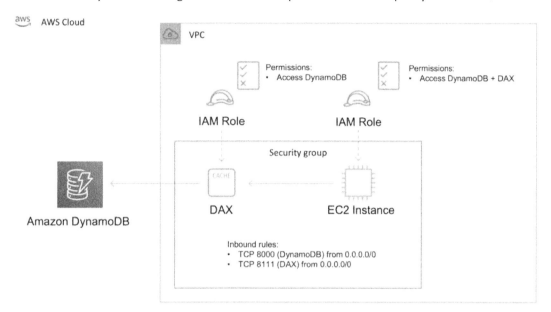

DAX VS ELASTICACHE

DAX is optimized for DynamoDB.

DAX does not support lazy loading (uses write-through caching).

With ElastiCache you have more management overhead (e.g. invalidation).

With ElastiCache you need to modify application code to point to cache.

ElastiCache supports more datastores.

DYNAMODB STREAMS

DynamoDB Streams captures a time-ordered sequence of item-level modifications in any DynamoDB table and stores this information in a log for up to 24 hours.

Applications can access this log and view the data items as they appeared before and after they were modified, in near-real time.

You can also use the CreateTable or UpdateTable API operations to enable or modify a stream.

Logs are encrypted at rest and stored for 24 hours.

Accessed using a dedicated endpoint.

By default, just the Primary key is recorded.

Before and after images can be captured.

Events are recorded in near real-time.

Applications can take actions based on contents.

A stream can be an event source for Lambda.

Lambda polls the DynamoDB stream and executes code based on a DynamoDB streams event.

Data is stored in stream for 24 hours only.

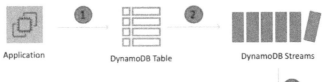

Application   DynamoDB Table   DynamoDB Streams

AWS Lambda   Amazon CloudWatch

1. Application inserts / updates /deletes item
2. A record is written to the DynamoDB stream
3. A Lambda function is triggered
4. The Lambda function writes to CloudWatch Logs

The StreamSpecification parameter determines how the stream is configured:

StreamEnabled — Specifies whether a stream is enabled (true) or disabled (false) for the table.

StreamViewType — Specifies the information that will be written to the stream whenever data in the table is modified:

- KEYS_ONLY — Only the key attributes of the modified item.
- NEW_IMAGE — The entire item, as it appears after it was modified.
- OLD_IMAGE — The entire item, as it appeared before it was modified.
- NEW_AND_OLD_IMAGES — Both the new and the old images of the item.

DYNAMODB TIME TO LIVE (TTL)

Automatically deletes an item after an expiry date / time.

Expired items are marked for deletion.

Great for removing irrelevant or old data such as:

- Session data.
- Event logs.
- Temporary data.

No extra cost and does not use WCU / RCU.

TTL is a background task operated by DynamoDB.

A TTL helps reduce storage and manage the table size over time.

The TTL is enabled per row (you define a TTL column and add the expiry date / time there).

DynamoDB typically deletes expired items within 48 hours of expiration.

Deleted items are also deleted from the LSI / GSI.

DynamoDB streams can help recover expired items.

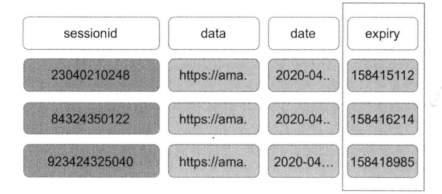

The item will be deleted when the expiry date (in Epoch format) expires

PROVISIONED THROUGHPUT EXCEEDED EXCEPTION

ProvisionedThroughputExceededException – indicates that your request rate is too high for the read /write capacity provisioned for the table.

SDK will automatically retry the requests until successful.

If you are not using the SDK you can:

- Reduce request frequency.
- Use Exponential Backoff.

EXPONENTIAL BACKOFF

Many components in a network can generate errors when overloaded.

In addition to simple retries all AWS SDKs use Exponential Backoff.

Progressively longer waits will occur between retries for improved flow control.

If after 1 minute this does not work, your request size may be exceeding the throughput for your read/write capacity.

If your workload is mainly reads consider offloading using DAX or ElastiCache.

If your workload is mainly writes consider increasing the WCUs for the table.

API CALLS

Writing data

- PutItem – create data or full replacement (consumes WCU).
- UpdateItem – update data, partial update of attributes (can use atomic counters).
- Conditional writes – accept a write / update only if conditions are met.

- DeleteItem – delete an individual row (can perform conditional delete).

- DeleteTable – delete a whole table (quicker than using DeleteItem on all items).

- BatchWriteItem – can put or delete up to 25 items in one call (max 16MB write / 400KB per item).

Batching allows you to save in latency by reducing the number of API calls.

Operations are done in parallel for better efficiency.

Reading data

- GetItem – read based on primary key (eventually consistent by default, can request strongly consistent read). Projection expression can be specified to include only certain attributes.

- BatchGetItem – up to 100 items, up to 16MB per item. Items are retrieved in parallel to minimize latency.

- Query – return items based on PartitionKey value and optionally a sort key. FilterExpression can be used for filtering. Returns up to 1MB of data or number of items specified in Limit. Can do pagination on results. Can query table, local secondary index, or a global secondary index.

- Scan – scans the entire table (inefficient). Returns up to 1MB of data – use pagination to view more results. Consumes a lot of RCU. Can use a ProjectionExpression + FilterExpression.

OPTIMISTIC LOCKING

Optimistic locking is a strategy to ensure that the client-side item that you are updating (or deleting) is the same as the item in Amazon DynamoDB.

Protects database writes from being overwritten by the writes of others, and vice versa.

CONDITIONAL UPDATES

To manipulate data in an Amazon DynamoDB table, you use the PutItem, UpdateItem, and DeleteItem operations.

You can optionally specify a condition expression to determine which items should be modified.

If the condition expression evaluates to true, the operation succeeds; otherwise, the operation fails.

SECURITY

VPC endpoints are available for DynamoDB.

Encryption at rest can be enabled using KMS.

Encryption in transit using SSL / TLS.

OTHER

Backup and restore feature available – no performance impact.

The AWS Database Migration Service (DMS) can be used to migrate to DynamoDB.

Can launch a local DynamoDB on your computer for development purposes.

AMAZON ELASTICACHE

GENERAL AMAZON ELASTICACHE CONCEPTS

Fully managed implementations of two popular in-memory data stores – Redis and Memcached.

ElastiCache is a web service that makes it easy to deploy and run Memcached or Redis protocol-compliant server nodes in the cloud.

The in-memory caching provided by ElastiCache can be used to significantly improve latency and throughput for many read-heavy application workloads or compute-intensive workloads.

It can be put in front of databases such as RDS and DynamoDB – sits between the application and the database.

Good if your database is particularly read-heavy and the data does not change frequently.

Also good for compute-heavy workloads such as recommendation engines and it can be used to store the results of I/O intensive database queries of compute-intensive calculations.

Elasticache can be used for storing session state.

Push-button scalability for memory, writes and reads.

In-memory key/value store.

Billed by node size and hours of use.

Elasticache EC2 nodes cannot be accessed from the Internet, nor can they be accessed by EC2 instances in other VPCs.

Exam tip: the key use cases for ElastiCache are offloading reads from a database, and storing the results of computations and session state. Also, remember that ElastiCache is an in-memory database and it's a managed service (so you can't run it on EC2).

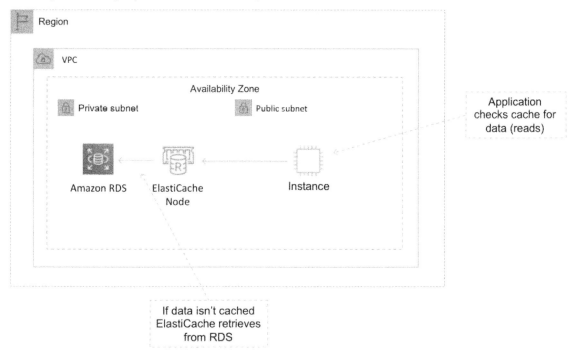

There are two types of engine you can choose from: Memcached, Redis

---

MEMCACHED

- Simplest model and can run large nodes.
- It can be scaled in and out and cache objects such as DBs.
- Widely adopted memory object caching system.
- Multi-threaded.

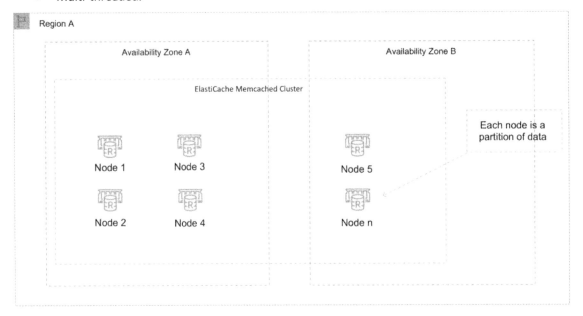

REDIS

- Open-source in-memory key-value store.
- Supports more complex data structures: sorted sets and lists.
- Supports master / slave replication and multi-AZ for cross-AZ redundancy.
- Supports automatic failover and backup/restore.

The following table provides a comparison of the different ElastiCache implementations:

Feature	Memcached	Redis (cluster mode disabled)	Redis (cluster mode enabled)
Data persistence	No	Yes	Yes
Data types	Simple	Complex	Complex
Data partitioning	Yes	No	Yes
Encryption	No	Yes	Yes
High availability (replication)	No	Yes	Yes
Multi-AZ	Yes, place nodes in multiple AZs. No failover or replication	Yes, with auto-failover. Uses read replicas (0-5 per shard)	Yes, with auto-failover. Uses read replicas (0-5 per shard)
Scaling	Up (node type); out (add nodes)	Single shard (can add replicas)	Add shards
Multithreaded	Yes	No	No
Backup and restore	No (and no snapshots)	Yes, automatic and manual snapshots	Yes, automatic and manual snapshots

The following diagram depicts Amazon ElastiCache Redis with Cluster Mode disabled:

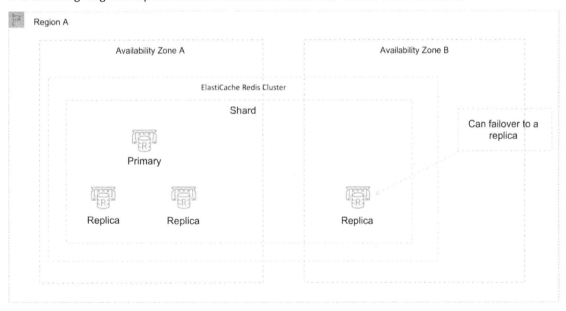

The following diagram depicts Amazon ElastiCache Redis with Cluster Mode enabled:

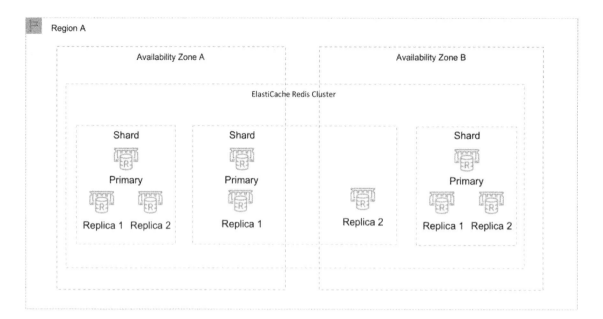

CACHING STRATEGIES

There are two caching strategies available: Lazy Loading and Write-Through:

Lazy Loading

- Loads the data into the cache only when necessary (if a cache miss occurs).

- Lazy loading avoids filling up the cache with data that won't be requested.

- If requested data is in the cache, ElastiCache returns the data to the application.

- If the data is not in the cache or has expired, ElastiCache returns a null.

- The application then fetches the data from the database and writes the data received into the cache so that it is available for next time.

- Data in the cache can become stale if Lazy Loading is implemented without other strategies (such as TTL).

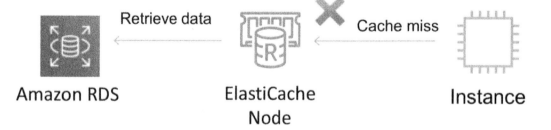

Write Through

- When using a write-through strategy, the cache is updated whenever a new write or update is made to the underlying database.

- Allows cache data to remain up-to-date.

- This can add wait time to write operations in your application.

- Without a TTL you can end up with a lot of cached data that is never read.

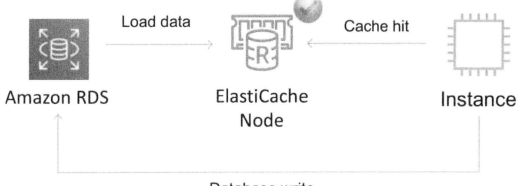

Load data → ElastiCache Node ← Cache hit

Amazon RDS ElastiCache Node Instance

Database write

DEALING WITH STALE DATA – TIME TO LIVE (TTL)

- The drawbacks of lazy loading and write through techniques can be mitigated by a TTL.

- The TTL specifies the number of seconds until the key (data) expires to avoid keeping stale data in the cache.

- When reading an expired key, the application checks the value in the underlying database.

- Lazy Loading treats an expired key as a cache miss and causes the application to retrieve the data from the database and subsequently write the data into the cache with a new TTL.

- Depending on the frequency with which data changes this strategy may not eliminate stale data – but helps to avoid it.

Exam tip: Compared to DynamoDB Accelerator (DAX) remember that DAX is optimized for DymamoDB specifically and only supports the write-through caching strategy (does not use lazy loading).

AWS DATABASE QUIZ QUESTIONS

Question 1: An application runs on a fleet of Auto Scaling Amazon EC2 instances and uses an RDS database back end. The traffic is extremely read-heavy and the database performance is being impacted by a large amount of traffic. What is the best way to scale the database for reads?

1. Add a multi-AZ standby

2. Add an Amazon DynamoDB DAX cluster

3. Add an RDS Read Replica

Question 2: An existing Amazon RDS database needs to be encrypted. How can a Developer enable encryption for the database?

1. Enable encryption in the RDS database settings in the AWS management console

2. Enable encryption using the AWS CLI

3. Create a snapshot, copy it, encrypt the copy and then create an encrypted DB from the snapshot

Question 3: Amazon DynamoDB is made up of which components?

1. Databases, items, and attributes

2. Documents, functions, and keys

3. Tables, items, and attributes

4. Keys, values, and annotations

Question 4: An application uses Amazon RDS with Amazon ElastiCache Redis. The application must ensure up-to-date data is retrieved from the cache with a minimum of read latency. Which caching strategy should be used?

1. Use lazy loading caching

2. Use write-through caching

Question 5: A team of Developers is deploying an application on AWS. The application will use Amazon ElastiCache in front of Amazon an RDS database. The team needs to ensure high availability and fault tolerance for the data in the cache. Which ElastiCache data store should they use?

1. Amazon ElastiCache Redis

2. Amazon ElastiCache Memcached

Question 6: An Amazon ElastiCache database stores session state data that is not required after 24 hours. How can the size of the database be better managed to reduce cost?

1. Use Redis with Cluster Mode Enabled

2. Use API calls to query the redundant data and remove it from the database

3. Use a Time to Live (TTL) attribute to remove the data after 24 hours.

Question 7: A company requires low-latency access to an Amazon RDS database from a different region to run some reports on a regular basis. The solution must be cost-effective. What's the best way to provide this access without impacting the performance of the main database?

1. Create a new copy of the database from a DB snapshot

2. Use a cross-region Multi-AZ database

3. Use a cross-region Read Replica

4. Use an Amazon ElastiCache cluster in the region where the reporting will take place that uses the main database

Question 8: What is the most efficient way to search for an attribute associated with a list of primary keys?

1. Scan

2. Query

Question 9: An Amazon DynamoDB table is very read-heavy and latency is suboptimal. How can the latency be reduced without impacting the applications' ability to respond quickly to all queries?

1. Add a DynamoDB Accelerator (DAX) cluster

2. Use a larger DynamoDB instance type

3. Use exponential backoff

Question 10: An Amazon DynamoDB table will record the results of an online game. The primary key strategy should allow the userid values to be stored together and then be sorted by timestamp. Which strategy should be used?

1. Use a composite key with the userid as the partition key and the timestamp as the sort key

2. Set the partition key to the userid as the timestamp as an attribute

3. Use a composite key with the timestamp as the partition key and the userid as the sort key

Question 11: A Developer needs to perform queries on an Amazon DynamoDB using non-key attributes. How can this be achieved?

1. Use a Local Secondary Index (LSI)

2. Use a Global Secondary Index (GSI)

Question 12: Which feature of Amazon DynamoDB enables reading and writing of multiple items across multiple tables as an all or nothing operation?

1. DynamoDB Accelerator (DAX)

2. DynamoDB Streams

3. DynamoDB Transactions

AWS DATABASE - QUIZ QUESTIONS & ANSWERS

Question 1: An application runs on a fleet of Auto Scaling Amazon EC2 instances and uses an RDS database back end. The traffic is extremely read-heavy and the database performance is being impacted by a large amount of traffic. What is the best way to scale the database for reads?

1. Add a multi-AZ standby

2. Add an Amazon DynamoDB DAX cluster

3. Add an RDS Read Replica

Question 1, Answer 3

Explanation:

1 is incorrect. A multi-AZ standby is used for disaster recovery rather than scaling reads.

2 is incorrect. DynamoDB DAX is a better fit for putting in front of a DynamoDB cluster to scale reads.

3 is correct. This is a good solution to scale reads. This is an example of scaling horizontally.

Question 2: An existing Amazon RDS database needs to be encrypted. How can a Developer enable encryption for the database?

1. Enable encryption in the RDS database settings in the AWS management console

2. Enable encryption using the AWS CLI

3. Create a snapshot, copy it, encrypt the copy and then create an encrypted DB from the snapshot

Question 2, Answer 3

Explanation:

1 is incorrect. You cannot enable encryption for an existing database.

2 is incorrect. You cannot enable encryption for an existing database.

3 is correct. You cannot encrypt an existing DB, you need to create a snapshot, copy it, encrypt the copy, then build an encrypted DB from the snapshot.

Question 3: Amazon DynamoDB is made up of which components?

1. Databases, items, and attributes

2. Documents, functions, and keys

3. Tables, items, and attributes

4. Keys, values, and annotations

Question 3, Answer 3

Explanation:

1 is incorrect. With DynamoDB you work with tables, not databases.

2 is incorrect. Functions are not part of DynamoDB, they are used with AWS Lambda.

3 is correct. DynamoDB is made up of: Tables. Items. Attributes.

4 is incorrect. DynamoDB is a key-value store. However, annotations are not a concept associated with DynamoDB (they're used with AWS X-Ray).

Question 4: An application uses Amazon RDS with Amazon ElastiCache Redis. The application must ensure up-to-date data is retrieved from the cache with a minimum of read latency. Which caching strategy should be used?

1. Use lazy loading caching

2. Use write-through caching

Question 4, Answer 2

Explanation:

1 is incorrect. This caching strategy loads the data into the cache only when necessary (if a cache miss occurs). Therefore, there could be more latency for reads.

2 is correct. When using a write through strategy, the cache is updated whenever a new write or update is made to the underlying database. This can add latency to writes but ensures the cache data is up-to-date.

Question 5: A team of Developers is deploying an application on AWS. The application will use Amazon ElastiCache in front of Amazon an RDS database. The team needs to ensure high availability and fault tolerance for the data in the cache. Which ElastiCache data store should they use?

1. Amazon ElastiCache Redis

2. Amazon ElastiCache Memcached

Question 5, Answer 1

Explanation:

1 is correct. Redis supports failover and replication.

2 is incorrect. Memcached does not support failover or replication.

Question 6: An Amazon ElastiCache database stores session state data that is not required after 24 hours. How can the size of the database be better managed to reduce cost?

1. Use Redis with Cluster Mode Enabled

2. Use API calls to query the redundant data and remove it from the database

3. Use a Time to Live (TTL) attribute to remove the data after 24 hours.

Question 6, Answer 3

Explanation:

1 is incorrect. This enables data partitioning in the Redis database, it does not assist with reducing database size by removing expired entries.

2 is incorrect. This is an inefficient way to solve this problem. A TTL is a better solution.

3 is correct. The TTL specifies the number of seconds until the key (data) expires to avoid keeping stale data in the cache.

Question 7: A company requires low-latency access to an Amazon RDS database from a different region to run some reports on a regular basis. The solution must be cost-effective. What's the best way to provide this access without impacting the performance of the main database?

1. Create a new copy of the database from a DB snapshot

2. Use a cross-region Multi-AZ database

3. Use a cross-region Read Replica

4. Use an Amazon ElastiCache cluster in the region where the reporting will take place that uses the main database

Question 7, Answer 3

Explanation:

1 is incorrect. This is not a good solution as the database will become out of sync.

2 is incorrect. You cannot deploy a multi-AZ database in another region.

3 is correct. This is a good use case for a cross-region Read Replica. It will provide low-latency access and remain up to date through synchronization.

4 is incorrect. This would be more costly than using a Read Replica.

Question 8: What is the most efficient way to search for an attribute associated with a list of primary keys?

1. Scan

2. Query

Question 8, Answer 2

Explanation:

1 is incorrect. A scan operation returns every item in a table. This is inefficient and expensive (RCUs).

2 is correct. A query operation finds items in your table based on the primary key attribute and a distinct value to search for. This is more efficient than a scan as a scan reads every item in the table.

Question 9: An Amazon DynamoDB table is very read-heavy and latency is suboptimal. How can the latency be reduced without impacting the applications' ability to respond quickly to all queries?

1. Add a DynamoDB Accelerator (DAX) cluster

2. Use a larger DynamoDB instance type

3. Use exponential backoff

Question 9, Answer 1

Explanation:

1 is correct. DAX is an in-memory caching service for DynamoDB and can deliver microsecond performance for millions of requests per second.

2 is incorrect. You cannot choose instance types for DynamoDB

3 is incorrect. This would reduce load on the database but that would impact the performance of the application

Question 10: An Amazon DynamoDB table will record the results of an online game. The primary key strategy should allow the userid values to be stored together and then be sorted by timestamp. Which strategy should be used?

1. Use a composite key with the userid as the partition key and the timestamp as the sort key

2. Set the partition key to the userid as the timestamp as an attribute

3. Use a composite key with the timestamp as the partition key and the userid as the sort key

Question 10, Answer 1

Explanation:

1 is correct. This strategy achieves the stated requirement. All items with the same Partition key are stored together, then sorted according to the Sort key value.

2 is incorrect. This would not work as this is not a composite key and you would not be able to have multiple entries for the userid.

3 is incorrect. This is backwards. The partition key should be the userid and the sort key should be the timestamp.

Question 11: A Developer needs to perform queries on an Amazon DynamoDB using non-key attributes. How can this be achieved?

1. Use a Local Secondary Index (LSI)

2. Use a Global Secondary Index (GSI)

Question 11, Answer 2

Explanation:

1 is incorrect. An LSI provides an alternative range key for your table, local to the hash key. However, it has the same partition key as your original table (just a different sort key).

2 is correct. A GSI is used to speed up queries on non-key attributes. It uses a different partition key as well as a different sort key.

Question 12: Which feature of Amazon DynamoDB enables reading and writing of multiple items across multiple tables as an all or nothing operation?

1. DynamoDB Accelerator (DAX)

2. DynamoDB Streams

3. DynamoDB Transactions

Question 12, Answer 3

Explanation:

1 is incorrect. DAX is a fully managed, clustered in-memory cache for DynamoDB.

2 is incorrect. DynamoDB Streams captures a time-ordered sequence of item-level modifications in any DynamoDB table and stores this information in a log for up to 24 hours.

3 is correct. DynamoDB Transactions enables reading and writing of multiple items across multiple tables as an all or nothing operation. It checks for a pre-requisite condition before writing to a table.

NETWORKING AND CONTENT DELIVERY

AMAZON VPC

GENERAL AMAZON VPC CONCEPTS

Amazon VPC lets you provision a logically isolated section of the Amazon Web Services (AWS) cloud where you can launch AWS resources in a virtual network that you define.

Analogous to having your own DC inside AWS.

Provides complete control over the virtual networking environment including selection of IP ranges, creation of subnets, and configuration of route tables and gateways.

A VPC is logically isolated from other VPCs on AWS.

Possible to connect the corporate data center to a VPC using a hardware VPN (site-to-site).

VPCs are region wide.

A default VPC is created in each region with a subnet in each AZ.

By default, you can create up to 5 VPCs per region.

You can define dedicated tenancy for a VPC to ensure instances are launched on dedicated hardware (overrides the configuration specified at launch).

A default VPC is automatically created for each AWS account the first time Amazon EC2 resources are provisioned.

The default VPC has all-public subnets.

Public subnets are subnets that have:

- "Auto-assign public IPv4 address" set to "Yes".
- The subnet route table has an attached Internet Gateway.

Instances in the default VPC always have both a public and private IP address.

AZs names are mapped to different zones for different users (i.e. the AZ "ap-southeast-2a" may map to a different physical zone for a different user).

Components of a VPC:

- **A Virtual Private Cloud:** A logically isolated virtual network in the AWS cloud. You define a VPC's IP address space from ranges you select.
- **Subnet:** A segment of a VPC's IP address range where you can place groups of isolated resources (maps to an AZ, 1:1).
- **Internet Gateway:** The Amazon VPC side of a connection to the public Internet.
- **NAT Gateway:** A highly available, managed Network Address Translation (NAT) service for your resources in a private subnet to access the Internet.
- **Hardware VPN Connection:** A hardware-based VPN connection between your Amazon VPC and your datacenter, home network, or co-location facility.
- **Virtual Private Gateway:** The Amazon VPC side of a VPN connection.
- **Customer Gateway:** Your side of a VPN connection.

- **Router:** Routers interconnect subnets and direct traffic between Internet gateways, virtual private gateways, NAT gateways, and subnets.
- **Peering Connection:** A peering connection enables you to route traffic via private IP addresses between two peered VPCs.
- **VPC Endpoints:** Enables private connectivity to services hosted in AWS, from within your VPC without using an an Internet Gateway, VPN, Network Address Translation (NAT) devices, or firewall proxies.
- **Egress-only Internet Gateway:** A stateful gateway to provide egress only access for IPv6 traffic from the VPC to the Internet.

Options for connecting to a VPC are:

- Hardware based VPN
- Direct Connect
- VPN CloudHub
- Software VPN

ROUTING

The VPC router performs routing between AZs within a region.

The VPC router connects different AZs together and connects the VPC to the Internet Gateway.

Each subnet has a route table the router uses to forward traffic within the VPC.

Route tables also have entries to external destinations.

Up to 200 route tables per VPC.

Up to 50 route entries per route table.

Each subnet can only be associated with one route table.

Can assign one route table to multiple subnets.

If no route table is specified a subnet will be assigned to the main route table at creation time.

Cannot delete the main route table.

You can manually set another route table to become the main route table.

There is a default rule that allows all VPC subnets to communicate with one another – this cannot be deleted or modified.

Routing between subnets is always possible because of this rule – any problems communicating is more likely to be security groups or NACLs.

SUBNETS AND SUBNET SIZING

Types of subnet:

- If a subnet's traffic is routed to an internet gateway, the subnet is known as a **public subnet.**
- If a subnet doesn't have a route to the internet gateway, the subnet is known as a **private subnet.**

- If a subnet doesn't have a route to the internet gateway, but has its traffic routed to a virtual private gateway for a VPN connection, the subnet is known as a **VPN-only subnet.**

The VPC is created with a master address range (CIDR block, can be anywhere from 16-28 bits), and subnet ranges are created within that range.

New subnets are always associated with the default route table.

Once the VPC is created you cannot change the CIDR block.

You cannot create additional CIDR blocks that overlap with existing CIDR blocks.

You cannot create additional CIDR blocks in a different RFC 1918 range.

Subnets with overlapping IP address ranges cannot be created.

The first 4 and last 1 IP addresses in a subnet are reserved.

Subnets are created within availability zones (AZs).

Each subnet must reside entirely within one Availability Zone and cannot span zones.

Availability Zones are distinct locations that are engineered to be isolated from failures in other Availability Zones.

Availability Zones are connected with low latency, high throughput, and highly redundant networking.

Can create private, public or VPN subnets.

Subnets map 1:1 to AZs and cannot span AZs.

You can only attach one Internet gateway to a custom VPC.

IPv6 addresses are all public and the range is allocated by AWS.

INTERNET GATEWAYS

An Internet Gateway is a horizontally scaled, redundant, and highly available VPC component that allows communication between instances in your VPC and the internet.

An Internet Gateway serves two purposes: .

- To provide a target in your VPC route tables for internet-routable traffic.
- To perform network address translation (NAT) for instances that have been assigned public IPv4 addresses.

Internet Gateways (IGW) must be created and then attached to a VPC, be added to a route table, and then associated with the relevant subnet(s).

No availability risk or bandwidth constraints.

If your subnet is associated with a route to the Internet, then it is a public subnet.

You cannot have multiple Internet Gateways in a VPC.

IGW is horizontally scaled, redundant and HA.

IGW performs NAT between private and public IPv4 addresses.

IGW supports IPv4 and IPv6.

IGWs must be detached before they can be deleted.

Can only attach 1 IGW to a VPC at a time.

Gateway terminology:

- Internet gateway (IGW) – AWS VPC side of the connection to the public Internet.

- Virtual private gateway (VPG) – VPC endpoint on the AWS side.

- Customer gateway (CGW) – representation of the customer end of the connection.

To enable access to or from the Internet for instances in a VPC subnet, you must do the following:

- Attach an Internet Gateway to your VPC.

- Ensure that your subnet's route table points to the Internet Gateway (see below).

- Ensure that instances in your subnet have a globally unique IP address (public IPv4 address, Elastic IP address, or IPv6 address).

- Ensure that your network access control and security group rules allow the relevant traffic to flow to and from your instance.

Must update subnet route table to point to IGW, either:

- To all destinations, e.g. 0.0.0.0/0 for IPv4 or ::/0for IPv6.

- To specific public IPv4 addresses, e.g. your company's public endpoints outside of AWS.

Egress-only Internet Gateway:

- Provides outbound Internet access for IPv6 addressed instances.

- Prevents inbound access to those IPv6 instances.

- IPv6 addresses are globally unique and are therefore public by default.

- Stateful – forwards traffic from instance to Internet and then sends back the response.

- Must create a custom route for ::/0 to the Egress-Only Internet Gateway.

- Use Egress-Only Internet Gateway instead of NAT for IPv6.

NAT INSTANCES

NAT instances are managed **by** you.

Used to enable private subnet instances to access the Internet.

NAT instance must live on a public subnet with a route to an Internet Gateway.

Private instances in private subnets must have a route to the NAT instance, usually the default route destination of 0.0.0.0/0.

When creating NAT instances always disable the source/destination check on the instance.

NAT instances must be in a single public subnet.

NAT instances need to be assigned to security groups.

Security groups for NAT instances must allow HTTP/HTTPS inbound from the private subnet and outbound to 0.0.0.0/0.

There needs to be a route from a private subnet to the NAT instance for it to work.

The amount of traffic a NAT instance can support is based on the instance type.

Using a NAT instance can lead to bottlenecks (not HA).

HA can be achieved by using Auto Scaling groups, multiple subnets in different AZ's and a script to automate failover.

Performance is dependent on instance size.

Can scale up instance size or use enhanced networking.

Can scale out by using multiple NATs in multiple subnets.

Can use as a bastion (jump) host.

Can monitor traffic metrics.

Not supported for IPv6 (use Egress-Only Internet Gateway).

NAT GATEWAYS

NAT gateways are managed **for** you by AWS.

Fully-managed NAT service that replaces the need for NAT instances on EC2.

Must be created in a public subnet.

Uses an Elastic IP address for the public IP.

Private instances in private subnets must have a route to the NAT instance, usually the default route destination of 0.0.0.0/0.

Created in a specified AZ with redundancy in that zone.

For multi-AZ redundancy, create NAT Gateways in each AZ with routes for private subnets to use the local gateway.

Up to 5 Gbps bandwidth that can scale up to 45 Gbps.

Can't use a NAT Gateway to access VPC peering, VPN or Direct Connect, so be sure to include specific routes to those in your route table.

NAT gateways are highly available in each AZ into which they are deployed.

They are preferred by enterprises.

No need to patch.

Not associated with any security groups.

Automatically assigned a public IP address.

Remember to update route tables and point towards your gateway.

More secure (e.g. you cannot access with SSH and there are no security groups to maintain).

No need to disable source/destination checks.

Egress only Internet gateways operate on IPv6 whereas NAT gateways operate on IPv4.

Port forwarding is not supported.

Using the NAT Gateway as a Bastion host server is not supported.

Traffic metrics are not supported.

The table below highlights the key differences between both types of gateway:

	NAT Gateway	NAT Instance
Managed	Managed by AWS	Managed by you
Availability	Highly available within an AZ	Not highly available (would require scripting)
Bandwidth	Up to 45 Gbps	Depends on the bandwidth of the EC2 instance type selected
Maintenance	Managed by AWS	Managed by you
Performance	Optimized for NAT	Amazon Linux AMI configured to perform NAT
Public IP	Elastic IP that cannot be detached	Elastic IP that can be detached
Security Groups	Cannot associate with a Security Group	Can associate with a Security Group
Bastion Host	Not supported	Can be used as a bastion host

SECURITY GROUPS

Security groups act like a firewall at the instance level.

Specifically, security groups operate at the network interface level.

Can only assign permit rules in a security group, cannot assign deny rules.

There is an implicit deny rule at the end of the security group.

All rules are evaluated until a permit is encountered or continues until the implicit deny.

Can control ingress and egress traffic.

Security groups are stateful.

By default, custom security groups do not have inbound allow rules (all inbound traffic is denied by default).

By default, default security groups do have inbound allow rules (allowing traffic from within the group).

All outbound traffic is allowed by default in custom and default security groups.

You cannot delete the security group that's created by default within a VPC.

You can use security group names as the source or destination in other security groups.

You can use the security group name as a source in its own inbound rules.

Security group members can be within any AZ or subnet within the VPC.

Security group membership can be changed whilst instances are running.

Any changes made will take effect immediately.

Up to 5 security groups can be added per EC2 instance interface.

There is no limit on the number of EC2 instances within a security group.

You cannot block specific IP addresses using security groups, use NACLs instead.

NETWORK ACL'S

Network ACL's function at the subnet level.

The VPC router hosts the network ACL function.

With NACLs you can have permit and deny rules.

Network ACLs contain a numbered list of rules that are evaluated in order from the lowest number until the explicit deny.

Recommended to leave spacing between network ACL numbers.

Network ACLs have separate inbound and outbound rules and each rule can allow or deny traffic.

Network ACLs are stateless, so responses are subject to the rules for the direction of traffic.

NACLs only apply to traffic that is ingress or egress to the subnet not to traffic within the subnet.

A VPC automatically comes with a default network ACL which allows all inbound/outbound traffic.

A custom NACL denies all traffic both inbound and outbound by default.

All subnets must be associated with a network ACL.

You can create custom network ACL's. By default, each custom network ACL denies all inbound and outbound traffic until you add rules.

Each subnet in your VPC must be associated with a network ACL. If you don't do this manually it will be associated with the default network ACL.

You can associate a network ACL with multiple subnets; however, a subnet can only be associated with one network ACL at a time.

Network ACLs do not filter traffic between instances in the same subnet.

NACLs are the preferred option for blocking specific IPs or ranges.

Security groups cannot be used to block specific ranges of IPs.

NACL is the first line of defense, the security group is the second line.

Also recommended to have software firewalls installed on your instances.

Changes to NACLs take effect immediately.

Security Group	Network ACL
Operates at the instance (interface) level	Operates at the subnet level
Supports allow rules only	Supports allow and deny rules
Stateful	Stateless
Evaluates all rules	Processes rules in order
Applies to an instance only if associated with a group	Automatically applies to all instances in the subnets its associated with

VPC PEERING

What	AWS-provided network connectivity between two VPCs
When	Multiple VPCs need to communicate or access each other's resources
Pros	Uses AWS backbone without traversing the Internet
Cons	Transitive peering is not supported
How	VPC peering request made; accepter accepts request (either within or across accounts)

A VPC peering connection is a networking connection between two VPCs that enables you to route traffic between them using private IPv4 addresses or IPv6 addresses.

Instances in either VPC can communicate with each other as if they are within the same network.

You can create a VPC peering connection between your own VPCs, or with a VPC in another AWS account.

The VPCs can be in different regions (also known as an inter-region VPC peering connection).

Data sent between VPCs in different regions is encrypted (traffic charges apply).

For inter-region VPC peering there are some limitations:

- You cannot create a security group rule that references a peer security group.
- Cannot enable DNS resolution.
- Maximum MTU is 1500 bytes (no jumbo frames support).
- Limited region support.

AWS uses the existing infrastructure of a VPC to create a VPC peering connection.

It is neither a gateway nor a VPN connection and does not rely on a separate piece of physical hardware.

There is no single point of failure for communication or a bandwidth bottleneck.

A VPC peering connection helps you to facilitate the transfer of data.

Can only have one peering connection between any two VPCs at a time.

Can peer with other accounts (within or between regions).

Cannot have overlapping CIDR ranges.

A VPC peering connection is a one to one relationship between two VPCs.

You can create multiple VPC peering connections for each VPC that you own, but transitive peering relationships are not supported.

You do not have any peering relationship with VPCs that your VPC is not directly peered with.

Limits are 50 VPC peers per VPC, up to 125 by request.

DNS is supported.

Must update route tables to configure routing.

Must update the inbound and outbound rules for VPC security group to reference security groups in the peered VPC.

When creating a VPC peering connection with another account you need to enter the account ID and VPC ID from the other account.

Need to accept the pending access request in the peered VPC.

The VPC peering connection can be added to route tables – shows as a target starting with "pcx-".

AWS PRIVATELINK

AWS PrivateLink simplifies the security of data shared with cloud-based applications by eliminating the exposure of data to the public Internet.

AWS PrivateLink provides private connectivity between VPCs, AWS services, and on-premises applications, securely on the Amazon network.

AWS PrivateLink makes it easy to connect services across different accounts and VPCs to significantly simplify the network architecture.

The table below provides more information on AWS PrivateLink and when to use it:

What	AWS-provided network connectivity between VPCs and/or AWS services using interface endpoints
When	Keep Private Subnets truly private by using the AWS backbone to reach other AWS or Marketplace services rather than the public Internet
Pros	Redundant; uses the AWS backbone
Cons	
How	Create endpoint for required AWS or Marketplace service in all required subnets; access via the provided DNS hostname

EXAM TIP: Know the difference between AWS PrivateLink and ClassicLink. ClassicLink allows you to link EC2-Classic instances to a VPC in your account, within the same region. EC2-Classic is an old platform from before VPCs were introduced and is not available to accounts created after December 2013. However, ClassicLink may come up in exam questions as a possible (incorrect) answer so you need to know what it is.

VPC ENDPOINTS

An Interface endpoint uses AWS PrivateLink and is an elastic network interface (ENI) with a private IP address that serves as an entry point for traffic destined to a supported service.

Using PrivateLink you can connect your VPC to supported AWS services, services hosted by other AWS accounts (VPC endpoint services), and supported AWS Marketplace partner services.

AWS PrivateLink access over Inter-Region VPC Peering:

- Applications in an AWS VPC can securely access AWS PrivateLink endpoints across AWS Regions using Inter-Region VPC Peering.

- AWS PrivateLink allows you to privately access services hosted on AWS in a highly available and scalable manner, without using public IPs, and without requiring the traffic to traverse the Internet.

- Customers can privately connect to a service even if the service endpoint resides in a different AWS Region.

- Traffic using Inter-Region VPC Peering stays on the global AWS backbone and never traverses the public Internet.

A gateway endpoint is a gateway that is a target for a specified route in your route table, used for traffic destined to a supported AWS service.

An interface VPC endpoint (interface endpoint) enables you to connect to services powered by AWS PrivateLink.

The table below highlights some key information about both types of endpoint:

	Interface Endpoint	Gateway Endpoint
What	Elastic Network Interface with a Private IP	A gateway that is a target for a specific route
How	Uses DNS entries to redirect traffic	Uses prefix lists in the route table to redirect traffic
Which services	API Gateway, CloudFormation, CloudWatch etc.	Amazon S3, DynamoDB
Security	Security Groups	VPC Endpoint Policies

By default, IAM users do not have permission to work with endpoints.

You can create an IAM user policy that grants users the permissions to create, modify, describe, and delete endpoints.

There's a long list of services that are supported by interface endpoints.

Gateway endpoints are only available for:

- Amazon DyanmoDB

- Amazon S3

EXAM TIP: Know which services use interface endpoints and gateway endpoints. The easiest way to remember this is that Gateway Endpoints are for Amazon S3 and DynamoDB only.

VPC FLOW LOGS

Flow Logs capture information about the IP traffic going to and from network interfaces in a VPC.

Flow log data is stored using Amazon CloudWatch Logs.

Flow logs can be created at the following levels:

- VPC.

- Subnet.

- Network interface.

You can't enable flow logs for VPC's that are peered with your VPC unless the peer VPC is in your account.

You can't tag a flow log.

You can't change the configuration of a flow log after it's been created.

After you've created a flow log, you cannot change its configuration (you need to delete and re-create).

Not all traffic is monitored, e.g. the following traffic is excluded:

- Traffic that goes to Route53.

- Traffic generated for Windows license activation.

- Traffic to and from 169.254.169.254 (instance metadata).

- Traffic to and from 169.254.169.123 for the Amazon Time Sync Service.

- DHCP traffic.

- Traffic to the reserved IP address for the default VPC router.

AMAZON CLOUDFRONT

GENERAL CLOUDFRONT CONCEPTS

CloudFront is a web service that gives businesses and web application developers an easy and cost-effective way to distribute content with low latency and high data transfer speeds.

CloudFront is a good choice for distribution of frequently accessed static content that benefits from edge delivery—like popular website images, videos, media files or software downloads.

Used for dynamic, static, streaming, and interactive content.

CloudFront is a global service:

- Ingress to upload objects.

- Egress to distribute content.

Amazon CloudFront provides a simple API that lets you:

- Distribute content with low latency and high data transfer rates by serving requests using a network of edge locations around the world.

- Get started without negotiating contracts and minimum commitments.

You can use a zone apex name on CloudFront.

CloudFront supports wildcard CNAME.

Supports wildcard SSL certificates, Dedicated IP, Custom SSL and SNI Custom SSL (cheaper). Supports Perfect Forward Secrecy which creates a new private key for each SSL session.

EDGE LOCATIONS AND REGIONAL EDGE CACHES

An edge location is the location where content is cached (separate to AWS regions/AZs).

Requests are automatically routed to the nearest edge location.

Edge locations are not tied to Availability Zones or regions.

Regional Edge Caches are located between origin web servers and global edge locations and have a larger cache.

Regional Edge Caches have larger cache-width than any individual edge location, so your objects remain in cache longer at these locations.

Regional Edge caches aim to get content closer to users.

Proxy methods PUT/POST/PATCH/OPTIONS/DELETE go directly to the origin from the edge locations and do not proxy through Regional Edge caches.

Dynamic content goes straight to the origin and does not flow through Regional Edge caches.

Edge locations are not just read only, you can write to them too.

The diagram below shows where Regional Edge Caches and Edge Locations are placed in relation to end users:

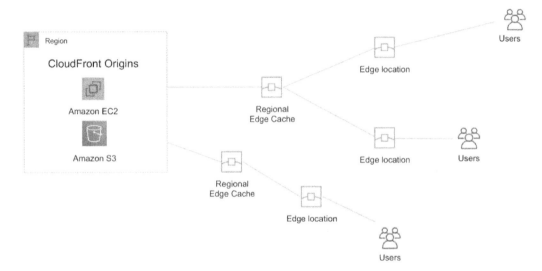

ORIGINS

An origin is the origin of the files that the CDN will distribute.

Origins can be either an S3 bucket, an EC2 instance, an Elastic Load Balancer, or Route 53 – can also be external (non-AWS).

When using Amazon S3 as an origin you place all of your objects within the bucket.

You can use an existing bucket and the bucket is not modified in any way.

By default, all newly created buckets are private.

You can setup access control to your buckets using:

- Bucket policies.
- Access Control Lists.

You can make objects publicly available or use CloudFront signed URLs.

A custom origin server is a HTTP server which can be an EC2 instance or an on-premise/non-AWS based web server.

When using an on-premise or non-AWS based web server you must specify the DNS name, ports and protocols that you want CloudFront to use when fetching objects from your origin.

Most CloudFront features are supported for custom origins except RTMP distributions (must be an S3 bucket).

When using EC2 for custom origins Amazon recommend:

- Use an AMI that automatically installs the software for a web server.
- Use ELB to handle traffic across multiple EC2 instances.
- Specify the URL of your load balancer as the domain name of the origin server.

S3 static website:

- Enter the S3 static website hosting endpoint for your bucket in the configuration.
- Example: http://<bucketname>.s3-website-<region>.amazonaws.com.

Objects are cached for 24 hours by default.

The expiration time is controlled through the TTL.

The minimum expiration time is 0.

Static websites on Amazon S3 are considered custom origins.

AWS origins are Amazon S3 buckets (not a static website).

CloudFront keeps persistent connections open with origin servers.

Files can also be uploaded to CloudFront.

High availability with Origin Failover:

- Can set up CloudFront with origin failover for scenarios that require high availability.
- Uses an origin group in which you designate a primary origin for CloudFront plus a second origin that CloudFront automatically switches to when the primary origin returns specific HTTP status code failure responses.
- Also works with Lambda@Edge functions.

DISTRIBUTIONS

To distribute content with CloudFront you need to create a distribution.

The distribution includes the configuration of the CDN including:

- Content origins.
- Access (public or restricted).
- Security (HTTP or HTTPS).
- Cookie or query-string forwarding.
- Geo-restrictions.
- Access logs (record viewer activity).

There are two types of distribution.

Web Distribution:

- Static and dynamic content including .html, .css, .php, and graphics files.
- Distributes files over HTTP and HTTPS.
- Add, update, or delete objects, and submit data from web forms.

- Use live streaming to stream an event in real time.

RTMP:

- Distribute streaming media files using Adobe Flash Media Server's RTMP protocol.
- Allows an end user to begin playing a media file before the file has finished downloading from a CloudFront edge location.
- Files must be stored in an S3 bucket.

To use CloudFront live streaming, create a web distribution.

For serving both the media player and media files you need two types of distributions:

- A web distribution for the media player.
- An RTMP distribution for the media files.

S3 buckets can be configured to create access logs and cookie logs which log all requests made to the S3 bucket.

Amazon Athena can be used to analyze access logs.

CloudFront is integrated with CloudTrail.

CloudTrail saves logs to the S3 bucket you specify.

CloudTrail captures information about all requests whether they were made using the CloudFront console, the CloudFront API, the AWS SDKs, the CloudFront CLI, or another service.

CloudTrail can be used to determine which requests were made, the source IP address, who made the request etc.

To view CloudFront requests in CloudTrail logs you must update an existing trail to include global services.

To delete a distribution, it must first be disabled (can take up to 15 minutes).

The diagram below depicts Amazon CloudFront Distributions and Origins:

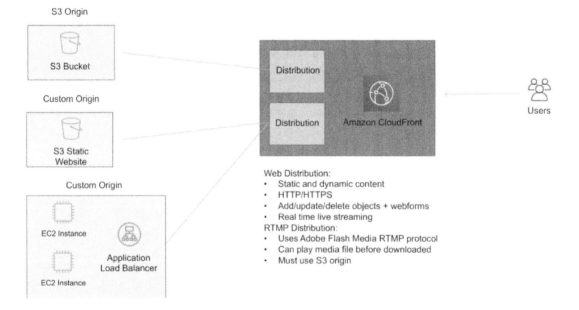

CACHE BEHAVIOR

Allows you to configure a variety of CloudFront functionality for a given URL path pattern.

For each cache behavior you can configure the following functionality:

- The path pattern (e.g. /images/*.jpg, /images*.php).
- The origin to forward requests to (if there are multiple origins).
- Whether to forward query strings.
- Whether to require signed URLs.
- Allowed HTTP methods.
- Minimum amount of time to retain the files in the CloudFront cache (regardless of the values of any cache-control headers).

The default cache behavior only allows a path pattern of /*.

Additional cache behaviors need to be defined to change the path pattern following creation of the distribution.

You can restrict access to content using the following methods:

- Restrict access to content using signed cookies or signed URLs.
- Restrict access to objects in your S3 bucket.

A special type of user called an Origin Access Identity (OAI) can be used to restrict access to content in an Amazon S3 bucket.

By using an OAI you can restrict users so they cannot access the content directly using the S3 URL, they must connect via CloudFront.

You can define the viewer protocol policy:

- HTTP and HTTPS
- Redirect HTTP to HTTPS
- HTTPS only

You can define the Allowed HTTP Methods:

- GET, HEAD
- GET, HEAD, OPTIONS
- GET, HEAD, OPTIONS, PUT, POST, PATCH, DELETE

For web distributions you can configure CloudFront to require that viewers use HTTPS.

Field-Level Encryption:

- Field-level encryption adds an additional layer of security on top of HTTPS that lets you protect specific data so that it is only visible to specific applications.
- Field-level encryption allows you to securely upload user-submitted sensitive information to your web servers.
- The sensitive information is encrypted at the edge closer to the user and remains encrypted throughout application processing.

Origin policy:

- HTTPS only.

- Match viewer – CloudFront matches the protocol with your custom origin.

- Use match viewer only if you specify Redirect HTTP to HTTPS or HTTPS only for the viewer protocol policy.

- CloudFront caches the object once even if viewers makes requests using HTTP and HTTPS.

Object invalidation:

- You can remove an object from the cache by invalidating the object.

- You cannot cancel an invalidation after submission.

- You cannot invalidate media files in the Microsoft Smooth Streaming format when you have enabled Smooth Streaming for the corresponding cache behavior.

Objects are cached for the TTL (always recorded in seconds, default is 24 hours, default max is 1 year).

Only caches for GET requests (not PUT, POST, PATCH, DELETE).

Dynamic content is cached.

Consider how often your files change when setting the TTL.

Invalidation can be used to immediately revoke cached objects – chargeable.

Deletions propagate.

RESTRICTIONS

Blacklists and whitelists can be used for geography – you can only use one at a time.

There are two options available for geo-restriction (geo-blocking):

- Use the CloudFront geo-restriction feature (use for restricting access to all files in a distribution and at the country level).

- Use a 3rd party geo-location service (use for restricting access to a subset of the files in a distribution and for finer granularity at the country level).

AWS WAF

AWS WAF is a web application firewall that lets you monitor HTTP and HTTPS requests that are forwarded to CloudFront and lets you control access to your content.

With AWS WAF you can shield access to content based on conditions in a web access control list (web ACL) such as:

- Origin IP address.

- Values in query strings.

CloudFront responds to requests with the requested content or an HTTP 403 status code (forbidden).

CloudFront can also be configured to deliver a custom error page.

Need to associate the relevant distribution with the web ACL.

SECURITY

PCI DSS compliant but recommended not to cache credit card information at edge locations.

HIPAA compliant as a HIPAA eligible service.

Distributed Denial of Service (DDoS) protection:

- CloudFront distributes traffic across multiple edge locations and filters requests to ensure that only valid HTTP(S) requests will be forwarded to backend hosts. CloudFront also supports geoblocking, which you can use to prevent requests from particular geographic locations from being served.

DOMAIN NAMES

CloudFront typically creates a domain name such as a232323.cloudfront.net.

Alternate domain names can be added using an alias record (Route 53).

For other service providers use a CNAME (cannot use the zone apex with CNAME).

Moving domain names between distributions:

- You can move subdomains yourself.
- For the root domain you need to use AWS support.

CHARGES

There is an option for reserved capacity over 12 months or longer (starts at 10TB of data transfer in a single region).

You pay for:

- Data Transfer Out to Internet.
- Data Transfer Out to Origin.
- Number of HTTP/HTTPS Requests.
- Invalidation Requests.
- Dedicated IP Custom SSL.
- Field level encryption requests.

You do not pay for:

- Data transfer between AWS regions and CloudFront.
- Regional edge cache.
- AWS ACM SSL/TLS certificates.
- Shared CloudFront certificates.

AMAZON ROUTE 53

GENERAL ROUTE 53 CONCEPTS

Amazon Route 53 is a highly available and scalable Domain Name System (DNS) service.

Route 53 offers the following functions:

- Domain name registry.

- DNS resolution.

- Health checking of resources.

Route 53 can perform any combination of these functions.

Route 53 provides a worldwide distributed DNS service.

Route 53 is located alongside all edge locations.

Health checks verify Internet connected resources are reachable, available and functional.

Route 53 can be used to route Internet traffic for domains registered with another domain registrar (any domain).

When you register a domain with Route 53 it becomes the authoritative DNS server for that domain and creates a public hosted zone.

To make Route 53 the authoritative DNS for an existing domain without transferring the domain create a Route 53 public hosted zone and change the DNS Name Servers on the existing provider to the Route 53 Name Servers.

Changes to Name Servers may not take effect for up to 48 hours due to the DNS record Time To Live (TTL) values.

You can transfer domains to Route 53 only if the Top Level Domain (TLD) is supported.

You can transfer a domain from Route 53 to another registrar by contacting AWS support.

You can transfer a domain to another account in AWS however it does not migrate the hosted zone by default (optional).

It is possible to have the domain registered in one AWS account and the hosted zone in another AWS account.

Primarily uses UDP port 53 (can use TCP).

AWS offer a 100% uptime SLA for Route 53.

You can control management access to your Amazon Route 53 hosted zone by using IAM.

There is a default limit of 50 domain names, but this can be increased by contacting support.

Private DNS is a Route 53 feature that lets you have authoritative DNS within your VPCs without exposing your DNS records (including the name of the resource and its IP address(es) to the Internet.

You can use the AWS Management Console or API to register new domain names with Route 53.

HOSTED ZONES

A hosted zone is a collection of records for a specified domain.

A hosted zone is analogous to a traditional DNS zone file; it represents a collection of records that can be managed together.

There are two types of zones:

- Public host zone – determines how traffic is routed on the Internet.
- Private hosted zone for VPC – determines how traffic is routed within VPC (resources are not accessible outside the VPC).

Amazon Route 53 automatically creates the Name Server (NS) and Start of Authority (SOA) records for the hosted zones.

Amazon Route 53 creates a set of 4 unique name servers (a delegation set) within each hosted zone.

You can create multiple hosted zones with the same name and different records.

NS servers are specified by Fully Qualified Domain Name (FQDN) but you can get the IP addresses from the command line (e.g. dig or nslookup).

For private hosted zones you can see a list of VPCs in each region and must select one.

For private hosted zones you must set the following VPC settings to "true":

- enableDnsHostname
- enableDnsSupport

You also need to create a DHCP options set.

You can extend an on-premises DNS to VPC.

You cannot extend Route 53 to on-premises instances.

You cannot automatically register EC2 instances with private hosted zones (would need to be scripted).

Health checks check the instance health by connecting to it.

Health checks can be pointed at:

- Endpoints
- Status of other health checks
- Status of a CloudWatch alarm

Endpoints can be IP addresses or domain names.

RECORDS

Amazon Route 53 currently supports the following DNS record types:

- A (address record)
- AAAA (IPv6 address record)
- CNAME (canonical name record)
- CAA (certification authority authorization)
- MX (mail exchange record)
- NAPTR (name authority pointer record
- NS (name server record)
- PTR (pointer record)
- SOA (start of authority record)
- SPF (sender policy framework)
- SRV (service locator)

- TXT (text record)
- Alias (an Amazon Route 53-specific virtual record)

The Alias record is a Route 53 specific record type.

Alias records are used to map resource record sets in your hosted zone to Amazon Elastic Load Balancing load balancers, Amazon CloudFront distributions, AWS Elastic Beanstalk environments, or Amazon S3 buckets that are configured as websites.

You can use Alias records to map custom domain names (such as api.example.com) both to API Gateway custom regional APIs and edge-optimized APIs and to Amazon VPC interface endpoints.

The Alias is pointed to the DNS name of the service.

You cannot set the TTL for Alias records for ELB, S3, or Elastic Beanstalk environment (uses the service's default).

Alias records work like a CNAME record in that you can map one DNS name (e.g. example.com) to another 'target' DNS name (e.g. elb1234.elb.amazonaws.com).

An Alias record can be used for resolving apex / naked domain names (e.g. example.com rather than sub.example.com).

A CNAME record can't be used for resolving apex / naked domain names.

Generally, use an Alias record where possible. The following table details the differences between Alias and CNAME records:

CNAME Records	Alias Records
Route 53 charges for CNAME queries	Route 53 doesn't charge for alias queries to AWS resources
You can't create a CNAME record at the top node of a DNS namespace (zone apex)	You can create an alias record at the zone apex (however you can't route to a CNAME at the zone apex)
A CNAME record redirects queries for a domain name regardless of record type	Route 53 follows the pointer in an alias record only when the record type also matches
A CNAME can point to any DNS record that is hosted anywhere	An alias record can only point to a CloudFront distribution, Elastic Beanstalk environment, ELB, S3 bucket as a static website, or to another record in the same hosted zone that you're creating the alias record in
A CNAME record is visible in the answer section of a reply from a Route 53 DNS server	An alias record is only visible in the Route 53 console or the Route 53 API
A CNAME record is followed by a recursive resolver	An alias record is only followed inside Route 53. This means that both the alias record and its target must exist in Route 53

Route 53 supports wildcard entries for all record types, except NS records.

ROUTING POLICIES

Routing policies determine how Route 53 responds to queries.

The following table highlights the key function of each type of routing policy:

Policy	What it Does
Simple	Simple DNS response providing the IP address associated with a name
Failover	If primary is down (based on health checks), routes to secondary destination
Geolocation	Uses geographic location you're in (e.g. Europe) to route you to the closest region
Geoproximity	Routes you to the closest region within a geographic area
Latency	Directs you based on the lowest latency route to resources
Multivalue answer	Returns several IP addresses and functions as a basic load balancer
Weighted	Uses the relative weights assigned to resources to determine which to route to

Simple:

- An A record is associated with one or more IP addresses
- Uses round robin
- Does not support health checks

The following diagram depicts an Amazon Route 53 Simple routing policy configuration:

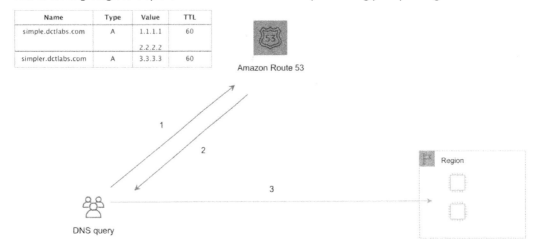

Failover:

- Failover to a secondary IP address.
- Associated with a health check.
- Used for active-passive.
- Routes only when the resource is healthy.
- Can be used with ELB.
- When used with Alias records set Evaluate Target Health to "Yes" and do not use health checks.

The following diagram depicts an Amazon Route 53 Failover routing policy configuration:

Name	Type	Value	Health	Record Type
failover.dctlabs.com	A	1.1.1.1	ID	Primary
failover.dctlabs.com	A	alb-id		Secondary

Amazon Route 53

Health Check required on Primary

Region – us-east-1

1.1.1.1

DNS query

Region – ap-southeast-2

ALB

Geo-location:

- Caters to different users in different countries and different languages.

- Contains users within a particular geography and offers them a customized version of the workload based on their specific needs.

- Geolocation can be used for localizing content and presenting some or all of your website in the language of your users.

- Can also protect distribution rights.

- Can be used for spreading load evenly between regions.

- If you have multiple records for overlapping regions, Route 53 will route to the smallest geographic region.

- You can create a default record for IP addresses that do not map to a geographic location.

The following diagram depicts an Amazon Route 53 Geolocation routing policy configuration:

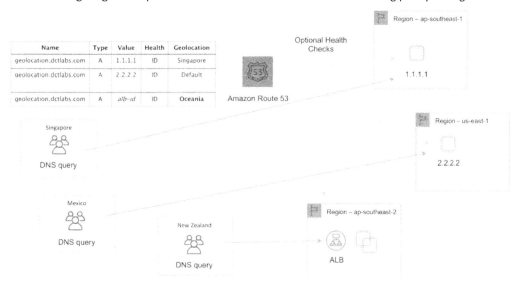

Name	Type	Value	Health	Geolocation
geolocation.dctlabs.com	A	1.1.1.1	ID	Singapore
geolocation.dctlabs.com	A	2.2.2.2	ID	Default
geolocation.dctlabs.com	A	alb-id	ID	Oceania

Amazon Route 53

Optional Health Checks

Region – ap-southeast-1

1.1.1.1

Singapore
DNS query

Region – us-east-1

2.2.2.2

Mexico
DNS query

New Zealand
DNS query

Region – ap-southeast-2

ALB

Geo-proximity routing policy (requires Route Flow):

- Use for routing traffic based on the location of resources and, optionally, shift traffic from resources in one location to resources in another.

Latency based routing:

- AWS maintains a database of latency from different parts of the world.

- Focused on improving performance by routing to the region with the lowest latency.

- You create latency records for your resources in multiple EC2 locations.

The following diagram depicts an Amazon Route 53 Latency based routing policy configuration:

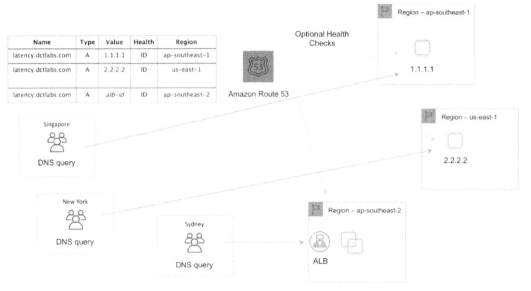

Multi-value answer routing policy:

- Use for responding to DNS queries with up to eight healthy records selected at random.

The following diagram depicts an Amazon Route 53 Multivalue routing policy configuration:

Weighted:

- Similar to simple but you can specify a weight per IP address.

- You create records that have the same name and type and assign each record a relative weight.

- Numerical value that favors one IP over another.

- To stop sending traffic to a resource you can change the weight of the record to 0.

The following diagram depicts an Amazon Route 53 Weighted routing policy configuration:

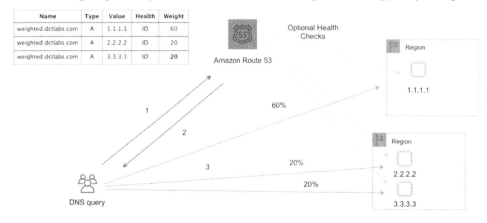

TRAFFIC FLOW

Route 53 Traffic Flow provides Global Traffic Management (GTM) services.

Traffic flow policies allow you to create routing configurations for resources using routing types such as failover and geolocation.

Create policies that route traffic based on specific constraints, including latency, endpoint health, load, geo-proximity and geography.

Scenarios include:

- Adding a simple backup page in Amazon S3 for a website.

- Building sophisticated routing policies that consider an end user's geographic location, proximity to an AWS region, and the health of each of your endpoints.

Amazon Route 53 Traffic Flow also includes a versioning feature that allows you to maintain a history of changes to your routing policies, and easily roll back to a previous policy version using the console or API.

ROUTE 53 RESOLVER

Route 53 Resolver is a set of features that enable bi-directional querying between on-premises and AWS over private connections.

Used for enabling DNS resolution for hybrid clouds.

Route 53 Resolver Endpoints:

- Inbound query capability is provided by Route 53 Resolver Endpoints, allowing DNS queries that originate on-premises to resolve AWS hosted domains.

- Connectivity needs to be established between your on-premises DNS infrastructure and AWS through a Direct Connect (DX) or a Virtual Private Network (VPN).

- Endpoints are configured through IP address assignment in each subnet for which you would like to provide a resolver.

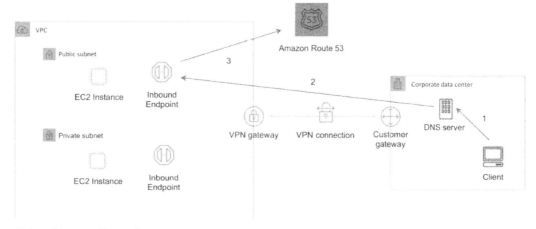

Conditional forwarding rules:

- Outbound DNS queries are enabled through the use of Conditional Forwarding Rules. .

- Domains hosted within your on-premises DNS infrastructure can be configured as forwarding rules in Route 53 Resolver.

- Rules will trigger when a query is made to one of those domains and will attempt to forward DNS requests to your DNS servers that were configured along with the rules.

- Like the inbound queries, this requires a private connection over DX or VPN.

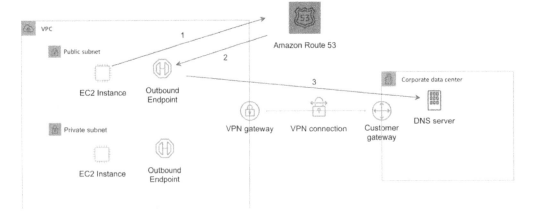

CHARGES

You pay per hosted zone per month (no partial months).

A hosted zone deleted within 12 hours of creation is not charged (queries are charges).

Additional charges for:

- Queries
- Traffic Flow
- Health Checks
- Route 53 Resolver ENIs + queries
- Domain names

Alias records are free of charge when the records are mapped to one of the following:

- Elastic Load Balancers
- Amazon CloudFront distributions
- AWS Elastic Beanstalk environments
- Amazon S3 buckets that are configured as website endpoints

Health checks are charged with different prices for AWS vs non-AWS endpoints.

You do not pay for the records that you add to your hosted zones.

Latency-based routing queries are more expensive.

Geo DNS and geo-proximity also have higher prices.

AMAZON API GATEWAY

GENERAL AMAZON API GATEWAY CONCEPTS

API Gateway is a fully managed service that makes it easy for developers to publish, maintain, monitor, and secure APIs at any scale.

API Gateway supports the following:

- Creating, deploying, and managing a REST application programming interface (API) to expose backend HTTP endpoints, AWS Lambda functions, or other AWS services.

- Creating, deploying, and managing a WebSocket API to expose AWS Lambda functions or other AWS services.

- Invoking exposed API methods through the frontend HTTP and WebSocket endpoints.

Together with Lambda, API Gateway forms the app-facing part of the AWS serverless infrastructure.

Back-end services include Amazon EC2, AWS Lambda or any web application (public or private endpoints).

API Gateway handles all of the tasks involved in accepting and processing up to hundreds of thousands of concurrent API calls.

API calls include traffic management, authorization and access control, monitoring, and API version management.

API Gateway provides a REST API that uses JSON.

API Gateway exposes HTTPS endpoints to define a RESTful API.

All of the APIs created with Amazon API Gateway expose HTTPS endpoints only (does not support unencrypted endpoints).

An API can present a certificate to be authenticated by the back-end.

Can send each API endpoint to a different target.

CloudFront is used as the public endpoint for API Gateway.

Using CloudFront behind the scenes, custom domains, and SNI are supported.

Supports API keys and Usage Plans for user identification, throttling or quota management.

Permissions to invoke a method are granted using IAM roles and policies or API Gateway custom authorizers.

By default API Gateway assigns an internal domain that automatically uses the API Gateway certificates.

When configuring your APIs to run under a custom domain name you can provide your own certificate.

AMAZON API GATEWAY FEATURES

The following table describes some of the core features of Amazon API Gateway.

API Gateway Feature	Benefit
Support for RESTful APIs and WebSocket APIs	With API Gateway, you can create RESTful APIs using either HTTP APIs or REST APIs
Private integrations with AWS ELB & AWS Cloud Map	With API Gateway, you can route requests to private resources in your VPC. Using HTTP APIs, you can build APIs for services behind private ALBs, private NLBs, and IP-based services registered in AWS Cloud Map, such as ECS tasks.
Metering	Define plans that meter and restrict third-party developer access to APIs
Security	API Gateway provides multiple tools to authorize access to APIs and control service operation access
Resiliency	Manage traffic with throttling so that backend operations can withstand traffic spikes
Operations Monitoring	API Gateway provides a metrics dashboard to monitor calls to services
Lifecycle Management	Operate multiple API versions and multiple stages for each version simultaneously so that existing applications can continue to call previous versions after new API versions are published
AWS Authorization	Support for signature version 4 for REST APIs and WebSocket APIs, IAM access policies, and authorization with bearer tokens (e.g. JWT, SAML) using Lambda functions.

ENDPOINTS

An API endpoint type is a hostname for an API in API Gateway that is deployed to a specific region.

The hostname is of the form {api-id}.execute-api.{region}.amazonaws.com.

The API endpoint type can be edge-optimized, regional, or private, depending on where the majority of your API traffic originates from.

Edge-Optimized Endpoint

- An edge-optimized API endpoint is best for geographically distributed clients. API requests are routed to the nearest CloudFront Point of Presence (POP). This is the default endpoint type for API Gateway REST APIs.

- Edge-optimized APIs capitalize the names of HTTP headers (for example, Cookie).

- CloudFront sorts HTTP cookies in natural order by cookie name before forwarding the request to your origin. For more information about the way CloudFront processes cookies, see Caching Content Based on Cookies.

- Any custom domain name that you use for an edge-optimized API applies across all regions.

Regional Endpoint

- A regional API endpoint is intended for clients in the same region.

- When a client running on an EC2 instance calls an API in the same region, or when an API is intended to serve a small number of clients with high demands, a regional API reduces connection overhead.

- For a regional API, any custom domain name that you use is specific to the region where the API is deployed.

- If you deploy a regional API in multiple regions, it can have the same custom domain name in all regions.

- You can use custom domains together with Amazon Route 53 to perform tasks such as latency-based routing.

- Regional API endpoints pass all header names through as-is.

Private Endpoint

- A private API endpoint is an API endpoint that can only be accessed from your Amazon Virtual Private Cloud (VPC) using an interface VPC endpoint, which is an endpoint network interface (ENI) that you create in your VPC.

- Private API endpoints pass all header names through as-is.

The following diagram depicts the three different Amazon API Gateway endpoint types:

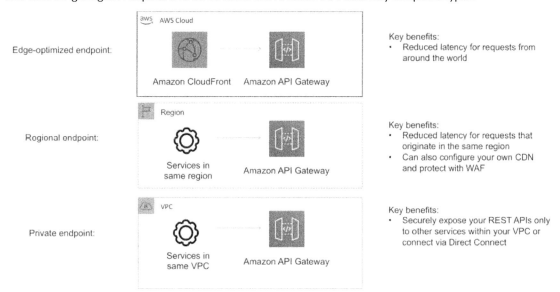

AMAZON API GATEWAY API'S

API Gateway REST API:

- A collection of HTTP resources and methods that are integrated with backend HTTP endpoints, Lambda functions, or other AWS services.

- This collection can be deployed in one or more stages.

- Typically, API resources are organized in a resource tree according to the application logic.

- Each API resource can expose one or more API methods that have unique HTTP verbs supported by API Gateway.

The following diagram depicts the structure of an API:

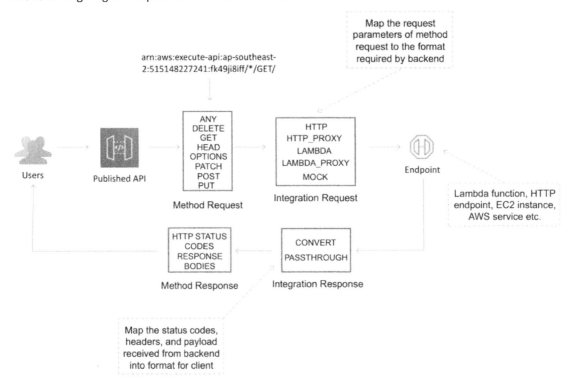

API Gateway WebSocket API:

- A collection of WebSocket routes and route keys that are integrated with backend HTTP endpoints, Lambda functions, or other AWS services.

- The collection can be deployed in one or more stages.

- API methods are invoked through frontend WebSocket connections that you can associate with a registered custom domain name.

METHODS

API Gateway Methods are HTTP methods associated with an API Gateway resource.

Each resource URL can have HTTP methods such as: GET, PUT, POST and DELETE.

AWS also offers the "ANY" method as a catch-all.

DEPLOYMENTS

Deployments are a snapshot of the APIs resources and methods.

Deployments must be created and associated with a stage in order for anyone to access the API.

STAGES AND STAGE VARIABLES

A stage is a logical reference to a lifecycle state of your REST or WebSocket API (for example, 'dev', 'prod', 'beta', 'v2').

API stages are identified by API ID and stage name.

Stage variables are like environment variables for API Gateway.

Stage variables can be used in:

- Lambda function ARN.
- HTTP endpoint.
- Parameter mapping templates.

Use cases for stage variables:

- Configure HTTP endpoints your stages talk to (dev, test, prod etc.).
- Pass configuration parameters to AWS Lambda through mapping templates.

Stage variables are passed to the "context" object in Lambda.

Stage variables are used with Lambda aliases.

You can create a stage variable to indicate the corresponding Lambda alias.

You can create canary deployments for any stage – choose the % of traffic the canary channel receives.

MAPPING TEMPLATES

Mapping templates can be used to modify request / responses.

Rename parameters.

Modify body content.

Add headers.

Map JSON to XML for sending to backend or back to client.

Uses Velocity Template Language (VTL).

Filter output results (remove unnecessary data).

CACHING

You can add caching to API calls by provisioning an Amazon API Gateway cache and specifying its size in gigabytes.

Caching allows you to cache the endpoint's response.

Caching can reduce the number of calls to the backend and improve the latency of requests to the API.

API Gateway caches responses for a specific amount of time (time to live or TTL).

The default TTL is 300 seconds (min 0, max 3600).

Caches are defined per stage.

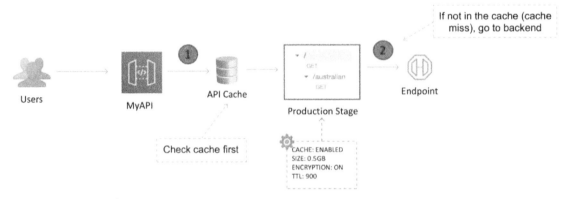

You can encrypt caches.

The cache capacity is between 0.5GB to 237GB.

It is possible to override cache settings for specific methods.

You are able to flush the entire cache (invalidate it) immediately if required.

Clients can invalidate the cache with the header: Cache-Control: max-age=0 .

API THROTTLING

API Gateway sets a limit on a steady-state rate and a burst of request submissions against all APIs in your account.

Limits:

- By default API Gateway limits the steady-state request rate to 10,000 requests per second.
- The maximum concurrent requests is 5,000 requests across all APIs within an AWS account.
- If you go over 10,000 requests per second or 5,000 concurrent requests you will receive a 429 Too Many Requests error response.

Upon catching such exceptions, the client can resubmit the failed requests in a way that is rate-limiting, while complying with the API Gateway throttling limits.

Amazon API Gateway provides two basic types of throttling-related settings:

- **Server-side** throttling limits are applied across all clients. These limit settings exist to prevent your API—and your account—from being overwhelmed by too many requests.

- **Per-client** throttling limits are applied to clients that use API keys associated with your usage policy as a client identifier.

API Gateway throttling-related settings are applied in the following order:

1. Per-client per-method throttling limits that you set for an API stage in a usage plan.

2. Per-client throttling limits that you set in a usage plan.

3. Default per-method limits and individual per-method limits that you set in API stage settings.

4. Account-level throttling.

INTEGRATIONS AND METHOD REQUESTS / RESPONSES

A method represents a client-facing interface by which the client calls the API to access back-end resources.

A Method resource is integrated with an Integration resource.

API methods are integrated with backend endpoints using API integrations.

Backend endpoints are known as "integration endpoints".

Integration request

The internal interface of a WebSocket API route or REST API method in API Gateway, in which you map the body of a route request or the parameters and body of a method request to the formats required by the backend.

Integration response

The internal interface of a WebSocket API route or REST API method in API Gateway, in which you map the status codes, headers, and payload that are received from the backend to the response format that is returned to a client app.

Method request

The public interface of a REST API method in API Gateway that defines the parameters and body that an app developer must send in requests to access the backend through the API

Method response

The public interface of a REST API that defines the status codes, headers, and body models that an app developer should expect in responses from the API.

MAPPING TEMPLATE

A script in Velocity Template Language (VTL) that transforms a request body from the frontend data format to the backend data format, or that transforms a response body from the backend data format to the frontend data format.

Mapping templates can be specified in the integration request or in the integration response. They can reference data made available at run time as context and stage variables.

The mapping can be as simple as an identity transform that passes the headers or body through the integration as-is from the client to the backend for a request.

The same is true for a response, in which the payload is passed from the backend to the client.

INTEGRATION TYPE

You choose an API integration type according to the types of integration endpoint you work with and how you want data to pass to and from the integration endpoint.

For a Lambda function, you can have the Lambda proxy integration, or the Lambda custom integration.

For an HTTP endpoint, you can have the HTTP proxy integration or the HTTP custom integration.

For an AWS service action, you have the AWS integration of the non-proxy type only. API Gateway also supports the mock integration, where API Gateway serves as an integration endpoint to respond to a method request.

The Lambda custom integration is a special case of the AWS integration, where the integration endpoint corresponds to the function-invoking action of the Lambda service.

Programmatically, you choose an integration type by setting the type property on the Integration resource.

For the Lambda proxy integration, the value is AWS_PROXY.

For the Lambda custom integration and all other AWS integrations, it is AWS.

For the HTTP proxy integration and HTTP integration, the value is HTTP_PROXY and HTTP, respectively.

For the mock integration, the type value is MOCK.

The following list summarizes the supported integration types:

AWS:

- This type of integration lets an API expose AWS service actions.

- In AWS integration, you must configure both the integration request and integration response and set up necessary data mappings from the method request to the integration request, and from the integration response to the method response.

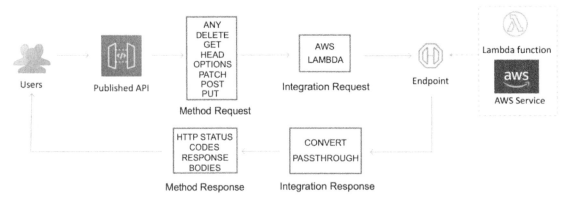

AWS_PROXY:

- This type of integration lets an API method be integrated with the Lambda function invocation action with a flexible, versatile, and streamlined integration setup.

- This integration relies on direct interactions between the client and the integrated Lambda function.

- With this type of integration, also known as the Lambda proxy integration, you do not set the integration request or the integration response.

- API Gateway passes the incoming request from the client as the input to the backend Lambda function.

- The integrated Lambda function takes the <u>input of this format</u> and parses the input from all available sources, including request headers, URL path variables, query string parameters, and applicable body.

- The function returns the result following this <u>output format</u>.

- This is the preferred integration type to call a Lambda function through API Gateway and is not applicable to any other AWS service actions, including Lambda actions other than the function-invoking action.

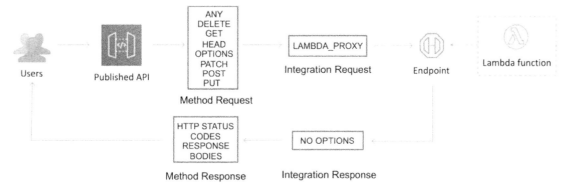

HTTP:

- This type of integration lets an API expose HTTP endpoints in the backend.

- With the HTTP integration, also known as the HTTP custom integration, you must configure both the integration request and integration response.

- You must set up necessary data mappings from the method request to the integration request, and from the integration response to the method response.

HTTP_PROXY:

- The HTTP proxy integration allows a client to access the backend HTTP endpoints with a streamlined integration setup on single API method.

- You do not set the integration request or the integration response.

- API Gateway passes the incoming request from the client to the HTTP endpoint and passes the outgoing response from the HTTP endpoint to the client.

MOCK:

- This type of integration lets API Gateway return a response without sending the request further to the backend.

- This is useful for API testing because it can be used to test the integration set up without incurring charges for using the backend and to enable collaborative development of an API.

- In collaborative development, a team can isolate their development effort by setting up simulations of API components owned by other teams by using the MOCK integrations.

- It is also used to return CORS-related headers to ensure that the API method permits CORS access.

- In fact, the API Gateway console integrates the OPTIONS method to support CORS with a mock integration.

- Gateway responses are other examples of mock integrations.

MOCK INTEGRATION

In a mock integration, API responses are generated from API Gateway directly, without the need for an integration backend.

As an API developer, you decide how API Gateway responds to a mock integration request.

For this, you configure the method's integration request and integration response to associate a response with a given status code.

MODEL

A data schema specifying the data structure of a request or response payload.

A model is required for generating a strongly typed SDK of an API.

It is also used to validate payloads.

A model is convenient for generating a sample mapping template to initiate creation of a production mapping template.

Although useful, a model is not required for creating a mapping template.

USAGE PLANS AND API KEYS

A usage plan specifies who can access one or more deployed API stages and methods — and also how much and how fast they can access them.

You can use a usage plan to configure throttling and quota limits, which are enforced on individual client API keys.

The plan uses API keys to identify API clients and meters access to the associated API stages for each key.

It also lets you configure throttling limits and quota limits that are enforced on individual client API keys.

API keys are alphanumeric string values that you distribute to app developer customers to grant access to your API.

You can use API keys together with usage plans or Lambda authorizers to control access to your APIs.

API Gateway can generate API keys on your behalf, or you can import them from a CSV file.

You can generate an API key in API Gateway, or import it into API Gateway from an external source.

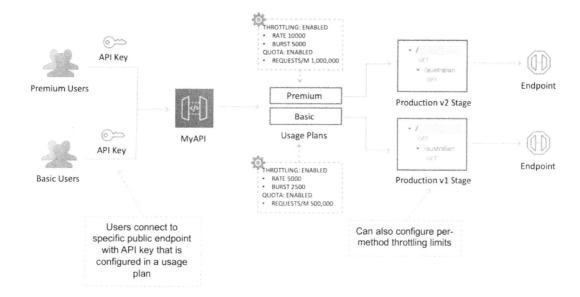

SAME ORIGIN POLICY

Used to prevent cross-site scripting attacks.

Web browser permits scripts in a first web page to access data in a second web page but only if the web pages have the same origin.

This is enforced by web browsers.

CROSS-ORIGIN RESOURCE SHARING (CORS)

Can enable Cross Origin Resource Sharing (CORS) for multiple domain use with Javascript/AJAX.

CORS is one way that the server at the other end (not the client code in the browser) can relax the same-origin policy.

CORS allows restricted resources (e.g. fonts) on a web page to be requested from another domain outside the domain from which the first resource was shared.

Using CORS:

- Can enable CORS on API Gateway if using JavaScript / AJAX.

- Can be used to enable requests from domains other than the APIs domain.

- Allows the sharing of resources between different domains.

- The method (GET, PUT, POST etc) for which you will enable CORS must be available in the API Gateway API before you enable CORS.

- If CORS is not enabled and an API resource received requests from another domain the request will be blocked.

- Enable CORS on the API resources using the selected methods under the API Gateway.

SECURITY

There are several mechanisms for controlling and managing access to an API.

These mechanisms include:

- Resource-based policies.
- Standard IAM Roles and Policies (identity-based policies).
- IAM Tags.
- Endpoint policies for interface VPC endpoints.
- Lambda authorizers.
- Amazon Cognito user pools.

IAM Resource-Based Policies

Amazon API Gateway resource policies are JSON policy documents that you attach to an API to control whether a specified principal (typically an IAM user or role) can invoke the API.

You can use API Gateway resource policies to allow your API to be securely invoked by:

- Users from a specified AWS account.
- Specified source IP address ranges or CIDR blocks.
- Specified virtual private clouds (VPCs) or VPC endpoints (in any account).
- You can use resource policies for all API endpoint types in API Gateway: private, edge-optimized, and Regional.

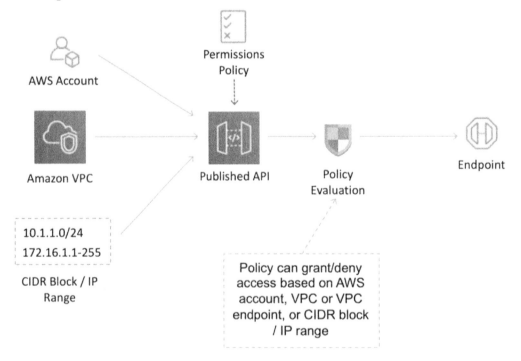

IAM Identity-Based Policies

You need to create IAM policies and attach to users / roles.

API Gateway verifies IAM permissions passed by the calling application.

Leverages sigv4 capability where IAM credentials are passed in headers.

Handles authentication and authorization.

Great for user / roles within your AWS account.

Lambda Authorizer

Use AWS Lambda to validate the token in the header being passed.

Option to cache the result of the authentication.

Lambda must return an IAM policy for the user.

You pay per Lambda invocation.

Handles authentication and authorization.

Good for using OAuth, SAML or 3rd party authentication.

1. Client calls API method, passing bearer token or request parameters.
2. API Gateway calls the Lambda authorizer.
3. Lambda function authenticates the user using:
   - Call OAuth provider to get token.
   - Call SAML provider to get assertion.
   - Generate IAM Policy based on request parameters.
4. If successful, Lambda grants access and returns IAM policy and a principal identifier.
5. API Gateway evaluates the policy:
   - If access is allowed, execute the method.
   - If access is denied, return status code (e.g. 403).

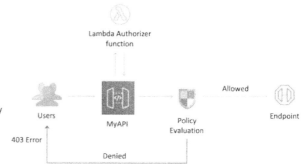

COGNITO USER POOLS

A user pool is a user directory in Amazon Cognito.

With a user pool, users can sign in to a web or mobile app through Amazon Cognito.

Users can also sign in through social identity providers like Google, Facebook, Amazon, or Apple, and through SAML identity providers.

Whether your users sign in directly or through a third party, all members of the user pool have a directory profile that you can access through a Software Development Kit (SDK).

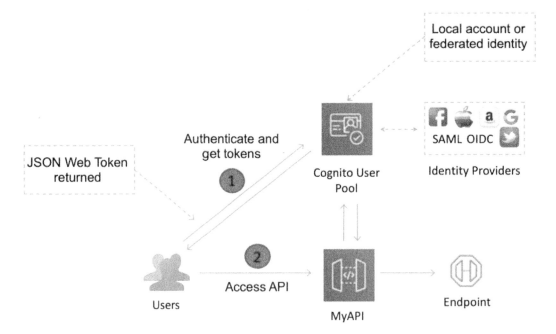

User pools provide:

- Sign-up and sign-in services.

- A built-in, customizable web UI to sign in users.

- Social sign-in with Facebook, Google, Login with Amazon, and Sign in with Apple, as well as sign-in with SAML identity providers from your user pool.

- User directory management and user profiles.

- Security features such as multi-factor authentication (MFA).

ADDITIONAL FEATURES AND BENEFITS

API Gateway provides several features that assist with creating and managing APIs:

- Metering – Define plans that meter and restrict third-party developer access to APIs.

- Security – API Gateway provides multiple tools to authorize access to APIs and control service operation access.

- Resiliency – Manage traffic with throttling so that backend operations can withstand traffic spikes.

- Operations Monitoring – API Gateway provides a metrics dashboard to monitor calls to services.

- Lifecycle Management – Operate multiple API versions and multiple stages for each version simultaneously so that existing applications can continue to call previous versions after new API versions are published.

API Gateway provides robust, secure, and scalable access to backend APIs and hosts multiple versions and release stages for your APIs.

You can create and distribute API Keys to developers.

Option to use AWS Sig-v4 to authorize access to APIs.

You can throttle and monitor requests to protect your backend.

API Gateway allows you to maintain a cache to store API responses.

SDK Generation for iOS, Android and JavaScript.

Reduced latency and distributed denial of service protection through the use of CloudFront.

Request/response data transformation and API mocking.

Resiliency through throttling rules based on the number of requests per second for each HTTP method (GET, PUT).

Throttling can be configured at multiple levels including Global and Service Call.

A cache can be created and specified in gigabytes (not enabled by default).

Caches are provisioned for a specific stage of your APIs.

Caching features include customizable keys and time-to-live (TTL) in seconds for your API data which enhances response times and reduces load on back-end services.

API Gateway can scale to any level of traffic received by an API.

LOGGING AND MONITORING

The Amazon API Gateway logs (near real time) back-end performance metrics such as API calls, latency, and error rates to CloudWatch.

You can monitor through the API Gateway dashboard (REST API) allowing you to visually monitor calls to the services.

API Gateway also meters utilization by third-party developers and the data is available in the API Gateway console and through APIs.

Amazon API Gateway is integrated with AWS CloudTrail to give a full auditable history of the changes to your REST APIs.

All API calls made to the Amazon API Gateway APIs to create, modify, delete, or deploy REST APIs are logged to CloudTrail.

Understanding the following metrics is useful for the exam:

- Monitor the IntegrationLatency metrics to measure the responsiveness of the backend.

- Monitor the Latency metrics to measure the overall responsiveness of your API calls.

- Monitor the CacheHitCount and CacheMissCount metrics to optimize cache capacities to achieve a desired performance.

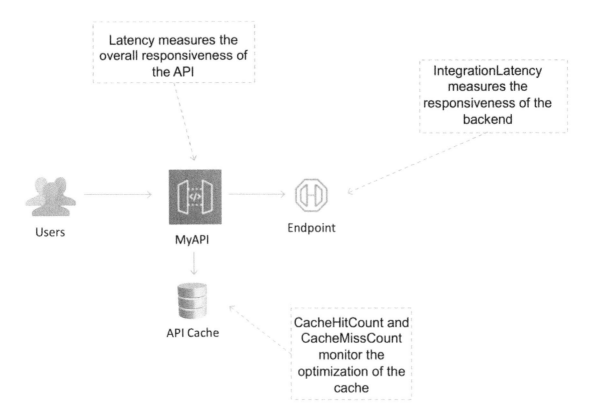

OPEN API / SWAGGER

Can import existing Swagger / Open API 3.0 definitions (written in YAML or JSON) to API Gateway.

This is a common way of defining REST APIs using API definition as code.

Can also export current APIs as Swagger / Open API 3.0 definition.

Uses the API Gateway Import API feature to import an API from an external definition.

With the import API you can either create a new API by submitting a POST request that includes a Swagger definition in the payload and endpoint configuration or you can update an existing API by using a PUT request that contains a Swagger definition, or merge a definition with an existing API.

You specify the options using a mode query parameter in the request URL.

CHARGES

With Amazon API Gateway, you only pay when your APIs are in use.

There are no minimum fees or upfront commitments.

You pay only for the API calls you receive and the amount of data transferred out.

There are no data transfer out charges for Private APIs (however, AWS PrivateLink charges apply when using Private APIs in Amazon API Gateway).

Amazon API Gateway also provides optional data caching charged at an hourly rate that varies based on the cache size you select.

The API Gateway free tier includes one million API calls per month for up to 12 months.

NETWORKING AND CONTENT DELIVERY QUIZ QUESTIONS

Question 1: At which level do you attach an Internet gateway?

1. Public Subnet

2. Private Subnet

3. Availability Zone

4. VPC

Question 2: What is the scope of a Virtual Private Cloud (VPC)?

1. Global

2. Regional

3. Availability Zone

Question 3: How should subnets be used for fault tolerance?

1. Create subnets that span multiple availability zones

2. Create subnets that have multiple Internet Gateways

3. Launch EC2 instances into subnets attached to a region

4. Launch EC2 instances into subnets created in different availability zones

Question 5: Your organization has a pre-production VPC and production VPC. You need to be able to setup routing between these VPCs using private IP addresses. How can this be done?

1. Configure a VPC endpoint

2. Add a route table entry for the opposite VPCs Internet gateway

3. Configure a peering connection

4. Use an Egress-only Internet gateway

Question 6: You created a new private subnet and created a route table with a path to a NAT gateway. However, EC2 instances launched into this subnet are not able to reach the Internet. Security Groups for the EC2 instances are setup correctly. What is the most likely explanation?

1. The security group for the NAT gateway is setup incorrectly.

2. You need to associate the new subnet with the new route table.

3. You need to add an entry for an Internet gateway.

Question 7: You need to apply a firewall to a group of EC2 instances launched in multiple subnets. Which option should be used?

1. Network Access Control List (ACL)

2. Operating system firewall

3. Security Group

4. IAM Policy

Question 8: A Developer needs to point the domain name dctlabs.com to the DNS name of an Elastic Load Balancer. Which type of record should be used?

1. MX record

2. A record

3. CNAME record

4. Alias record

Question 9: A company hosts copies of the same data in Amazon S3 buckets around the world and needs to ensure that customers connect to the nearest S3 bucket. Which Route 53 routing policy should be used?

1. Simple

2. Failover

3. Latency

4. Weighted

Question 10: A media organization offers news in local languages around the world. Which Route 53 routing policy should be used to direct readers to the website with the correct language?

1. Latency

2. Geolocation

3. Multivalue answer

4. Weighted

Question 11: A Developer needs to create a DNS record in AWS Route 53 for a website running on an Amazon EC2 instance. The record should map the domain name www.dctlabs.com to dctlabs.com. Which record type should the Developer use?

1. CNAME

2. NS

3. PTR

4. TXT

Question 12: A Developer is deploying an Amazon S3 Static Website. The website will have the domain name dctlabs.com. How can the developer setup an AWS Route 53 DNS record that points users to the bucket using the URL HTTP://dctlabs.com?

1. Add a CNAME record for dctlabs.com that points to the S3 static website endpoint

2. Add an Alias record that points to the S3 static website endpoint

3. Add an Alias record that points to the S3 static website IP address

Question 13: Which services form the app-facing part of the AWS serverless infrastructure?

1. Amazon ECS and Amazon API Gateway

2. AWS Lambda and Amazon SNS

3. Amazon API Gateway and Amazon Kinesis

4. AWS Lambda and Amazon API Gateway

Question 14: A Developer is configuring the integration between AWS Lambda and an Amazon API Gateway method. The Developer wants to pass the raw request as-is to the Lambda function. Which integration type should be used?

1. Use a Mock integration

2. Use a Lambda proxy integration

3. Use an AWS Service integration

Question 15: Which type of Amazon API Gateway endpoint is ideal for geographically distributed clients?

1. Edge-Optimized Endpoint

2. Regional Endpoint

3. Private Endpoint

Question 16: A Developer has created an Amazon API Gateway REST API. The API is ready for testing. How can the Developer publish the API so the test applications can access it?

1. Deploy a method

2. Deploy with a mapping template

3. Deploy to a stage

Question 17: A company has deployed a REST API using Amazon API Gateway. Their customers pay for different tiers of access and the company needs to be able to specify different usage limits for each tier. How can this be achieved?

1. Create different usage plans with the relevant limits and provide API keys to the customers

2. Create different usage plans with the relevant limits and provide access keys to the customers

3. Create separate IAM policies that provide the necessary permissions and assign them to different API stages

Question 18: A Developer wants to implement a bearer token system for authorizing access to a REST API running on Amazon API Gateway. The system should return an IAM policy as output and use JSON web tokens. What should the Developer implement?

1. An API authorizer

2. A Lambda authorizer

3. An IAM authorizer

NETWORKING AND CONTENT DELIVERY - QUIZ QUESTIONS & ANSWERS

Question 1: At which level do you attach an Internet gateway?

1. Public Subnet

2. Private Subnet

3. Availability Zone

4. VPC

Question 1, Answer 4

Explanation:

1 is incorrect. You do not attach Internet gateways to subnets.

2 is incorrect. You do not attach Internet gateways to subnets.

3 is incorrect. You do not attach Internet gateways to AZs.

4 is correct. Internet Gateways are attached to the VPC. You then need to add entries to the route tables for your public subnets to point to the IGW.

Question 2: What is the scope of a Virtual Private Cloud (VPC)?

1. Global

2. Regional

3. Availability Zone

Question 2, Answer 2

Explanation:

1 is incorrect. VPCs are not global.

2 is correct. VPCs are regional. You create VPCs in each region separately.

3 is incorrect. An availability zone exists within a region and a VPC can span subnets attached to all AZs in the region.

Question 3: How should subnets be used for fault tolerance?

1. Create subnets that span multiple availability zones

2. Create subnets that have multiple Internet Gateways

3. Launch EC2 instances into subnets attached to a region

4. Launch EC2 instances into subnets created in different availability zones

Question 3, Answer 4

Explanation:

1 is incorrect. Subnets cannot span multiple AZs.

2 is incorrect. You cannot have multiple IGWs attached to a VPC.

3 is incorrect. You cannot attach a subnet to a region.

4 is correct. You should create multiple subnets each within a different AZ and launch EC2 instances running your application across these subnets.

Question 5: Your organization has a pre-production VPC and production VPC. You need to be able to setup routing between these VPCs using private IP addresses. How can this be done?

1. Configure a VPC endpoint

2. Add a route table entry for the opposite VPCs Internet gateway

3. Configure a peering connection

4. Use an Egress-only Internet gateway

Question 5, Answer 3

Explanation:

1 is incorrect. A VPC endpoint can be used for sharing resources between VPCs but it is not used for direct routing between private IP addresses.

2 is incorrect. You cannot route between VPCs by using Internet gateways.

3 is correct. A peering connection enables you to route traffic via private IP addresses between two peered VPCs.

4 is incorrect. An egress-only Internet gateway is used for IPv6 traffic.

Question 6: You created a new private subnet and created a route table with a path to a NAT gateway. However, EC2 instances launched into this subnet are not able to reach the Internet. Security Groups for the EC2 instances are setup correctly. What is the most likely explanation?

1. The security group for the NAT gateway is setup incorrectly.

2. You need to associate the new subnet with the new route table.

3. You need to add an entry for an Internet gateway.

Question 6, Answer 2

Explanation:

1 is incorrect. NAT gateways do not have security groups.

2 is correct. By default new subnets are associated with the default route table. You need to assign the new route table in order for the instances to see the route to the NAT gateway.

3 is incorrect. You cannot use an Internet Gateway with a private subnet as the instances will not have public IP addresses.

Question 7: You need to apply a firewall to a group of EC2 instances launched in multiple subnets. Which option should be used?

1. Network Access Control List (ACL)

2. Operating system firewall

3. Security Group

4. IAM Policy

Question 7, Answer 3

Explanation:

1 is incorrect. Network ACLs are applied at the subnet level and will apply to all instances in the subnet, not just the group of EC2 instances.

2 is incorrect. Operating system-level firewalls require more administrative effort to maintain and are not the best option on AWS.

3 is correct. A Security Group can be applied to the group of EC2 instances. You can specify what ports and protocols are allowed to reach the instances and from what sources.

4 is incorrect. An IAM Policy is not a firewall.

Question 8: A Developer needs to point the domain name dctlabs.com to the DNS name of an Elastic Load Balancer. Which type of record should be used?

1. MX record

2. A record

3. CNAME record

4. Alias record

Question 8, Answer 4

Explanation:

1 is incorrect. An MX record is a mail exchanger record for email servers.

2 is incorrect. An A record simply points a name to an IP address.

3 is incorrect. A CNAME record cannot be pointed at a domain apex record like dctlabs.com.

4 is correct. An Alias record can be used with domain apex records and can point to an ELB.

Question 9: A company hosts copies of the same data in Amazon S3 buckets around the world and needs to ensure that customers connect to the nearest S3 bucket. Which Route 53 routing policy should be used?

1. Simple

2. Failover

3. Latency

4. Weighted

Question 9, Answer 3

Explanation:

1 is incorrect. The simple routing policy does not perform any routing based on location or latency.

2 is incorrect. The failover routing policy uses primary and secondary records for high availability.

3 is correct. The latency routing policy directs based on the lowest latency to the AWS resource. Latency increases over distance so this should ensure customers connect to the closest S3 bucket.

4 is incorrect. The weighted policy uses relative weights not location or latency.

Question 10: A media organization offers news in local languages around the world. Which Route 53 routing policy should be used to direct readers to the website with the correct language?

1. Latency

2. Geolocation

3. Multivalue answer

4. Weighted

Question 10, Answer 2

Explanation:

1 is incorrect. The latency routing policy directs based on latency (distance) but does not allow you to specify geographic locations.

2 is correct. In this case you need to identify specific geographic locations and associate them with the correct language version.

3 is incorrect. This routing policy returns multiple answers for load balancing.

4 is incorrect. The weighted policy uses relative weights not geographic information.

Question 11: A Developer needs to create a DNS record in AWS Route 53 for a website running on an Amazon EC2 instance. The record should map the domain name www.dctlabs.com to dctlabs.com. Which record type should the Developer use?

1. CNAME

2. NS

3. PTR

4. TXT

Question 11, Answer 1

Explanation:

1 is correct. This is the only record type shown that can be used for this use case.

2 is incorrect. This is a name server record.

3 is incorrect. This is a pointer record that points an IP address to a DNS name.

4 is incorrect. This is a text record.

Question 12: A Developer is deploying an Amazon S3 Static Website. The website will have the domain name dctlabs.com. How can the developer setup an AWS Route 53 DNS record that points users to the bucket using the URL HTTP://dctlabs.com?

1. Add a CNAME record for dctlabs.com that points to the S3 static website endpoint

2. Add an Alias record that points to the S3 static website endpoint

3. Add an Alias record that points to the S3 static website IP address

Question 12, Answer 2

Explanation:

1 is incorrect. You cannot create a CNAME for the zone apex (e.g. dctlabs.com rather than www.dctlabs.com).

2 is correct. You can create an Alias record that points to endpoints including Amazon Elastic Load Balancing load balancers, Amazon CloudFront distributions, AWS Elastic Beanstalk environments, or Amazon S3 buckets that are configured as websites.

3 is incorrect. You cannot point an Alias record to an IP address and there is no IP address for an S3 static website anyway.

Question 13: Which services form the app-facing part of the AWS serverless infrastructure?

1. Amazon ECS and Amazon API Gateway

2. AWS Lambda and Amazon SNS

3. Amazon API Gateway and Amazon Kinesis

4. AWS Lambda and Amazon API Gateway

Question 13, Answer 4

Explanation:

1 is incorrect. Amazon ECS is not an app-facing part of the AWS serverless infrastructure.

2 is incorrect. Amazon SNS is not an app-facing part of the AWS serverless infrastructure.

3 is incorrect. Amazon Kinesis is not an app-facing part of the AWS serverless infrastructure.

4 is correct. Together with Lambda, API Gateway forms the app-facing part of the AWS serverless infrastructure.

Question 14: A Developer is configuring the integration between AWS Lambda and an Amazon API Gateway method. The Developer wants to pass the raw request as-is to the Lambda function. Which integration type should be used?

1. Use a Mock integration

2. Use a Lambda proxy integration

3. Use an AWS Service integration

Question 14, Answer 2

Explanation:

1 is incorrect. This is used more for testing and will not integrate with the Lambda function.

2 is correct. In Lambda proxy integration, when a client submits an API request, API Gateway passes to the integrated Lambda function the raw request as-is, except that the order of the request parameters is not preserved.

4 is incorrect. This can be used to integrate with other AWS services but should not be used for Lambda

Question 15: Which type of Amazon API Gateway endpoint is ideal for geographically distributed clients?

1. Edge-Optimized Endpoint

2. Regional Endpoint

3. Private Endpoint

Question 15, Answer 1

Explanation:

1 is correct. An edge-optimized API endpoint is best for geographically distributed clients. API requests are routed to the nearest CloudFront Point of Presence (POP). This is the default endpoint type for API Gateway REST APIs.

2 is incorrect. A regional API endpoint is intended for clients in the same region.

3 is incorrect. A private API endpoint is an API endpoint that can only be accessed from your Amazon Virtual Private Cloud (VPC) using an interface VPC endpoint, which is an endpoint network interface (ENI) that you create in your VPC.

Question 16: A Developer has created an Amazon API Gateway REST API. The API is ready for testing. How can the Developer publish the API so the test applications can access it?

1. Deploy a method

2. Deploy with a mapping template

3. Deploy to a stage

Question 16, Answer 3

Explanation:

1 is incorrect. API Gateway Methods are HTTP methods associated with an API Gateway resource. You do not deploy to a method.

2 is incorrect. Mapping templates can be used to modify request / responses. They are not used for deploying the API for testing.

3 is correct. A stage is a logical reference to a lifecycle state of your REST or WebSocket API (for example, 'dev', 'prod', 'beta', 'v2'). The API should be deployed to a test stage.

Question 17: A company has deployed a REST API using Amazon API Gateway. Their customers pay for different tiers of access and the company needs to be able to specify different usage limits for each tier. How can this be achieved?

1. Create different usage plans with the relevant limits and provide API keys to the customers

2. Create different usage plans with the relevant limits and provide access keys to the customers

3. Create separate IAM policies that provide the necessary permissions and assign them to different API stages

Question 17, Answer 1

Explanation:

1 is correct. A usage plan specifies who can access one or more deployed API stages and methods — and also how much and how fast they can access them. You can use a usage plan to configure throttling and quota limits, which are enforced on individual client API keys. The plan uses API keys to identify API clients and meters access to the associated API stages for each key.

2 is incorrect. Access keys are not associated with usage plans.

3 is incorrect. You cannot assign usage limits using IAM policies.

Question 18: A Developer wants to implement a bearer token system for authorizing access to a REST API running on Amazon API Gateway. The system should return an IAM policy as output and use JSON web tokens. What should the Developer implement?

1. An API authorizer

2. A Lambda authorizer

3. An IAM authorizer

Question 18, Answer 2

Explanation:

1 is incorrect. There's no such thing as an API authorizer.

2 is correct. A Lambda authorizer (formerly known as a custom authorizer) is an API Gateway feature that uses a Lambda function to control access to your API. A Lambda authorizer is useful if you want to implement a custom authorization scheme that uses a bearer token authentication strategy such as OAuth or SAML, or that uses request parameters to determine the caller's identity. When a client makes a request to one of your API's methods, API Gateway calls your Lambda authorizer, which takes the caller's identity as input and returns an IAM policy as output.

3 is incorrect. You can configure IAM to authorize access to your API however it does not use tokens.

AWS DEVELOPER TOOLS

AWS CODECOMMIT

GENERAL AWS CODECOMMIT CONCEPTS

AWS CodeCommit is a fully-managed source control service that hosts secure Git-based repositories.

Git is an Open Source distributed source control system:

- Centralized repository for all of your code, binaries, images, and libraries.

- Tracks and manages code changes.

- Maintains version history.

- Manages updates from multiple sources.

- Enables collaboration.

It makes it easy for teams to collaborate on code in a secure and highly scalable ecosystem.

CodeCommit eliminates the need to operate your own source control system or worry about scaling its infrastructure.

You can use CodeCommit to securely store anything from source code to binaries, and it works seamlessly with your existing Git tools.

Provides version control for version changes that happen over time.

You can easily commit, branch, and merge your code.

CodeCommit repositories are private.

CodeCommit scales seamlessly.

CodeCommit is integrated with Jenkins, CodeBuild and other CI tools.

CodeCommit is one of the AWS continuous integration tools (CodeBuild compiles and test code):

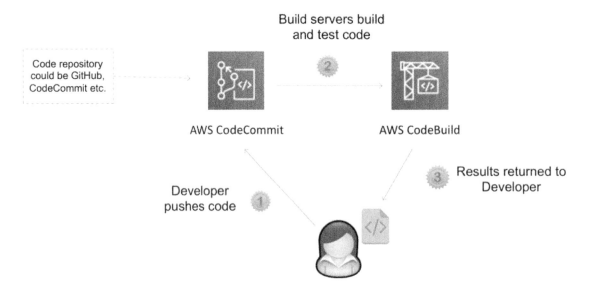

ENCRYPTION

You can transfer your files to and from AWS CodeCommit using HTTPS or SSH.

Repositories are automatically encrypted at rest through AWS Key Management Service (AWS KMS) using customer-specific keys.

AUTHENTICATION AND ACCESS CONTROL

AWS CodeCommit uses AWS Identity and Access Management to control and monitor who can access data as well as how, when, and where they can access it.

CodeCommit also helps monitor your repositories via AWS CloudTrail and AWS CloudWatch.

AUTHENTICATION

You need to configure your Git client to communicate with CodeCommit repositories.

As part of this configuration, you provide IAM credentials that CodeCommit can use to authenticate you.

IAM supports CodeCommit with three types of credentials:

- Git credentials, an IAM -generated user name and password pair you can use to communicate with CodeCommit repositories over HTTPS.
- SSH keys, a locally generated public-private key pair that you can associate with your IAM user to communicate with CodeCommit repositories over SSH.
- AWS access keys, which you can use with the credential helper included with the AWS CLI to communicate with CodeCommit repositories over HTTPS.

AUTHORIZATION

IAM policies for authorizing access for users/roles to repositories.

CodeCommit only supports identity-based policies, not resource-based policies.

You can attach tags to CodeCommit resources or pass tags in a request to CodeCommit.

To control access based on tags, you provide tag information in the condition element of a policy using the codecommit:ResourceTag/key-name, aws:RequestTag/key-name, or aws:TagKeys condition keys.

NOTIFICATIONS

You can trigger notifications in CodeCommit using AWS SNS or AWS Lambda or AWS CloudWatch Event rules.

Notifications are in relation to pull request and comment events – triggers are related to pushing to a branch or creating / deleting a branch.

Use cases for notifications SNS / AWS Lambda:

- Deletion of branches.
- Trigger for pushes that happen in the master branch.
- Notify external build system.

- Trigger AWS Lambda function to perform codebase analysis.

Use cases for CloudWatch Event Rules:

- Trigger for pull request updates (created / updated / deleted / commented).
- Commit comment events.
- CloudWatch Event Rules go into an SNS Topic.

AWS CODEBUILD

GENERAL AWS CODEBUILD CONCEPTS

AWS CodeBuild is a fully managed continuous integration (CI) service that compiles source code, runs tests, and produces software packages that are ready to deploy.

With CodeBuild, you don't need to provision, manage, and scale your own build servers.

CodeBuild scales continuously and processes multiple builds concurrently, so your builds are not left waiting in a queue.

CodeBuild is an alternative to other build tools such as Jenkins.

CodeBuild scales continuously and processes multiple builds concurrently.

You pay based on the time it takes to complete the builds.

AWS CodeBuild runs your builds in preconfigured build environments that contain the operating system, programming language runtime, and build tools (e.g., Apache Maven, Gradle, npm) required to complete the task.

It is possible to extend capabilities by leveraging your own Docker images.

CodeBuild is integrated with KMS for encryption of build artifacts, IAM for build permissions, VPC for network security, and CloudTrail for logging API calls.

CodeBuild takes source code from GitHub, CodeCommit, CodePipleine, S3 etc.

Build instructions can be defined in the code (buildspec.yml).

Output logs can be sent to Amazon S3 & AWS CloudWatch Logs.

There are metrics to monitor CodeBuild statistics.

You can use CloudWatch alarms to detect failed builds and trigger SNS notifications.

Builds can be defined within CodePipeline or CodeBuild itself.

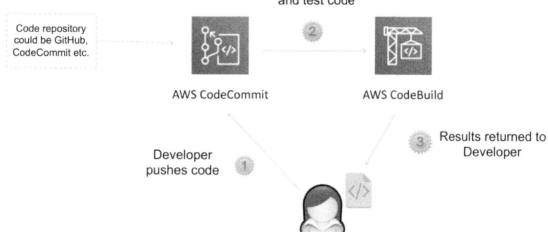

BENEFITS OF CODEBUILD

Fully managed by AWS.

On-demand and scales seamlessly.

Pre-configured environments for many programming languages.

CODEBUILD CONCEPTS

Build project – defines how CodeBuild will run a build defines settings including:

-
    - Location of the source code.
    - The build environment to use.
    - The build commands to run.
    - Where to store the output of the build.

Build environment – the operating system, language runtime, and tools that CodeBuild uses for the build.

Build Specification – a YAML file that describes the collection of commands and settings for CodeBuild to run a build.

PRECONFIGURED BUILD ENVIRONMENTS

AWS CodeBuild provides build environments for Java, Python, Node.js, Ruby, Go, Android, .NET Core for Linux, and Docker.

Customized build environments

You can bring your own build environments to use with AWS CodeBuild, such as for the Microsoft .NET Framework.

You can package the runtime and tools for your build into a Docker image and upload it to a public Docker Hub repository or Amazon EC2 Container Registry (Amazon ECR).

When you create a new build project, you can specify the location of your Docker image, and CodeBuild will pull the image and use it as the build project configuration.

Specifying build commands

You can define the specific commands that you want AWS CodeBuild to perform, such as installing build tool packages, running unit tests, and packaging your code.

The build specification is a YAML file that lets you choose the commands to run at each phase of the build and other settings.

You can override the default buildspec file name and location.

CodeBuild helps you get started quickly with sample build specification files for common scenarios, such as builds using Apache Maven, Gradle, or npm.

The code sample shows the contents of a buildspec.yml file that is being used to build a Docker image and push it to Amazon Elastic Container Registry (ECR):

```
version: 0.2

phases:
install:

runtime-versions:

docker: 18

pre_build:

commands:

- echo Logging in to Amazon ECR...

- $(aws ecr get-login --no-include-email --region $AWS_DEFAULT_REGION)
build:

commands:

- echo Build started on `date`

- echo Building the Docker image...

- docker build -t $IMAGE_REPO_NAME:$IMAGE_TAG .
```

```
-                    docker          tag          $IMAGE_REPO_NAME:$IMAGE_TAG
$AWS_ACCOUNT_ID.dkr.ecr.$AWS_DEFAULT_REGION.amazonaws.com/$IMAGE_REPO_NAME:$IMAG
E_TAG
```

post_build:

commands:

- echo Build completed on `date`

- echo Pushing the Docker image...

```
-                              docker                              push
$AWS_ACCOUNT_ID.dkr.ecr.$AWS_DEFAULT_REGION.amazonaws.com/$IMAGE_REPO_NAME:$IMAG
E_TAG
```

Exam tip: You must have a buildspec.yml file at the root of your source code.

You can define environment variables:

- Plaintext variables.
- Secure secrets using the SSM Parameter store.

Phases:

- Install: install dependencies you may need for the build.
- Pre-build: final commands to execute before build.
- Build: actual build commands.
- Post build: finishing touches (e.g. zip file output).

Artifacts: these get uploaded to S3 (encrypted with KMS).

Cache: files to cache (usually dependencies) to S3 for future builds.

CODEBUILD LOCAL BUILD

In case you need to do deep troubleshooting beyond analyzing log files.

Can run CodeBuild locally on your computer using Docker.

Leverages the CodeBuild agent.

AWS CODEDEPLOY

GENERAL AWS CODEDEPLOY CONCEPTS

CodeDeploy is a deployment service that automates application deployments to Amazon EC2 instances, on-premises instances, serverless Lambda functions, or Amazon ECS services.

You can deploy a nearly unlimited variety of application content, including:

- Serverless AWS Lambda functions.
- Web and configuration files.
- Executables.
- Packages.
- Scripts.
- Multimedia files.

CodeDeploy can deploy application content that runs on a server and is stored in Amazon S3 buckets, GitHub repositories, or Bitbucket repositories.

CodeDeploy can also deploy a serverless Lambda function.

You do not need to make changes to your existing code before you can use CodeDeploy.

Can be used to automatically deploy applications to many EC2 instances.

Similar open source tools include Ansible, Terraform, Chef, Puppet etc.

Integrates with various CI/CD tools including Jenkins, GitHub, Atlassian, AWS CodePipeline as well as config management tools like Ansible, Puppet and Chef.

CodeDeploy is a fully managed service.

There's lots of flexibility to define any kind of deployment.

CodeDeploy can be connected to CodePipeline and use artifacts from there.

CodeDeploy can use re-use existing setup tools, works with any application, auto scaling integration.

CODEDEPLOY APPLICATION

An AWS CodeDeploy application contains information about what to deploy and how to deploy it.

Need to choose the compute platform:

- EC2/On-premises.
- AWS Lambda.
- Amazon ECS.

EC2/On-Premises:

- Amazon EC2 cloud instances, on-premises servers, or both.
- Deployments that use the EC2/On-Premises compute platform manage the way in which traffic is directed to instances by using an in-place or blue/green deployment type.

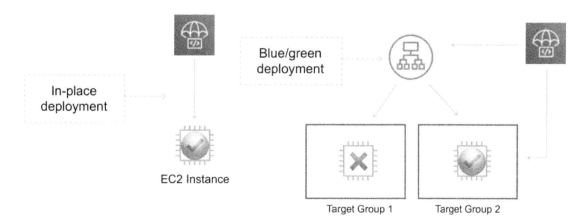

AWS Lambda:

- Used to deploy applications that consist of an updated version of a Lambda function.
- You can manage the way in which traffic is shifted to the updated Lambda function versions during a deployment by choosing a canary, linear, or all-at-once configuration.

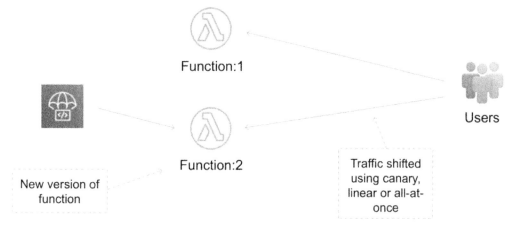

Amazon ECS:

- Used to deploy an Amazon ECS containerized application as a task set.
- CodeDeploy performs a blue/green deployment by installing an updated version of the application as a new replacement task set.
- CodeDeploy reroutes production traffic from the original application task set to the replacement task set.
- The original task set is terminated after a successful deployment.
- You can manage the way in which traffic is shifted to the updated task set during a deployment by choosing a canary, linear, or all-at-once configuration.

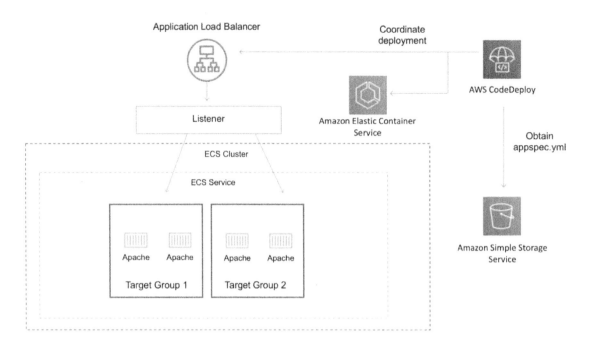

DEPLOYMENT GROUP

Each deployment group belongs to one application and specifies:

- A deployment configuration – a set of deployment rules as well as success / failure conditions used during a deployment.

- Notifications configuration for deployment events.

- Amazon CloudWatch alarms to monitor a deployment.

- Deployment rollback configuration.

Deployment Type

CodeDeploy provides two deployment type options – in-place and blue/green.

In-place deployment:

- The application on each instance in the deployment group is stopped, the latest application revision is installed, and the new version of the application is started and validated.

- You can use a load balancer so that each instance is deregistered during its deployment and then restored to service after the deployment is complete.

- Only deployments that use the EC2/On-Premises compute platform can use in-place deployments.

Exam tip: AWS Lambda and Amazon ECS deployments cannot use an in-place deployment type.

Blue/green on an EC2/On-Premises compute platform:

- The instances in a deployment group (the original environment) are replaced by a different set of instances (the replacement environment) using these steps:

  - Instances are provisioned for the replacement environment.

  - The latest application revision is installed on the replacement instances.

  - An optional wait time occurs for activities such as application testing and system verification.

  - Instances in the replacement environment are registered with an Elastic Load Balancing load balancer, causing traffic to be rerouted to them.

  - Instances in the original environment are deregistered and can be terminated or kept running for other uses.

Note: If you use an EC2/On-Premises compute platform, be aware that blue/green deployments work with Amazon EC2 instances only.

Blue/green on an AWS Lambda compute platform:

- Traffic is shifted from your current serverless environment to one with your updated Lambda function versions.

- You can specify Lambda functions that perform validation tests and choose the way in which the traffic shifting occurs.

- All AWS Lambda compute platform deployments are blue/green deployments.

- For this reason, you do not need to specify a deployment type.

Blue/green on an Amazon ECS compute platform:

- Traffic is shifted from the task set with the original version of an application in an Amazon ECS service to a replacement task set in the same service.

- You can set the traffic shifting to linear or canary through the deployment configuration.

- The protocol and port of a specified load balancer listener is used to reroute production traffic.

- During a deployment, a test listener can be used to serve traffic to the replacement task set while validation tests are run.

Deployment on Amazon EC2:

EC2 instances are identified by CodeDeploy by using tags or an Auto Scaling Group name.

Select any combination of Amazon EC2 Auto Scaling groups, Amazon EC2 instances, and on-premises instances to add to this deployment

☑ **Amazon EC2 Auto Scaling groups**
0 unique matched instances. Click here for details ↗

You can select up to 10 Amazon EC2 Auto Scaling groups to deploy your application revision to.

[▼]

☑ **Amazon EC2 instances**
0 unique matched instances. Click here for details ↗

You can add up to three groups of tags for EC2 instances to this deployment group.
One tag group: Any instance identified by the tag group will be deployed to.
Multiple tag groups: Only instances identified by all the tag groups will be deployed to.

Tag group 1

Key	Value - *optional*	
🔍	🔍	Remove tag

Each Amazon EC2 instance must have the correct IAM instance profile attached.

The CodeDeploy agent must be installed and running on each instance.

The agent continuously polls for work to do.

CodeDeploy sends the appspec.yml file (which must be at the root of your source code).

The application code is pulled from GitHub or S3.

EC2 will run the deployment instructions.

CodeDeploy agent will report of success / failure of deployment on the instance.

EC2 instances are grouped by deployment group (e.g. dev, test, prod).

Note: CodeDeploy does not provision the resources – it deploys applications not EC2 instances.

APPSPEC FILE

The application specification file (AppSpec file) is a YAML-formatted or JSON-formatted file used by CodeDeploy to manage a deployment.

The AppSpec file defines the deployment actions you want AWS CodeDeploy to execute.

The name of the AppSpec file for an EC2/On-Premises deployment must be appspec.yml. The name of the AppSpec file for an Amazon ECS or AWS Lambda deployment must be appspec.yaml.

The following code sample shows the format of an appspec.yml file for an Amazon EC2 instance with WordPress:

 version: 0.0

os: linux

```yaml
files:

- source: /

destination: /var/www/html/WordPress

hooks:

BeforeInstall:

- location: scripts/install_dependencies.sh

timeout: 300

runas: root

AfterInstall:

- location: scripts/change_permissions.sh

timeout: 300

runas: root

ApplicationStart:

- location: scripts/start_server.sh

- location: scripts/create_test_db.sh

timeout: 300

runas: root

ApplicationStop:
```

- location: scripts/stop_server.sh

timeout: 300

runas: root

The *files* section specifies how to source and copy from S3 / GitHub to the filesystem.

hooks are a set of instructions to be run to deploy the new version (hooks have timeouts).

APPSPEC.YAML FOR ECS

The Amazon ECS task definition file must be specified with its ARN in the TaskDefinition instruction in the AppSpec file.

The container and port in your replacement task set where your Application Load Balancer or Network Load Balancer reroutes traffic during a deployment must be specified with the LoadBalancerInfo instruction in the AppSpec file.

Here is an example of an AppSpec file written in YAML for deploying an Amazon ECS service

```
version: 0.0

Resources:

- TargetService:

Type: AWS::ECS::Service

Properties:

TaskDefinition:        "arn:aws:ecs:us-east-1:111222333444:task-definition/my-task-definition-family-name:1"

LoadBalancerInfo:

ContainerName: "SampleApplicationName"

ContainerPort: 80

# Optional properties

PlatformVersion: "LATEST"
```

NetworkConfiguration:

AwsvpcConfiguration:

Subnets: ["subnet-1234abcd","subnet-5678abcd"]

SecurityGroups: ["sg-12345678"]

AssignPublicIp: "ENABLED"

Hooks:

- BeforeInstall: "LambdaFunctionToValidateBeforeInstall"

- AfterInstall: "LambdaFunctionToValidateAfterTraffic"

- AfterAllowTestTraffic: "LambdaFunctionToValidateAfterTestTrafficStarts"

- BeforeAllowTraffic: "LambdaFunctionToValidateBeforeAllowingProductionTraffic"

- AfterAllowTraffic: "LambdaFunctionToValidateAfterAllowingProductionTraffic"

Note: The hooks are different for each type of compute platform and not all available hooks are shown. For more information on the available hooks for each compute platform please read the AWS documentation here.

APPSPEC.YAML FOR AWS LAMBDA

The format of the AppSpec.yaml file for use with AWS Lambda is as follows:

version: 0.0

Resources:

- myLambdaFunction:

Type: AWS::Lambda::Function

Properties:

Name: "myLambdaFunction"

Alias: "myLambdaFunctionAlias"

CurrentVersion: "1"

TargetVersion: "2"

Hooks:

- BeforeAllowTraffic: "LambdaFunctionToValidateBeforeTrafficShift"

- AfterAllowTraffic: "LambdaFunctionToValidateAfterTrafficShift"

The following hooks are available for use:

- BeforeAllowTraffic – used to specify the tasks or functions you want to run before traffic is routed to the newly deployed Lambda function.
- AfterAllowTraffic – used to specify the tasks or functions you want to run after the traffic has been routed to the newly deployed Lambda function.

REVISION

When updating to a new version a Revision includes everything needed to deploy the new version: AppSpec file, application files, executables and config files.

DEPLOYMENT CONFIGURATION

In-place deployment (EC2 only)

Here's how it works:

1. First, you create deployable content on your local development machine or similar environment, and then you add an application specification file (AppSpec file). The AppSpec file is unique to CodeDeploy. It defines the deployment actions you want CodeDeploy to execute. You bundle your deployable content and the AppSpec file into an archive file, and then upload it to an Amazon S3 bucket or a GitHub repository. This archive file is called an application revision (or simply a revision).

2. Next, you provide CodeDeploy with information about your deployment, such as which Amazon S3 bucket or GitHub repository to pull the revision from and to which set of Amazon EC2 instances to deploy its contents. CodeDeploy calls a set of Amazon EC2 instances a deployment group. A deployment group contains individually tagged Amazon EC2 instances, Amazon EC2 instances in Amazon EC2 Auto Scaling groups, or both. Each time you successfully upload a new application revision that you want to deploy to the deployment group, that bundle is set as the target revision for the deployment group. In other

words, the application revision that is currently targeted for deployment is the target revision. This is also the revision that is pulled for automatic deployments.

3. Next, the CodeDeploy agent on each instance polls CodeDeploy to determine what and when to pull from the specified Amazon S3 bucket or GitHub repository.

4. Finally, the CodeDeploy agent on each instance pulls the target revision from the Amazon S3 bucket or GitHub repository and, using the instructions in the AppSpec file, deploys the contents to the instance.

CodeDeploy keeps a record of your deployments so that you can get deployment status, deployment configuration parameters, instance health, and so on.

BLUE/GREEN DEPLOYMENTS

A blue/green deployment is used to update your applications while minimizing interruptions caused by the changes of a new application version. CodeDeploy provisions your new application version alongside the old version before rerouting your production traffic.

AWS Lambda: Traffic is shifted from one version of a Lambda function to a new version of the same Lambda function.

Amazon ECS: Traffic is shifted from a task set in your Amazon ECS service to an updated, replacement task set in the same Amazon ECS service.

EC2/On-Premises: Traffic is shifted from one set of instances in the original environment to a replacement set of instances.

Note: All AWS Lambda and Amazon ECS deployments are blue/green. An EC2/On-Premises deployment can be in-place or blue/green.

For Amazon ECS and AWS Lambda there are three ways traffic can be shifted during a deployment:

- Canary: Traffic is shifted in two increments. You can choose from predefined canary options that specify the percentage of traffic shifted to your updated Amazon ECS task set / Lambda function in the first increment and the interval, in minutes, before the remaining traffic is shifted in the second increment.

- Linear: Traffic is shifted in equal increments with an equal number of minutes between each increment. You can choose from predefined linear options that specify the percentage of traffic shifted in each increment and the number of minutes between each increment.

- All-at-once: All traffic is shifted from the original Amazon ECS task set / Lambda function to the updated Amazon ECS task set / Lambda function all at once.

For Amazon EC2 you can choose how your replacement environment is specified:

Copy an existing Amazon EC2 Auto Scaling group:

- During the blue/green deployment, CodeDeploy creates the instances for your replacement environment during the deployment.

- With this option, CodeDeploy uses the Amazon EC2 Auto Scaling group you specify as a template for the replacement environment, including the same number of running instances and many other configuration options.

Choose instances manually:

- You can specify the instances to be counted as your replacement using Amazon EC2 instance tags, Amazon EC2 Auto Scaling group names, or both.

- If you choose this option, you do not need to specify the instances for the replacement environment until you create a deployment.

AWS CODEPIPELINE

GENERAL AWS CODEPIPELINE CONCEPTS

AWS CodePipeline is a fully managed continuous delivery service that helps you automate your release pipelines for fast and reliable application and infrastructure updates.

CodePipeline automates the build, test, and deploy phases of your release process every time there is a code change, based on the release model you define.

CodePipeline enables you to rapidly and reliably deliver features and updates.

You can easily integrate AWS CodePipeline with third-party services such as GitHub or with your own custom plugin. With AWS CodePipeline, you only pay for what you use.

There are no upfront fees or long-term commitments.

Uses a user-defined software release process.

A fast and reliable way to quickly release new features and bug fixes.

CodePipeline provides tooling integrations for many AWS and third-party software at each stage of the pipeline including:

- Source stage – S3, CodeCommit, Github, ECR, Bitbucket Cloud (beta).
- Build – CodeBuild, Jenkins.
- Deploy stage – CloudFormation, CodeDeploy, ECS, Elastic Beanstalk, AWS Service Catalog, S3.

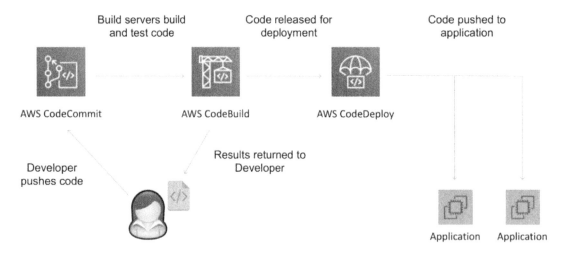

KEY CODEPIPELINE CONCEPTS

Pipelines:

- A workflow that describes how software changes go through the release process.

Artifacts:

- Files or changes that will be worked on by the actions and stages in the pipeline.

- Each pipeline stage can create "artifacts".
- Artifacts are passed, stored in Amazon S3 and then passed on to the next stage.

Stages:

- Pipelines are broken up into stages, e.g. build stage, deployment stage.
- Each stage can have sequential actions and or parallel actions.
- Stage examples would be build, test, deploy, load test etc.
- Manual approval can be defined at any stage.

Actions:

- Stages contain at least one action, these actions take some action on artifacts and will have artifacts as either an input, and output, or both.

Transitions:

- The progressing from one stage to another inside of a pipeline.

The diagram below shows a pipeline with a manual approval stage:

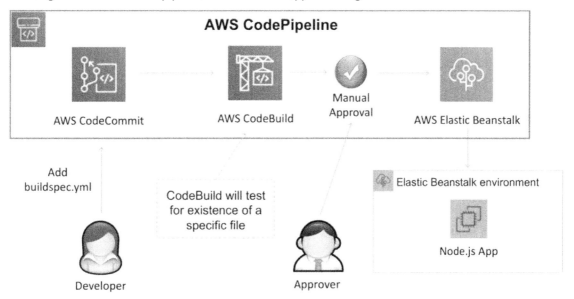

Every code change pushed to your code repository automatically enters the workflow and triggers the set of actions defined for each stage of the pipeline.

CodePipeline state changes happen in AWS CloudWatch Events which can create SNS notifications.

Notifications may include failed pipelines or cancelled stages.

If CodePipeline fails a stage, your pipeline stops and you can get information in the console.

You can also audit API calls with AWS CloudTrail.

If CodePipeline cannot perform an action, check that the IAM service role attached to the pipeline has the correct permissions.

AWS CODESTAR

GENERAL AWS CODESTAR CONCEPTS

AWS CodeStar enables you to quickly develop, build, and deploy applications on AWS. AWS CodeStar provides a unified user interface, enabling you to easily manage your software development activities in one place.

With AWS CodeStar, you can set up your entire continuous delivery toolchain in minutes, allowing you to start releasing code faster.

AWS CodeStar makes it easy for your whole team to work together securely, allowing you to easily manage access and add owners, contributors, and viewers to your projects.

Each AWS CodeStar project comes with a project management dashboard, including an integrated issue tracking capability powered by Atlassian JIRA Software.

With the AWS CodeStar project dashboard, you can easily track progress across your entire software development process, from your backlog of work items to teams' recent code deployments.

Exam tip: If an exam scenario requires a unified development toolchain, and mentions collaboration between team members, synchronization, and centralized management of the CI/CD pipeline this will be CodeStar rather than CodePipeline or CodeCommit.

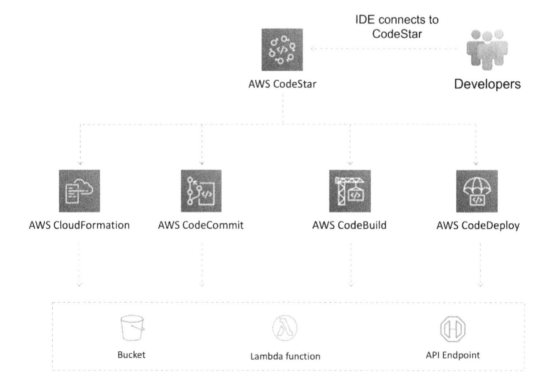

BENEFITS AND FEATURES

Project templates for various projects and programming languages:

- With AWS CodeStar project templates, you can easily develop a variety of applications including websites, web applications, web services, and Alexa skills.

- AWS CodeStar project templates include the code for getting started on supported programming languages including Java, JavaScript, PHP, Ruby, and Python.

Work across your team securely:

- AWS CodeStar enables you to collaborate across your team in a secure manner.

- AWS CodeStar simplifies the process of setting up project access for teams because it provides built-in role-based policies that follow AWS security best practices.

- You can easily manage access for project owners, contributors, and viewers without needing to manually configure your own policy for each service.

Support for multiple Integrated Development Environments (IDEs):

- Integrates natively with the AWS Cloud9 cloud-based IDE.

- Can also choose from a number of popular IDEs such as Microsoft Visual Studio and Eclipse.

CodeStar integrates with several other AWS services including:

- CodeCommit.

- CodeBuild.

- CodeDeploy.

- CodePipeline.

- CloudWatch.

PRICING

There is no additional charge for AWS CodeStar.

You pay for AWS resources (e.g. EC2 instances, Lambda executions or S3 buckets) used to in your CodeStar projects.

You only pay for what you use, as you use it; there are no minimum fees and no upfront commitments.

AWS CLOUD9

GENERAL AWS CLOUD9 CONCEPTS

AWS Cloud9 is a cloud-based integrated development environment (IDE) that lets you write, run, and debug your code with just a browser.

It includes a code editor, debugger, and terminal.

Cloud9 comes prepackaged with essential tools for popular programming languages, including JavaScript, Python, PHP, and more, so you don't need to install files or configure your development machine to start new projects.

Since your Cloud9 IDE is cloud-based, you can work on your projects from your office, home, or anywhere using an internet-connected machine.

Cloud9 also provides a seamless experience for developing serverless applications enabling you to easily define resources, debug, and switch between local and remote execution of serverless applications.

With Cloud9, you can quickly share your development environment with your team, enabling you to pair program and track each other's inputs in real time.

BENEFITS

Code with just a browser:

- AWS Cloud9 gives you the flexibility to run your development environment on a managed Amazon EC2 instance or any existing Linux server that supports SSH.

- This means that you can write, run, and debug applications with just a browser, without needing to install or maintain a local IDE.

- The Cloud9 code editor and integrated debugger include helpful, time-saving features such as code hinting, code completion, and step-through debugging.

- The Cloud9 terminal provides a browser-based shell experience enabling you to install additional software, do a git push, or enter commands.

Code together in real-time:

- AWS Cloud9 makes collaborating on code easy.

- You can share your development environment with your team in just a few clicks and pair program together.

- While collaborating, your team members can see each other type in real time, and instantly chat with one another from within the IDE.

Build serverless applications with ease:

- AWS Cloud9 makes it easy to write, run, and debug serverless applications.

- It preconfigures the development environment with all the SDKs, libraries, and plug-ins needed for serverless development.

- Cloud9 also provides an environment for locally testing and debugging AWS Lambda functions.

- This allows you to iterate on your code directly, saving you time and improving the quality of your code.

Direct terminal access to AWS:

- AWS Cloud9 comes with a terminal that includes sudo privileges to the managed Amazon EC2 instance that is hosting your development environment and a preauthenticated AWS Command Line Interface.

- This makes it easy for you to quickly run commands and directly access AWS services.

Start new projects quickly:

- AWS Cloud9 makes it easy for you to start new projects.

- Cloud9's development environment comes prepackaged with tooling for over 40 programming languages, including Node.js, JavaScript, Python, PHP, Ruby, Go, and C++.

- This enables you to start writing code for popular application stacks within minutes by eliminating the need to install or configure files, SDKs, and plug-ins for your development machine.

- Because Cloud9 is cloud-based, you can easily maintain multiple development environments to isolate your project's resources.

AWS X-RAY

GENERAL AWS X-RAY CONCEPTS

AWS X-Ray helps developers analyze and debug production, distributed applications, such as those built using a microservices architecture.

With X-Ray, you can understand how your application and its underlying services are performing to identify and troubleshoot the root cause of performance issues and errors.

X-Ray provides an end-to-end view of requests as they travel through your application, and shows a map of your application's underlying components.

You can use X-Ray to analyze both applications in development and in production, from simple three-tier applications to complex microservices applications consisting of thousands of services.

AWS X-Ray supports applications running on:

- Amazon Elastic Compute Cloud (Amazon EC2).
- Amazon EC2 Container Service (Amazon ECS).
- AWS Lambda.
- AWS Elastic Beanstalk.

X-Ray on EC2 / On-premise:

- Linux system must run the X-Ray daemon.
- IAM instance role if EC2, other AWS credentials on on-premise instance.

X-Ray on Lambda:

- Make sure the X-Ray integration is ticked in the Lambda configuration (Lambda will run the daemon).
- IAM role is the Lambda role.

X-Ray on Elastic Beanstalk:

- Set configuration in the Elastic Beanstalk console.
- Or use the Beanstalk extension (.ebextensions/xray-daemon.config)

X-Ray on ECS/EKS/Fargate:

- Create a Docker image that runs the daemon or use the official X-Ray Docker image.
- Ensure port mappings and network settings are correct and IAM task roles are defined.

The X-Ray SDK captures metadata for requests made to MySQL and PostgreSQL databases (self-hosted, Amazon RDS, Amazon Aurora), and Amazon DynamoDB.

It also captures metadata for requests made to Amazon Simple Queue Service and Amazon Simple Notification Service.

The X-Ray SDK is installed in your application and forwards to the X-Ray daemon which forwards to the X-Ray API.

You can then visualize what is happening in the X-Ray console.

The X-Ray SDK provides:

- Interceptors to add your code to trace incoming HTTP requests.
- Client handlers to instrument AWS SDK client that your application uses to call other AWS services.
- An HTTP client to use to instrument calls to other internal and external HTTP web services.

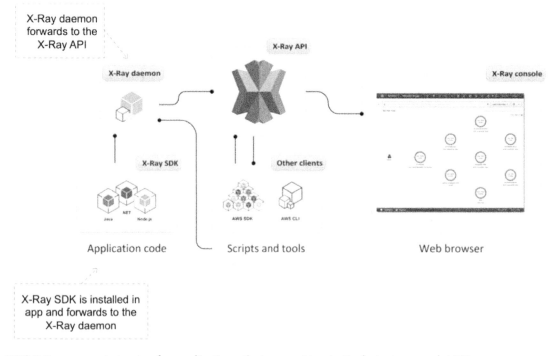

AWS X-Ray supports tracing for applications that are written in Node.js, Java, and .NET.

Code must be instrumented to use the AWS X-Ray SDK.

The IAM role must be correct to send traces to X-Ray.

The X-Ray daemon agent has a config to send traces cross account:

- Make sure the IAM permissions are correct – the agent will assume a role.
- This allows to have a central account for all your application tracing.

KEY X-RAY TERMINOLOGY

Trace:

- An X-Ray trace is a set of data points that share the same trace ID.

Segments:

- An X-Ray segment encapsulates all the data points for a single component (for example, authorization service) of the distributed application.
- Segments include system-defined and user-defined data in the form of annotations and are composed of one or more sub-segments that represent remote calls made from the service.

Subsegments:

- Subsegments provide more granular timing information and details about downstream calls that your application made to fulfill the original request.
- A subsegment can contain additional details about a call to an AWS service, an external HTTP API, or an SQL database.
- You can even define arbitrary subsegments to instrument specific functions or lines of code in your application.
- For services that don't send their own segments, like Amazon DynamoDB, X-Ray uses subsegments to generate inferred segments and downstream nodes on the service map.
- This lets you see all of your downstream dependencies, even if they don't support tracing, or are external.

Annotations:

- An X-Ray annotation is system-defined or user-defined data associated with a segment.
- System-defined annotations include data added to the segment by AWS services, whereas user-defined annotations are metadata added to a segment by a developer.
- A segment can contain multiple annotations.
- These are key / value pairs used to index traces and use with filters.
- Use annotations to record information on segments or subsegments that you want indexed for search.

Sampling:

- To provide a performant and cost-effective experience, X-Ray does not collect data for every request that is sent to an application.
- Instead, it collects data for a statistically significant number of requests.
- X-Ray should not be used as an audit or compliance tool because it does not guarantee data completeness.

Metadata:

- Key / value pairs, not indexed and not used for searching.

Exam tip: Remember that annotations can be used for adding system or user-defined data to segments and subsegments that you want to index for search. Metadata is not indexed and cannot be used for searching.

ANNOTATIONS AND FILTERING

AWS X-Ray lets you add annotations to data emitted from specific components or services in your application.

You can use this to append business-specific metadata that help you better diagnose issues.

You can also view and filter data for traces by properties such as annotation value, average latencies, HTTP response status, timestamp, database table used, and more.

X-RAY SDK

The X-Ray SDK is installed in your application and forwards to the X-Ray daemon which forwards to the X-Ray API.

You can then visualize what is happening in the X-Ray console.

The X-Ray SDK provides:

- Interceptors to add your code to trace incoming HTTP requests.

- Client handlers to instrument AWS SDK client that your application uses to call other AWS services.

- An HTTP client to use to instrument calls to other internal and external HTTP web services.

Code must be instrumented to use the AWS X-Ray SDK.

The IAM role must be correct to send traces to X-Ray.

AWS DEVELOPER TOOLS QUIZ QUESTIONS

Question 1: Which AWS service can be used as a centralized repository for all of your code, binaries, images, and libraries?

1. AWS CodeCommit

2. AWS CodeBuild

3. AWS CodeDeploy

Question 2: Which file should be used to specify build instructions with AWS CodeBuild?

1. appspec.yml

2. buildspec.yml

3. template.json

Question 3: A Development team is attempting to build a continuous integration and delivery (CI/CD) software development and release process. Which AWS service can the team use that will automate the build, test, and deploy phases of the release process?

1. AWS Cloud9

2. AWS CodeDeploy

3. AWS CodePipeline

Question 4: AWS CodeDeploy is being used to deploy an update to an AWS Lambda function. The update is critical and must be implemented as quickly as possible without testing. What is the FASTEST deployment option?

1. In-place

2. Blue/green

Question 5: A Developer is deploying an update to an Amazon ECS cluster. The Developer would like to shift 20 percent of traffic in the first increment, then after an interval shift the remaining traffic in the second increment. Which traffic shifting option should the Developer use?

1. All-at-once

2. Linear

3. Canary

Question 6: Which file is used by AWS CodeDeploy to define the deployment actions to execute for an Amazon EC2 deployment?

1. appspec.yml

2. appspec.yaml

3. appspec.json

Question 7: Which service can be used for monitoring the CPU utilization of Amazon EC2 instances?

1. AWS CloudTrail

2. AWS X-Ray

3. Amazon CloudWatch

Question 8: A Developer needs to add data to AWS X-Ray segments that are indexed and searchable. What should be used to add the data?

1. User-defined annotations

2. System-defined annotations

3. Metadata

4. Subsegments

AWS DEVELOPER TOOLS - QUIZ QUESTIONS & ANSWERS

Question 1: Which AWS service can be used as a centralized repository for all of your code, binaries, images, and libraries?

1. AWS CodeCommit

2. AWS CodeBuild

3. AWS CodeDeploy

Question 1, Answer 1

Explanation:

1 is correct. AWS CodeCommit is a fully-managed source control service that hosts secure Git-based repositories. It can be used a centralized repository for all of your code, binaries, images, and libraries.

2 is incorrect. AWS CodeBuild is a fully managed continuous integration (CI) service that compiles source code, runs tests, and produces software packages that are ready to deploy.

3 is incorrect. CodeDeploy is a deployment service that automates application deployments to Amazon EC2 instances, on-premises instances, serverless Lambda functions, or Amazon ECS services.

Question 2: Which file should be used to specify build instructions with AWS CodeBuild?

1. appspec.yml

2. buildspec.yml

3. template.json

Question 2, Answer 2

Explanation:

1 is incorrect. The appspec.yml file is a file used with AWS CodeDeploy

2 is correct. Build instructions can be defined in the code with the buildspec.yml file.

3 is incorrect. This is not a file you would use with CodeBuild. This is a file you may use with AWS CloudFormation.

Question 3: A Development team is attempting to build a continuous integration and delivery (CI/CD) software development and release process. Which AWS service can the team use that will automate the build, test, and deploy phases of the release process?

1. AWS Cloud9

2. AWS CodeDeploy

3. AWS CodePipeline

Question 3, Answer 3

Explanation:

1 is incorrect. AWS Cloud9 is a cloud-based integrated development environment (IDE) that lets you write, run, and debug your code with just a browser.

2 is incorrect. CodeDeploy is a deployment service that automates application deployments to Amazon EC2 instances, on-premises instances, serverless Lambda functions, or Amazon ECS services.

3 is correct. AWS CodePipeline is a fully managed continuous delivery service that helps you automate your release pipelines for fast and reliable application and infrastructure updates.

Question 4: AWS CodeDeploy is being used to deploy an update to an AWS Lambda function. The update is critical and must be implemented as quickly as possible without testing. What is the FASTEST deployment option?

1. In-place

2. Blue/green

Question 4, Answer 2

Explanation:

1 is incorrect. You cannot use this deployment type for AWS Lambda.

2 is correct. AWS Lambda and Amazon ECS deployments cannot use an in-place deployment type, only blue/green.

Question 5: A Developer is deploying an update to an Amazon ECS cluster. The Developer would like to shift 20 percent of traffic in the first increment, then after an interval shift the remaining traffic in the second increment. Which traffic shifting option should the Developer use?

1. All-at-once

2. Linear

3. Canary

Question 5, Answer 3

Explanation:

1 is incorrect. With this option all traffic is shifted from the original Amazon ECS task set / Lambda function to the updated Amazon ECS task set / Lambda function all at once.

2 is incorrect. With this option traffic is shifted in equal increments with an equal number of minutes between each increment. You can choose from predefined linear options that specify the percentage of traffic shifted in each increment and the number of minutes between each increment.

3 is correct. With this option traffic is shifted in two increments. You can choose from predefined canary options that specify the percentage of traffic shifted to your updated Amazon ECS task set / Lambda function in the first increment and the interval, in minutes, before the remaining traffic is shifted in the second increment.

Question 6: Which file is used by AWS CodeDeploy to define the deployment actions to execute for an Amazon EC2 deployment?

1. appspec.yml

2. appspec.yaml

3. appspec.json

Question 6, Answer 1

Explanation:

1 is correct. The name of the AppSpec file for an EC2/On-Premises deployment must be appspec..

2 is incorrect. Oops, one letter wrong! The name of the AppSpec file for an Amazon ECS or AWS Lambda deployment must be appspec.yaml.

3 is incorrect. This is not a valid file extension for an appspec file used with AWS CodeDeploy.

Question 7: Which service can be used for monitoring the CPU utilization of Amazon EC2 instances?

1. AWS CloudTrail

2. AWS X-Ray

3. Amazon CloudWatch

Question 7, Answer 3

Explanation:

1 is incorrect. CloudTrail is an auditing service used for monitoring API activity.

2 is incorrect. AWS X-Ray is used for tracing distributed applications. It does track some latency statistics but for performance metrics on CPU this is not the correct service to use.

3 is correct. Amazon CloudWatch is a monitoring service for AWS cloud resources and the applications you run on AWS.

Question 8: A Developer needs to add data to AWS X-Ray segments that are indexed and searchable. What should be used to add the data?

1. User-defined annotations

2. System-defined annotations

3. Metadata

4. Subsegments

Question 8, Answer 1

Explanation:

1 is correct. System-defined annotations include data added to the segment by AWS services, whereas user-defined annotations are metadata added to a segment by a developer. A segment can contain multiple annotations. These are key / value pairs used to index traces and use with filters.

2 is incorrect. System-defined annotations include data added to the segment by AWS services, whereas user-defined annotations are metadata added to a segment by a developer.

3 is incorrect. Metadata are Key / value pairs, and are not indexed and not used for searching.

4 is incorrect. Subsegments provide more granular timing information and details about downstream calls that your application made to fulfill the original request

AWS MANAGEMENT AND GOVERNANCE

AWS ORGANIZATIONS

AWS Organizations helps you centrally govern your environment as you grow and scale your workloads on AWS.

Organizations helps you to centrally manage billing; control access, compliance, and security; and share resources across your AWS accounts.

Using AWS Organizations, you can automate account creation, create groups of accounts to reflect your business needs, and apply policies for these groups for governance.

You can also simplify billing by setting up a single payment method for all of your AWS accounts.

Through integrations with other AWS services, you can use Organizations to define central configurations and resource sharing across accounts in your organization.

AWS Organizations is available to all AWS customers at no additional charge.

The AWS Organizations API enables automation for account creation and management.

Available in two feature sets:

- Consolidated billing.
- All features.

By default, organizations support consolidated billing features.

Consolidated billing separates paying accounts and linked accounts.

You can use AWS Organizations to set up a single payment method for all the AWS accounts in your organization through consolidated billing.

With consolidated billing, you can see a combined view of charges incurred by all your accounts.

Can also take advantage of pricing benefits from aggregated usage, such as volume discounts for Amazon EC2 and Amazon S3.

Limit of 20 linked accounts for consolidated billing (default).

Policies can be assigned at different points in the hierarchy.

Can help with cost control through volume discounts.

Unused reserved EC2 instances are applied across the group.

Paying accounts should be used for billing purposes only.

Billing alerts can be setup at the paying account which shows billing for all linked accounts.

CORE CONCEPTS

Some of the core concepts you need to understand are listed here:

AWS Organization – An organization is a collection of AWS accounts that you can organize into a hierarchy and manage centrally.

AWS Account – An AWS account is a container for your AWS resources.

Master Account – A master account is the AWS account you use to create your organization.

Member Account – A member account is an AWS account, other than the master account, that is part of an organization.

Administrative Root – An administrative root is the starting point for organizing your AWS accounts. The administrative root is the top-most container in your organization's hierarchy.

Organizational Unit (OU) – An organizational unit (OU) is a group of AWS accounts within an organization. An OU can also contain other OUs enabling you to create a hierarchy.

Policy – A policy is a "document" with one or more statements that define the controls that you want to apply to a group of AWS accounts. AWS Organizations supports a specific type of policy called a Service Control Policy (SCP). An SCP defines the AWS service actions, such as Amazon EC2 RunInstances, that are available for use in different accounts within an organization.

MIGRATING ACCOUNTS BETWEEN ORGANIZATIONS

Accounts can be migrated between organizations.

You must have root or IAM access to both the member and master accounts.

Use the AWS Organizations console for just a few accounts.

Use the AWS Organizations API or AWS Command Line Interface (AWS CLI) if there are many accounts to migrate.

Billing history and billing reports for all accounts stay with the master account in an organization.

Before migration download any billing or report history for any member accounts that you want to keep.

When a member account leaves an organization, all charges incurred by the account are charged directly to the standalone account.

Even if the account move only takes a minute to process, it is likely that some charges will be incurred by the member account.

RESOURCE GROUPS

You can use resource groups to organize your AWS resources.

In AWS, a resource is an entity that you can work with.

Resource groups make it easier to manage and automate tasks on large numbers of resources at one time.

Resource groups allow you to group resources and then tag them.

The Tag Editor assists with finding resources and adding tags.

You can access Resource Groups through any of the following entry points:

- On the navigation bar of the AWS Management Console.
- In the AWS Systems Manager console, from the left navigation pane entry for Resource Groups.
- By using the Resource Groups API, in AWS CLI commands or AWS SDK programming languages.

A resource group is a collection of AWS resources that are all in the same AWS region, and that match criteria provided in a query.

In Resource Groups, there are two types of queries on which you can build a group.

Both query types include resources that are specified in the format AWS::service::resource.

- **Tag-based** – Tag-based queries include lists of resources and tags. Tags are keys that help identify and sort your resources within your organization. Optionally, tags include values for keys.

- **AWS CloudFormation stack-based** – In an AWS CloudFormation stack-based query, you choose an AWS CloudFormation stack in your account in the current region, and then choose resource types within the stack that you want to be in the group. You can base your query on only one AWS CloudFormation stack.

Resource groups can be nested; a resource group can contain existing resource groups in the same region.

AMAZON CLOUDWATCH

GENERAL AMAZON CLOUDWATCH CONCEPTS

Amazon CloudWatch is a monitoring service for AWS cloud resources and the applications you run on AWS.

It is used to collect and track metrics, collect and monitor log files, and set alarms.

With CloudWatch you can:

- Gain system-wide visibility into resource utilization.

- Monitor application performance.

- Monitor operational health.

CloudWatch alarms monitor metrics and automatically initiate actions.

CloudWatch Logs centralizes logs from systems, applications, and AWS services.

CloudWatch Events delivers a stream of system events that describe changes in AWS resources.

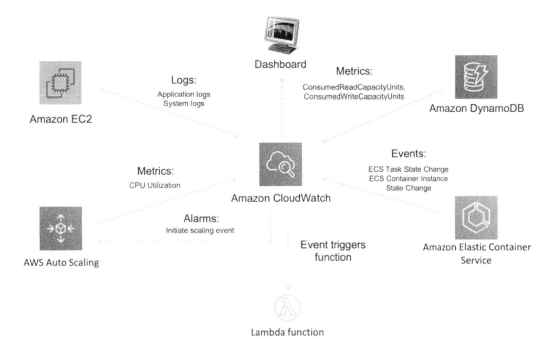

CloudWatch is accessed via API, command-line interface, AWS SDKs, and the AWS Management Console.

CloudWatch integrates with IAM.

Can automatically react to changes in your AWS resources.

CloudWatch vs CloudTrail:

CloudWatch	CloudTrail
Performance monitoring	Auditing
Log events across AWS services – think operations	Log API activity across AWS services – think activities
Higher-level comprehensive monitoring and eventing	More low-level granular
Log from multiple accounts	Log from multiple accounts
Logs stored indefinitely	Logs stored to S3 or CloudWatch indefinitely
Alarms history for 14 days	No native alarming; can use CloudWatch alarms

Used to collect and track metrics, collect and monitor log files, and set alarms.

Automatically react to changes in your AWS resources.

With CloudWatch you can monitor resources such as:

- EC2 instances.
- DynamoDB tables.
- RDS DB instances.
- Custom metrics generated by applications and services.
- Any log files generated by your applications.

Gain system-wide visibility into resource utilization.

Monitor application performance.

Monitor operational health.

CloudWatch is accessed via API, command-line interface, AWS SDKs, and the AWS Management Console.

CloudWatch integrates with IAM.

METRICS

Metrics are the fundamental concept in CloudWatch.

A metric represents a time-ordered set of data points that are published to CloudWatch.

AWS services send metrics to CloudWatch.

You can also send your own custom metrics to CloudWatch.

Metrics exist within a region.

Metrics cannot be deleted but automatically expire after 15 months.

Metrics are uniquely defined by a name, a namespace, and zero or more dimensions.

CloudWatch retains metric data as follows:

- Data points with a period of less than 60 seconds are available for 3 hours. These data points are high-resolution custom metrics.

- Data points with a period of 60 seconds (1 minute) are available for 15 days.

- Data points with a period of 300 seconds (5 minute) are available for 63 days.

- Data points with a period of 3600 seconds (1 hour) are available for 455 days (15 months).

CUSTOM METRICS

You can publish your own metrics to CloudWatch using the AWS CLI or an API.

You can view statistical graphs of your published metrics with the AWS Management Console.

CloudWatch stores data about a metric as a series of data points.

Each data point has an associated time stamp.

You can even publish an aggregated set of data points called a statistic set.

HIGH-RESOLUTION METRICS

Each metric is one of the following:

- Standard resolution, with data having a one-minute granularity

- High resolution, with data at a granularity of one second

Metrics produced by AWS services are standard resolution by default.

When you publish a custom metric, you can define it as either standard resolution or high resolution.

When you publish a high-resolution metric, CloudWatch stores it with a resolution of 1 second, and you can read and retrieve it with a period of 1 second, 5 seconds, 10 seconds, 30 seconds, or any multiple of 60 seconds.

High-resolution metrics can give you more immediate insight into your application's sub-minute activity.

Keep in mind that every PutMetricData call for a custom metric is charged, so calling PutMetricData more often on a high-resolution metric can lead to higher charges.

If you set an alarm on a high-resolution metric, you can specify a high-resolution alarm with a period of 10 seconds or 30 seconds, or you can set a regular alarm with a period of any multiple of 60 seconds.

There is a higher charge for high-resolution alarms with a period of 10 or 30 seconds.

NAMESPACE

A namespace is a container for CloudWatch metrics.

Metrics in different namespaces are isolated from each other, so that metrics from different applications are not mistakenly aggregated into the same statistics.

The following table provides some examples of namespaces for several AWS services:

Service	Namespace
Amazon API Gateway	AWS/ApiGateway
Amazon CloudFront	AWS/CloudFront
AWS CloudHSM	AWS/CloudHSM
Amazon CloudWatch Logs	AWS/Logs
AWS CodeBuild	AWS/CodeBuild
Amazon Cognito	AWS/Cognito
Amazon DynamoDB	AWS/DynamoDB
Amazon EC2	AWS/EC2
AWS Elastic Beanstalk	AWS/ElasticBeanstalk

DIMENSIONS

In custom metrics, the –dimensions parameter is common.

A dimension further clarifies what the metric is and what data it stores.

You can have up to 10 dimensions in one metric, and each dimension is defined by a name and value pair.

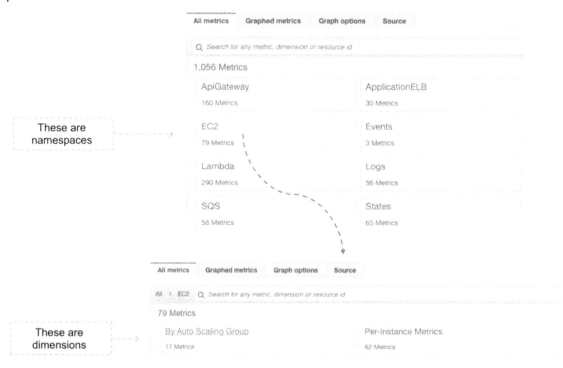

How you specify a dimension is different when you use different commands.

With put-metric-data, you specify each dimension as MyName=MyValue, and with get-metric-statistics or put-metric-alarm you use the format Name=MyName, Value=MyValue.

For example, the following command publishes a Buffers metric with two dimensions named InstanceId and InstanceType.

aws cloudwatch put-metric-data --metric-name Buffers --namespace MyNameSpace --unit Bytes --value 231434333 --dimensions InstanceId=1-23456789,InstanceType=m1.small

This command retrieves statistics for that same metric. Separate the Name and Value parts of a single dimension with commas, but if you have multiple dimensions, use a space between one dimension and the next.

aws cloudwatch get-metric-statistics --metric-name Buffers --namespace MyNameSpace --dimensions Name=InstanceId,Value=1-23456789   Name=InstanceType,Value=m1.small   --start-time   2016-10-15T04:00:00Z --end-time 2016-10-19T07:00:00Z --statistics Average --period 60

If a single metric includes multiple dimensions, you must specify a value for every defined dimension when you use get-metric-statistics. For example, the Amazon S3 metric BucketSizeBytes includes the dimensions BucketName and StorageType, so you must specify both dimensions with get-metric-statistics.

aws cloudwatch get-metric-statistics --metric-name BucketSizeBytes --start-time 2017-01-23T14:23:00Z --end-time 2017-01-26T19:30:00Z --period 3600 --namespace AWS/S3 --statistics Maximum --dimensions Name=BucketName,Value=MyBucketName Name=StorageType,Value=StandardStorage --output table

PUBLISHING SINGLE DATA POINTS

To publish a single data point for a new or existing metric, use the put-metric-data command with one value and time stamp.

For example, the following actions each publish one data point.

aws cloudwatch put-metric-data --metric-name PageViewCount --namespace MyService --value 2 --timestamp 2016-10-20T12:00:00.000Z

aws cloudwatch put-metric-data --metric-name PageViewCount --namespace MyService --value 4 --timestamp 2016-10-20T12:00:01.000Z

aws cloudwatch put-metric-data --metric-name PageViewCount --namespace MyService --value 5 --timestamp 2016-10-20T12:00:02.000Z

STATISTICS

Statistics are metric data aggregations over specified periods of time.

CloudWatch provides statistics based on the metric data points provided by your custom data or provided by other AWS services to CloudWatch.

Statistic	Description
Minimum	The lowest value observed during the specified period. You can use this value to determine low volumes of activity for your application.
Maximum	The highest value observed during the specified period. You can use this value to determine high volumes of activity for your application.
Sum	All values submitted for the matching metric added together. This statistic can be useful for determining the total volume of a metric.
Average	The value of Sum / SampleCount during the specified period. By comparing this statistic with the Minimum and Maximum, you can determine the full scope of a metric and how close the average use is to the Minimum and Maximum. This comparison helps you to know when to increase or decrease your resources as needed.
SampleCount	The count (number) of data points used for the statistical calculation.
pNN.NN	The value of the specified percentile. You can specify any percentile, using up to two decimal places (for example, p95.45). Percentile statistics are not available for metrics that include any negative values. For more information, see Percentiles.

CLOUDWATCH ALARMS

You can use an alarm to automatically initiate actions on your behalf.

An alarm watches a single metric over a specified time period, and performs one or more specified actions, based on the value of the metric relative to a threshold over time.

The action is a notification sent to an Amazon SNS topic or an Auto Scaling policy.

You can also add alarms to dashboards.

Alarms invoke actions for sustained state changes only.

CloudWatch alarms do not invoke actions simply because they are in a particular state.

The state must have changed and been maintained for a specified number of periods.

CLOUDWATCH LOGS

Amazon CloudWatch Logs lets you monitor and troubleshoot your systems and applications using your existing system, application and custom log files.

You can use Amazon CloudWatch Logs to monitor, store, and access your log files from Amazon Elastic Compute Cloud (Amazon EC2) instances, AWS CloudTrail, Route 53, and other sources.

Features:

- **Monitor logs from Amazon EC2 instances** – monitors application and system logs and can trigger notifications.

- **Monitor CloudTrail Logged Events** – alarms can be created in CloudWatch based on API activity captured by CloudTrail.

- **Log retention** – by default, logs are retained indefinitely. Configurable per log group from 1 day to 10 years.

CloudWatch Logs can be used for real time application and system monitoring as well as long term log retention.

CloudWatch Logs keeps logs indefinitely by default.

CloudTrail logs can be sent to CloudWatch Logs for real-time monitoring.

CloudWatch Logs metric filters can evaluate CloudTrail logs for specific terms, phrases or values.

CLOUDWATCH LOGS AGENT

The CloudWatch Logs agent provides an automated way to send log data to CloudWatch Logs from Amazon EC2 instances.

There is now a unified CloudWatch agent that collects both logs and metrics.

The unified CloudWatch agent includes metrics such as memory and disk utilization.

The unified CloudWatch agent enables you to do the following:

- Collect more system-level metrics from Amazon EC2 instances across operating systems. The metrics can include in-guest metrics, in addition to the metrics for EC2 instances.

- Collect system-level metrics from on-premises servers. These can include servers in a hybrid environment as well as servers not managed by AWS.

- Retrieve custom metrics from your applications or services using the StatsD and collected protocols.

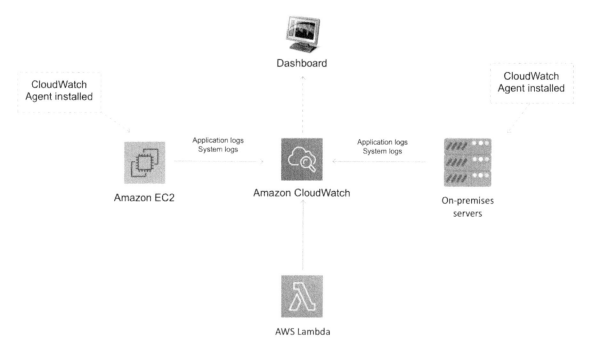

CLOUDWATCH EVENTS

Amazon CloudWatch Events delivers a near real-time stream of system events that describe changes in AWS resources.

Can use CloudWatch Events to schedule automated actions that self-trigger at certain times using cron or rate expressions

Can match events and route them to one or more target functions or streams.

Targets include:

- Amazon EC2 instances.

- AWS Lambda functions.

- Streams in Amazon Kinesis Data Streams.

- Delivery streams in Amazon Kinesis Data Firehose.

- Log groups in Amazon CloudWatch Logs.

- Amazon ECS tasks.

- Systems Manager Run Command.

- Systems Manager Automation.

- AWS Batch jobs.

- Step Functions state machines.

- Pipelines in CodePipeline.

- CodeBuild projects.

- Amazon Inspector assessment templates.

- Amazon SNS topics.

- Amazon SQS queues.

In the following example, an EC2 instance changes state (terminated) and the event is sent to CloudWatch Events which forwards the event to the target (SQS queue).

USEFUL API ACTIONS

It is useful to understand the following API actions for the Developer Associate exam. You should check these out and other API actions on the AWS website as well prior to your exam.

GetMetricData

- Retrieve as many as 500 different metrics in a single request.

PutMetricData

- Publishes metric data points to Amazon CloudWatch.

- CloudWatch associates the data points with the specified metric.

- If the specified metric does not exist, CloudWatch creates the metric.

GetMetricStatistics

- Gets statistics for the specified metric.

- CloudWatch aggregates data points based on the length of the period that you specify.

- Maximum number of data points returned from a single call is 1,440.

PutMetricAlarm

- Creates or updates an alarm and associates it with the specified metric, metric math expression, or anomaly detection model.

- Alarms based on anomaly detection models cannot have Auto Scaling actions.

AWS CLOUDFORMATION

GENERAL AWS CLOUDFORMATION CONCEPTS

AWS CloudFormation is a service that allows you to manage, configure and provision your AWS infrastructure as code.

AWS CloudFormation provides a common language for you to describe and provision all the infrastructure resources in your cloud environment.

Resources are defined using a CloudFormation template.

CloudFormation interprets the template and makes the appropriate API calls to create the resources you have defined.

Supports YAML or JSON.

CloudFormation can be used to provision a broad range of AWS resources.

Think of CloudFormation as deploying infrastructure as code.

CloudFormation has some similarities with AWS Elastic Beanstalk though they are also quite different as detailed in the table below:

CloudFormation	Elastic Beanstalk
"Template–driven provisioning"	"Web apps made easy"
Deploys infrastructure using code	Deploys applications on EC2 (PaaS)
Can be used to deploy almost any AWS service	Deploys web applications based on Java, .NET, PHP, Node.js, Python, Ruby, Go, and Docker
Uses JSON or YAML template files	Uses ZIP or WAR files
Similar to Terraform	Similar to Google App Engine

KEY BENEFITS

Infrastructure is provisioned consistently, with fewer mistakes (human error).

Less time and effort than configuring resources manually.

You can use version control and peer review for your CloudFormation templates.

Free to use (you're only charged for the resources provisioned).

It can be used to manage updates and dependencies.

It can be used to rollback and delete the entire stack as well.

KEY CONCEPTS

The following table describes the key concepts associated with AWS CloudFormation:

Component	Description
Templates	The JSON or YAML text file that contains the instructions for building out the AWS environment
Stacks	The entire environment described by the template and created, updated, and deleted as a single unit
StackSets	AWS CloudFormation StackSets extends the functionality of stacks by enabling you to create, update, or delete stacks across multiple accounts and regions with a single operation
Change Sets	A summary of proposed changes to your stack that will allow you to see how those changes might impact your existing resources before implementing them
Templates	The JSON or YAML text file that contains the instructions for building out the AWS environment

TEMPLATES

A template is a YAML or JSON template used to describe the end-state of the infrastructure you are either provisioning or changing.

After creating the template, you upload it to CloudFormation directly or using Amazon S3.

CloudFormation reads the template and makes the API calls on your behalf.

The resulting resources are called a "Stack".

Logical IDs are used to reference resources within the template.

Physical IDs identify resources outside of AWS CloudFormation templates, but only after the resources have been created.

TEMPLATE ELEMENTS

Mandatory:

- List of resources and associated configuration values.

Not mandatory:

- Template parameters (limited to 60).
- Output values (limited to 60).
- List of data tables.

TEMPLATE COMPONENTS

Resources – the *required* Resources section declares the AWS resources that you want to include in the stack, such as an Amazon EC2 instance or an Amazon S3 bucket.

- Mandatory.

- Represent AWS components that will be created.

- Resources are declared and can reference each other.

The following example YAML code declares an EC2 instance as a resource:

```
Resources:
 MyEC2Instance:
  Type: "AWS::EC2::Instance"
  Properties:
   ImageId: "ami-0ff8a91507f77f867"
```

Parameters – use the *optional* Parameters section to customize your templates. Parameters enable you to input custom values to your template each time you create or update a stack.

- Provide inputs to your CloudFormation template.

- Useful for template reuse.

The following example declares a parameter named InstanceTypeParameter. This parameter lets you specify the Amazon EC2 instance type for the stack to use when you create or update the stack.

Note: the InstanceTypeParameter has a default value of t2.micro. This is the value that AWS CloudFormation uses to provision the stack unless another value is provided.

```
Parameters:
 InstanceTypeParameter:
  Type: String
  Default: t2.micro
  AllowedValues:
   - t2.micro
   - m1.small
   - m1.large
  Description: Enter t2.micro, m1.small, or m1.large. Default is t2.micro.
```

Pseudo Parameters

Pseudo parameters are parameters that are predefined by AWS CloudFormation. You do not declare them in your template. Use them the same way as you would a parameter, as the argument for the Ref function.

Examples include:

- AWS::AccountId – Returns the AWS account ID of the account in which the stack is being created.

- AWS::NotificationARNs – Returns the list of notification Amazon Resource Names (ARNs) for the current stack.

- AWS::Region – Returns a string representing the AWS Region in which the encompassing resource is being created.

- AWS::StackId – Returns the ID of the stack as specified with the aws cloudformation create-stack command.

Mappings – the *optional* Mappings section matches a key to a corresponding set of named values.

- Fixed variables.

- Good for differentiating between regions, environments, AMIs etc.

- Need to know the values in advance.

- For user-specific values use parameters instead.

The following example has region keys that are mapped to two sets of values: one named HVM64 and the other HVMG2.

RegionMap:

  us-east-1:

  HVM64: ami-0ff8a91507f77f867

  HVMG2: ami-0a584ac55a7631c0c

  us-west-1:

  HVM64: ami-0bdb828fd58c52235

  HVMG2: ami-066ee5fd4a9ef77f1

Exam tip: with mappings you can, for example, set values based on a region. You can create a mapping that uses the region name as a key and contains the values you want to specify for each specific region.

Outputs – the *optional* Outputs section declares output values that you can import into other stacks (to create cross-stack references), return in response (to describe stack calls), or view on the AWS CloudFormation console.

- Outputs can be imported into other stacks.

- Can view the outputs in the console or using the AWS CLI.

- Cannot delete a Stack if it's outputs are being referenced by another CloudFormation Stack.

In the following example YAML code, the output named StackVPC returns the ID of a VPC, and then exports the value for cross-stack referencing with the name VPCID appended to the stack's name

Outputs:

  StackVPC:

  Description: The ID of the VPC

  Value: !Ref MyVPC

  Export:

  Name: !Sub "${AWS::StackName}-VPCID"

Conditions – the *optional* Conditions section contains statements that define the circumstances under which entities are created or configured.

- Control the creation of resources based on a condition.

- Applied to resources and outputs.

In the sample YAML code below, resources are created only if the EnvType parameter is equal to prod:

Conditions:

  CreateProdResources: !Equals [!Ref EnvType, prod]

Transform – the optional Transform section specifies one or more macros that AWS CloudFormation uses to process your template.

The transform section can be used to reference additional code stored in S3, such as Lambda code or reusable snippets of CloudFormation code.

The AWS::Serverless transform, which is a macro hosted by AWS CloudFormation, takes an entire template written in the AWS Serverless Application Model (AWS SAM) syntax and transforms and expands it into a compliant AWS CloudFormation template.

In the following example, the template uses AWS SAM syntax to simplify the declaration of a Lambda function and its execution role:

Transform: AWS::Serverless-2016-10-31

Resources:

  MyServerlessFunctionLogicalID:

    Type: AWS::Serverless::Function

    Properties:

      Handler: index.handler

      Runtime: nodejs8.10

      CodeUri: 's3://testBucket/mySourceCode.zip'

INTRINSIC FUNCTIONS

AWS CloudFormation provides several built-in functions that help you manage your stacks. Use intrinsic functions in your templates to assign values to properties that are not available until runtime.

EXAM TIP: At a minimum, know the intrinsic functions listed below for the exam. The full list can be found at: https://docs.aws.amazon.com/AWSCloudFormation/latest/UserGuide/intrinsic-function-reference.html

Ref

- Fn::Ref (or !Ref in YAML),
- The intrinsic function Ref returns the value of the specified parameter or resource.
- When you specify a parameter's logical name, it returns the value of the parameter.
- When you specify a resource's logical name, it returns a value that you can typically use to refer to that resource, such as a physical ID.

The following resource declaration for an Elastic IP address needs the instance ID of an EC2 instance and uses the Ref function to specify the instance ID of the MyEC2Instance resource:

MyEIP:

  Type: "AWS::EC2::EIP"

  Properties:

InstanceId: !Ref MyEC2Instance

Fn::GetAtt

- The Fn::GetAtt intrinsic function returns the value of an attribute from a resource in the template.

- Full syntax (YAML): Fn::GetAtt: [logicalNameOfResource, attributeName]

- Short form (YAML): !GetAtt logicalNameOfResource.attributeName

The following example template returns the SourceSecurityGroup.OwnerAlias and SourceSecurityGroup.GroupName of the load balancer with the logical name myELB.

AWSTemplateFormatVersion: 2010-09-09

Resources:

 myELB:

  Type: AWS::ElasticLoadBalancing::LoadBalancer

  Properties:

   AvailabilityZones:

    - eu-west-1a

   Listeners:

    - LoadBalancerPort: '80'

     InstancePort: '80'

     Protocol: HTTP

 myELBIngressGroup:

  Type: AWS::EC2::SecurityGroup

  Properties:

   GroupDescription: ELB ingress group

   SecurityGroupIngress:

    - IpProtocol: tcp

     FromPort: '80'

     ToPort: '80'

     SourceSecurityGroupOwnerId: !GetAtt myELB.SourceSecurityGroup.OwnerAlias

     SourceSecurityGroupName: !GetAtt myELB.SourceSecurityGroup.GroupName

Fn::FindInMap

- The intrinsic function Fn::FindInMap returns the value corresponding to keys in a two-level map that is declared in the Mappings section.

- Full syntax (YAML): Fn::FindInMap: [MapName, TopLevelKey, SecondLevelKey]

- Short form (YAML): !FindInMap [MapName, TopLevelKey, SecondLevelKey]

The following example shows how to use Fn::FindInMap for a template with a Mappings section that contains a single map, RegionMap, that associates AMIs with AWS regions:

```
Mappings:
  RegionMap:
    us-east-1:
      HVM64: "ami-0ff8a91507f77f867"
      HVMG2: "ami-0a584ac55a7631c0c"
    us-west-1:
      HVM64: "ami-0bdb828fd58c52235"
      HVMG2: "ami-066ee5fd4a9ef77f1"
Resources:
  myEC2Instance:
    Type: "AWS::EC2::Instance"
    Properties:
      ImageId: !FindInMap
        - RegionMap
        - !Ref 'AWS::Region'
        - HVM64
      InstanceType: m1.small
```

Fn::ImportValue

- The intrinsic function Fn::ImportValue returns the value of an output exported by another stack.
- You typically use this function to create cross-stack references.

```
Fn::ImportValue:
  !Sub "${NetworkStackName}-SecurityGroupID"
```

Fn::Join

- Full syntax (YAML): Fn::Join: [delimiter, [comma-delimited list of values]]
- Short form (YAML): !Join [delimiter, [comma-delimited list of values]]

The following example uses Fn::Join to construct a string value. It uses the Ref function with the Partition parameter and the AWS::AccountId pseudo parameter.

```
!Join
  - ''
  - - 'arn:'
    - !Ref Partition
    - ':s3:::elasticbeanstalk-*-'
    - !Ref 'AWS::AccountId'
```

Fn::Sub

- The intrinsic function Fn::Sub substitutes variables in an input string with values that you specify.

- In your templates, you can use this function to construct commands or outputs that include values that aren't available until you create or update a stack.

The following example uses a mapping to substitute the ${Domain} variable with the resulting value from the Ref function:

Name: !Sub

  - www.${Domain}

  - { Domain: !Ref RootDomainName }

STACKS AND STACK SETS

Stacks:

- Deployed resources based on templates.
- Create, update and delete stacks using templates.
- Deployed through the Management Console, CLI or APIs.

Stack creation errors:

- Automatic rollback on error is enabled by default.
- You will be charged for resources provisioned even if there is an error.

Updating stacks:

- AWS CloudFormation provides two methods for updating stacks: direct update or creating and executing change sets.
- When you directly update a stack, you submit changes and AWS CloudFormation immediately deploys them.
- Use direct updates when you want to quickly deploy your updates.
- With change sets, you can preview the changes AWS CloudFormation will make to your stack, and then decide whether to apply those changes.

Stack Sets:

- AWS CloudFormation StackSets extends the functionality of stacks by enabling you to create, update, or delete stacks across multiple accounts and regions with a single operation.
- Using an administrator account, you define and manage an AWS CloudFormation template, and use the template as the basis for provisioning stacks into selected target accounts across specified regions.
- An administrator account is the AWS account in which you create stack sets.
- A stack set is managed by signing in to the AWS administrator account in which it was created.
- A target account is the account into which you create, update, or delete one or more stacks in your stack set.

Before you can use a stack set to create stacks in a target account, you must set up a trust relationship between the administrator and target accounts.

CloudFormation Nested Stacks:

- Nested stacks allow re-use of CloudFormation code for common use cases.
- For example standard configuration for a load balancer, web server, application server etc.

- Instead of copying out the code each time, create a standard template for each common use case and reference from within your CloudFormation template.

BEST PRACTICES

AWS provides Python "helper scripts" which can help you install software and start services on your EC2 instances.

- Use CloudFormation to make changes to your landscape rather than going directly into the resources.
- Make use of Change Sets to identify potential trouble spots in your updates.
- Use Stack Policies to explicitly protect sensitive portions of your stack.
- Use a version control system such as CodeCommit or GitHub to track changes to templates.

SERVERLESS APPLICATION MODEL (SAM)

Use SAM for deploying serverless applications using CloudFormation.

SAM is an extension to CloudFormation used to define serverless applications.

Simplified syntax for defining serverless resources: APIs, Lambda Functions, DynamoDB Tables etc.

Use the SAM CLI to package your deployment code, upload it to S3 and deploy your serverless application.

CHARGES

- There is no additional charge for AWS CloudFormation.
- You pay for AWS resources (such as Amazon EC2 instances, Elastic Load Balancing load balancers, etc.) created using AWS CloudFormation in the same manner as if you created them manually.
- You only pay for what you use, as you use it; there are no minimum fees and no required upfront commitments.

SNIPPETS

https://docs.aws.amazon.com/AWSCloudFormation/latest/UserGuide/CHAP_TemplateQuickRef.html

AWS CLOUDTRAIL

GENERAL AWS CLOUDTRAIL CONCEPTS

AWS CloudTrail is a web service that records activity made on your account.

A CloudTrail trail can be created which delivers log files to an Amazon S3 bucket.

CloudTrail is about logging and saves a history of API calls for your AWS account.

It enables governance, compliance, and operational and risk auditing of your AWS account.

Events include actions taken in the AWS Management Console, AWS Command Line Interface, and AWS SDKs and APIs.

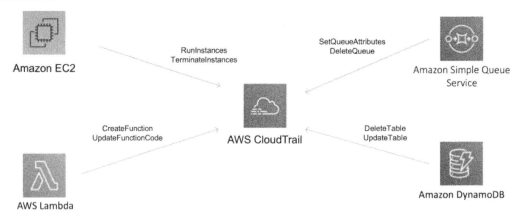

CloudTrail provides visibility into user activity by recording actions taken on your account.

API history enables security analysis, resource change tracking, and compliance auditing.

Logs API calls made via:

- AWS Management Console.
- AWS SDKs.
- Command line tools.
- Higher-level AWS services (such as CloudFormation).

CloudTrail records account activity and service events from most AWS services and logs the following records:

- The identity of the API caller.
- The time of the API call.
- The source IP address of the API caller.
- The request parameters.
- The response elements returned by the AWS service.

CloudTrail is enabled on your AWS account when you create it.

CloudTrail is per AWS account.

You can create two types of trails for an AWS account:

- A trail that applies to all regions – records events in all regions and delivers to an S3 bucket.
- A trail that applies to a single region – records events in a single region and delivers to an S3 bucket. Additional single trails can use the same or a different S3 bucket.

Trails can be configured to log data events and management events:

- **Data events:** These events provide insight into the resource operations performed on or within a resource. These are also known as data plane operations.
- **Management events:** Management events provide insight into management operations that are performed on resources in your AWS account. These are also known as control plane operations. Management events can also include non-API events that occur in your account.

Example data events include:

- Amazon S3 object-level API activity (for example, GetObject, DeleteObject, and PutObject API operations).

- AWS Lambda function execution activity (the Invoke API).

Example management events include:

- Configuring security (for example, IAM AttachRolePolicy API operations).

- Registering devices (for example, Amazon EC2 CreateDefaultVpc API operations).

- Configuring rules for routing data (for example, Amazon EC2 CreateSubnet API operations).

- Setting up logging (for example, AWS CloudTrail CreateTrail API operations).

- CloudTrail log files are encrypted using S3 Server Side Encryption (SSE).

You can also enable encryption using SSE KMS for additional security.

A single KMS key can be used to encrypt log files for trails applied to all regions.

You can consolidate logs from multiple accounts using an S3 bucket:

1. Turn on CloudTrail in the paying account.

2. Create a bucket policy that allows cross-account access.

3. Turn on CloudTrail in the other accounts and use the bucket in the paying account.

You can integrate CloudTrail with CloudWatch Logs to deliver data events captured by CloudTrail to a CloudWatch Logs log stream.

CloudTrail log file integrity validation feature allows you to determine whether a CloudTrail log file was unchanged, deleted, or modified since CloudTrail delivered it to the specified Amazon S3 bucket.

CloudWatch vs CloudTrail:

CloudWatch	CloudTrail
Performance monitoring	Auditing
Log events across AWS services – think operations	Log API activity across AWS services – think activities
Higher-level comprehensive monitoring and eventing	More low-level granular
Log from multiple accounts	Log from multiple accounts
Logs stored indefinitely	Logs stored to S3 or CloudWatch indefinitely
Alarms history for 14 days	No native alarming; can use CloudWatch alarms

AWS SYSTEMS MANAGER PARAMETER STORE

GENERAL AWS SYSTEMS MANAGER PARAMETER STORE CONCEPTS

AWS Systems Manager Parameter Store provides secure, hierarchical storage for configuration data management and secrets management.

It is highly scalable, available, and durable,

You can store data such as passwords, database strings, and license codes as parameter values.

You can store values as plaintext (unencrypted data) or ciphertext (encrypted data).

You can then reference values by using the unique name that you specified when you created the parameter.

There are no additional charges for using SSM Parameter Store. However, there is a limit of 10,000 parameters per account.

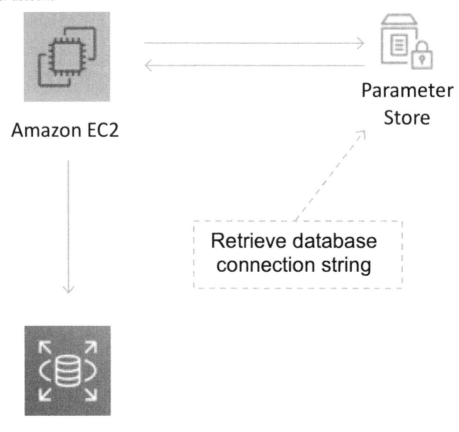

BENEFITS AND FEATURES

Use a secure, scalable, hosted secrets management service with no servers to manage.

Improve your security posture by separating your data from your code.

Store configuration data and secure strings in hierarchies and track versions.

Control and audit access at granular levels.

Configure change notifications and trigger automated actions for both parameters and parameter policies.

Tag parameters individually, and then secure access from different levels, including operational, parameter, Amazon EC2 tag, and path levels.

Reference AWS Secrets Manager secrets by using Parameter Store parameters.

Use Parameter Store parameters with other Systems Manager capabilities and AWS services to retrieve secrets and configuration data from a central store.

Can store strings such as licence keys to pass to EC2 instances.

Parameters can be encrypted using KMS.

Data can then be referenced by the name of the value stored.

SERVICES SUPPORT

The growing list of AWS services that support Parameter Store parameters includes the following:

- Amazon Elastic Compute Cloud (Amazon EC2).
- Amazon Elastic Container Service (Amazon ECS).
- AWS Lambda.
- AWS CloudFormation.
- AWS CodeBuild.
- AWS CodeDeploy.

You can also configure integration with the following AWS services for encryption, notification, monitoring, and auditing:

- AWS Key Management Service (AWS KMS).
- Amazon Simple Notification Service (Amazon SNS).
- Amazon CloudWatch.
- AWS CloudTrail.

AWS MANAGEMENT AND GOVERNANCE QUIZ QUESTIONS

Question 1: How can a Developer view proposed changes to an AWS CloudFormation stack before committing to implementing the change?

1. Use a Stack Set

2. Use a Change Set

3. Use a JSON template rather than YAML

Question 2: Which component of an AWS CloudFormation template is mandatory and is used to declare the AWS services that will be created?

1. Resources

2. Parameters

3. Mappings

4. Conditions

Question 3: Which Transform header indicates a template is using AWS Serverless Application Model (SAM) syntax?

1. AWS::Serverless-2016-10-31

2. AWS::Include

3. AWS::SAM-2016-10-31

Question 4: A Developer needs to create a CloudFormation that contains multiple values for each specific region. Which template component should be used to specify the possible values?

1. Outputs

2. Pseudo Parameters

3. Mappings

Question 5: A Developer needs to track custom metrics with a resolution of 1 second. Which type of metric should be used?

1. Standard resolution

2. High resolution

3. Detailed monitoring

Question 6: How can a Developer configure Amazon CloudTrail to log events from all AWS regions to a single Amazon S3 bucket?

1. Configure a Trail and apply it to all regions and specify a single S3 bucket

2. Use Amazon CloudWatch Logs to capture the API activity in a single S3 bucket

3. Create a trail in each region and use cross-region replication to copy data to a single S3 bucket

Question 7: How can a Developer monitor the memory usage of an Amazon EC2 instance?

1. Use Amazon CloudWatch with a standard metric

2. Use Amazon CloudWatch with a custom metric

3. Use Amazon CloudWatch with a custom dimension

Question 8: A manager needs to receive email notification of state changes in Amazon EC2. Which AWS services can assist with this?

1. Use Amazon CloudWatch Events with an Amazon SNS Topic

2. Use Amazon CloudWatch Alarms with an Amazon SNS Topic

3. Use Amazon CloudTrail Logs with an AWS Lambda function

AWS MANAGEMENT AND GOVERNANCE - QUIZ QUESTIONS & ANSWERS

Question 1: How can a Developer view proposed changes to an AWS CloudFormation stack before committing to implementing the change?

1. Use a Stack Set

2. Use a Change Set

3. Use a JSON template rather than YAML

Question 1, Answer 2

Explanation:

1 is incorrect. AWS CloudFormation StackSets extends the functionality of stacks by enabling you to create, update, or delete stacks across multiple accounts and regions with a single operation.

2 is correct. Change sets provide a summary of proposed changes to your stack that allows you to see how those changes might impact existing resources before implementing them.

3 is incorrect. It does not matter whether you use JSON or YAML for your template files and this does not help you view proposed changes.

Question 2: Which component of an AWS CloudFormation template is mandatory and is used to declare the AWS services that will be created?

1. Resources

2. Parameters

3. Mappings

4. Conditions

Question 2, Answer 1

Explanation:

1 is correct. The required Resources section declares the AWS resources that you want to include in the stack, such as an Amazon EC2 instance or an Amazon S3 bucket.

2 is incorrect. Use the optional Parameters section to customize your templates. Parameters enable you to input custom values to your template each time you create or update a stack.

3 is incorrect. The optional Mappings section matches a key to a corresponding set of named values.

4 is incorrect. The optional Conditions section contains statements that define the circumstances under which entities are created or configured.

Question 3: Which Transform header indicates a template is using AWS Serverless Application Model (SAM) syntax?

1. AWS::Serverless-2016-10-31

2. AWS::Include

3. AWS::SAM-2016-10-31

Question 3, Answer 1

Explanation:

1 is correct. The AWS::Serverless transform, which is a macro hosted by AWS CloudFormation, takes an entire template written in the AWS Serverless Application Model (AWS SAM) syntax and transforms and expands it into a compliant AWS CloudFormation template.

2 is incorrect. Use the AWS::Include transform, which is a macro hosted by AWS CloudFormation, to insert boilerplate content into your templates.

3 is incorrect. This is not a valid transform header.

Question 4: A Developer needs to create a CloudFormation that contains multiple values for each specific region. Which template component should be used to specify the possible values?

1. Outputs

2. Pseudo Parameters

3. Mappings

Question 4, Answer 3

Explanation:

1 is incorrect. The optional Outputs section declares output values that you can import into other stacks (to create cross-stack references), return in response (to describe stack calls), or view on the AWS CloudFormation console.

2 is incorrect. Pseudo parameters are parameters that are predefined by AWS CloudFormation. You do not declare them in your template. Use them the same way as you would a parameter, as the argument for the Ref function.

3 is correct. The optional Mappings section matches a key to a corresponding set of named values. With mappings you can, for example, set values based on a region. You can create a mapping that uses the region name as a key and contains the values you want to specify for each specific region.

Question 5: A Developer needs to track custom metrics with a resolution of 1 second. Which type of metric should be used?

1. Standard resolution

2. High resolution

3. Detailed monitoring

Question 5, Answer 2

Explanation:

1 is incorrect. Standard resolution has a granularity of 1 minute.

2 is correct. High resolution has a granularity of 1 second.

3 is incorrect. Detailed monitoring is associated with services such as Amazon EC2 to enable monitoring with a granularity of 1 minute.

Question 6: How can a Developer configure Amazon CloudTrail to log events from all AWS regions to a single Amazon S3 bucket?

1. Configure a Trail and apply it to all regions and specify a single S3 bucket

2. Use Amazon CloudWatch Logs to capture the API activity in a single S3 bucket

3. Create a trail in each region and use cross-region replication to copy data to a single S3 bucket

Question 6, Answer 1

Explanation:

1 is correct. Trails can be enabled per region or a trail can be applied to all regions. When you apply a trail to all regions you can specify a single S3 bucket.

2 is incorrect. Amazon CloudWatch Logs does not capture API activity.

3 is incorrect. This is inefficient and unnecessary. It's better to apply a trail to all regions and specify a single S3 bucket.

Question 7: How can a Developer monitor the memory usage of an Amazon EC2 instance?

1. Use Amazon CloudWatch with a standard metric

2. Use Amazon CloudWatch with a custom metric

3. Use Amazon CloudWatch with a custom dimension

Question 7, Answer 2

Explanation:

1 is incorrect. Standard metrics do not monitor memory usage.

2 is correct. A custom metric can be created to monitor memory usage.

3 is incorrect. A custom metric should be used not a custom dimension. A dimension further clarifies what the metric is and what data it stores.

Question 8: A manager needs to receive email notification of state changes in Amazon EC2. Which AWS services can assist with this?

1. Use Amazon CloudWatch Events with an Amazon SNS Topic

2. Use Amazon CloudWatch Alarms with an Amazon SNS Topic

3. Use Amazon CloudTrail Logs with an AWS Lambda function

Question 8, Answer 1

Explanation:

1 is correct. Amazon CloudWatch Events delivers a near real-time stream of system events that describe changes in AWS resources. Destinations include Amazon SNS topics which would be ideal for sending the notification.

2 is incorrect. CloudWatch Alarms monitors performance metrics not state changes.

3 is incorrect. CloudTrail monitors API activity rather than state changes.

AWS ANALYTICS

AMAZON KINESIS

GENERAL AMAZON KINESIS CONCEPTS

Amazon Kinesis makes it easy to collect, process, and analyze real-time, streaming data so you can get timely insights and react quickly to new information.

Collection of services for processing streams of various data.

Data is processed in "shards" – with each shard able to ingest 1000 records per second.

There is a default limit of 500 shards, but you can request an increase to unlimited shards.

A record consists of a partition key, sequence number, and data blob (up to 1 MB).

Transient data store – default retention of 24 hours, but can be configured for up to 7 days.

The Kinesis family includes Kinesis Data Streams, Kinesis Data Firehose, Kinesis Data Analytics and Kinesis Video Streams (out of scope).

Examples of streaming data:

- Purchases from online stores.
- Stock prices.
- Game data (statistics and results as the gamer plays).
- Social network data.
- Geospatial data (think uber.com).
- IoT sensor data.

The following Kinesis services are in scope for the exam:

- Kinesis Streams.
- Kinesis Firehose.
- Kinesis Analytics.

KINESIS DATA STREAMS

Producers send data to Kinesis, data is stored in Shards for 24 hours (by default, up to 7 days).

Consumers then take the data and process it – data can then be saved into another AWS service.

One shard provides a capacity of 1MB/sec data input and 2MB/sec data output.

One shard can support up to 1000 PUT records per second.

The following diagram shows producers placing records in a stream and then consumers processing records from the stream. There are multiple options for destinations.

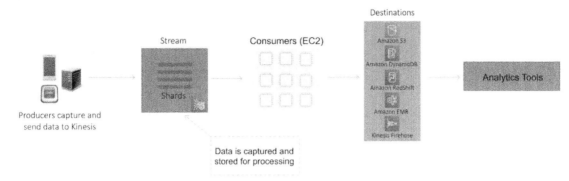

The total capacity of the stream is the sum of the capacities of its shards.

Kinesis Data Streams supports resharding, which lets you adjust the number of shards in your stream to adapt to changes in the rate of data flow through the stream.

There are two types of resharding operations: shard split and shard merge.

- In a shard split, you divide a single shard into two shards.

- In a shard merge, you combine two shards into a single shard.

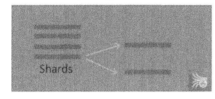

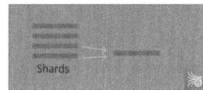

Splitting increases the number of shards in your stream and therefore increases the data capacity of the stream.

Splitting increases the cost of your stream (you pay per-shard).

Merging reduces the number of shards in your stream and therefore decreases the data capacity—and cost—of the stream.

KINESIS DATA FIREHOSE

Producers send data to Firehose.

There are no Shards, it's completely automated (scalability is elastic).

Firehose data is sent to another AWS service for storing, data can be optionally processed using AWS Lambda.

Data sent to RedShift must go to S3 first.

Fully managed service.

Near real-time (60 seconds latency).

Load data into RedShift, S3, Elasticsearch, or Splunk.

Automatic scaling.

Supports many data formats (pay for conversion).

You pay for the amount of data going through Firehose.

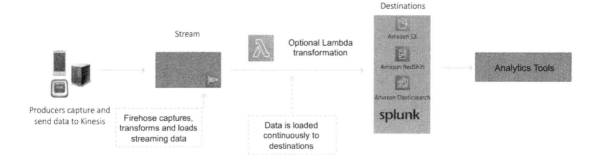

KINESIS DATA ANALYTICS

Use SQL query to query data within Kinesis (Streams and Firehose).

Data is then stored in S3, RedShift or an Elasticsearch cluster.

Use for real-time analytics on Kinesis streams using SQL.

Provides auto scaling.

Fully managed service.

Continuous: real-time.

You pay for the actual consumption rate.

Can create streams out of the real-time queries.

KINESIS CLIENT LIBRARY

Kinesis Client Library is a Java library that helps read records from a Kinesis Stream with distributed applications sharing the read workload.

The KCL is different from the Kinesis Data Streams API that is available in the AWS SDKs.

- The Kinesis Data Streams API helps you manage many aspects of Kinesis Data Streams (including creating streams, resharding, and putting and getting records).

- The KCL provides a layer of abstraction specifically for processing data in a consumer role.

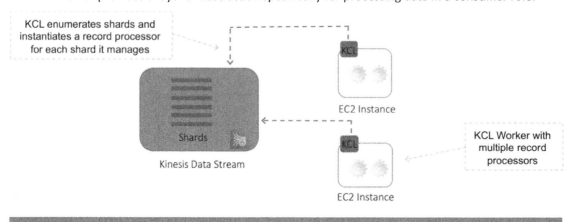

The KCL acts as an intermediary between your record processing logic and Kinesis Data Streams.

When you start a KCL application, it calls the KCL to instantiate a worker. The KCL performs the following tasks:

- Connects to the stream.
- Enumerates the shards.
- Coordinates shard associations with other workers (if any).
- Instantiates a record processor for every shard it manages.
- Pulls data records from the stream.
- Pushes the records to the corresponding record processor.
- Checkpoints processed records.
- Balances shard-worker associations when the worker instance count changes.
- Balances shard-worker associations when shards are split or merged.

The KCL ensures that for every shard there is a record processor.

Manages the number of record processors relative to the number of shards & consumers.

If you have only one consumer, the KCL will create all the record processors on a single consumer.

Each shard is processed by exactly one KCL worker and has exactly one corresponding record processor, so you never need multiple instances to process one shard.

However, one worker can process any number of shards, so it's fine if the number of shards exceeds the number of instances.

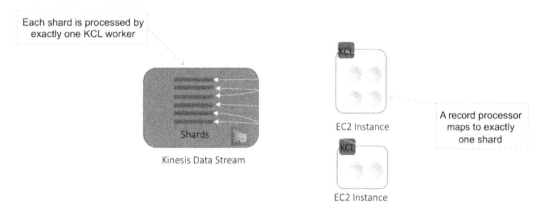

If you have two consumers it will load balance and create half the processors on one instance and half on another.

Scaling out consumers:

- With KCL, generally you should ensure that the number of instances does not exceed the number of shards (except for failure or standby purposes).
- Each shard can be read by only one KCL instance.
- You never need multiple instances to handle the processing of one shard.

However, one worker can process multiple shards.

Example:

- 4 shards = max 4 KCL instances.

- 6 shards = max 6 KCL instances.

Progress is checkpointed into DynamoDB (IAM access required).

KCL can run on EC2, Elastic Beanstalk, and on-premises servers.

Records are read in order at the shard level.

SECURITY

Control access / authorization using IAM policies.

Encryption in flight using HTTPS endpoints.

Encryption at rest using KMS.

Possible to encrypt / decrypt data on the client side.

VPC endpoints available for Kinesis to access within a VPC.

SQS VS SNS VS KINESIS

SQS:

- Consumers pull data.
- Data is deleted after being consumed.
- Can have as many workers (consumers) as you need.
- No need to provision throughput.
- No ordering guarantee (except with FIFO queues).
- Individual message delay.

SNS:

- Push data to many subscribers.
- Up to 10,000,000 subscribers.
- Data is not persisted (lost if not deleted).
- Pub/sub.
- Up to 10,000,000 topics.
- No need to provision throughput.
- Integrates with SQS for fan-out architecture pattern.

Kinesis:

- Consumers pull data.
- As many consumers as you need.
- Possible to replay data.
- Meant for real-time big data, analytics, and ETL.
- Ordering at the shard level.
- Data expires after X days.
- Must provision throughput.

AWS SECURITY, IDENTITY AND COMPLIANCE

AMAZON IAM

GENERAL AMAZON IAM CONCEPTS

IAM is used to securely control individual and group access to AWS resources.

IAM makes it easy to provide multiple users secure access to AWS resources.

IAM can be used to manage:

- Users.
- Groups.
- Access policies.
- Roles.
- User credentials.
- User password policies.
- Multi-factor authentication (MFA).
- API keys for programmatic access (CLI).

Provides centralized control of your AWS account.

Enables shared access to your AWS account.

By default new users are created with NO access to any AWS services – they can only login to the AWS console.

Permission must be explicitly granted to allow a user to access an AWS service.

IAM users are individuals who have been granted access to an AWS account.

Each IAM user has three main components:

- A user-name.
- A password.
- Permissions to access various resources.

You can apply granular permissions with IAM.

You can assign users individual security credentials such as access keys, passwords, and multi-factor authentication devices.

IAM is not used for application-level authentication.

Identity Federation (including AD, Facebook etc.) can be configured allowing secure access to resources in an AWS account without creating an IAM user account.

Multi-factor authentication (MFA) can be enabled/enforced for the AWS account and for individual users under the account.

MFA uses an authentication device that continually generates random, six-digit, single-use authentication codes.

You can authenticate using an MFA device in the following three ways:

- Through the **AWS Management Console** – the user is prompted for a user name, password and authentication code.

- Using the **AWS API** – restrictions are added to IAM policies and developers can request temporary security credentials and pass MFA parameters in their AWS STS API requests.

- Using the **AWS CLI** by obtaining temporary security credentials from STS (aws sts get-session-token).

It is a best practice to use MFA for all users and to use U2F or hardware MFA devices for all privileged users.

IAM is universal (global) and does not apply to regions.

IAM is eventually consistent.

IAM replicates data across multiple data centres around the world.

The "root account" is the account created when you setup the AWS account. It has complete Admin access and is the only account that has this access by default.

It is a best practice to not use the root account for anything other than billing.

Power user access allows all permissions except the management of groups and users in IAM.

Temporary security credentials consist of the AWS access key ID, secret access key, and security token.

IAM can assign temporary security credentials to provide users with temporary access to services/resources.

To sign-in you must provide your account ID or account alias in addition to a user name and password.

The sign-in URL includes the account ID or account alias, e.g:

https://**My_AWS_Account_ID**.signin.aws.amazon.com/console/.

Alternatively you can sign-in at the following URL and enter your account ID or alias manually:

https://console.aws.amazon.com/.

IAM integrates with many different AWS services.

IAM supports PCI DSS compliance.

AWS recommend that you use the AWS SDKs to make programmatic API calls to IAM.

However, you can also use the IAM Query API to make direct calls to the IAM web service.

IAM INFRASTRUCTURE ELEMENTS

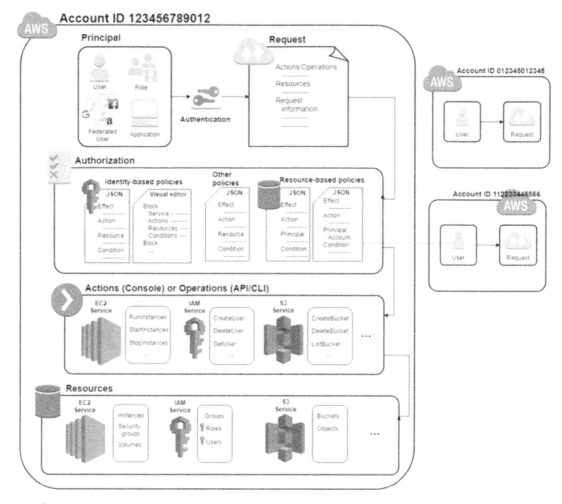

Principals:

- An entity that can take an action on an AWS resource.

- Your administrative IAM user is your first principal.

- You can allow users and services to assume a role.

- IAM supports federated users.

- IAM supports programmatic access to allow an application to access your AWS account.

- IAM users, roles, federated users, and applications are all AWS principals.

Requests:

- Principals send requests via the Console, CLI, SDKs, or APIs.

- Requests are:

    - Actions (or operations) that the principal wants to perform.

    - Resources upon which the actions are performed.

    - Principal information including the environment from which the request was made.

- Request context – AWS gathers the request information:

- Principal (requester).
- Aggregate permissions associated with the principal.
- Environment data, such as IP address, user agent, SSL status etc.
- Resource data, or data that is related to the resource being requested.

Authentication:

- A principal sending a request must be authenticated to send a request to AWS.
- To authenticate from the console, you must sign in with your user name and password.
- To authenticate from the API or CLI, you must provide your access key and secret key.

Authorization:

- IAM uses values from the request context to check for matching policies and determines whether to allow or deny the request.
- IAM policies are stored in IAM as JSON documents and specify the permissions that are allowed or denied.
- IAM policies can be:
    - User (identity) based policies.
    - Resource-based policies.
- IAM checks each policy that matches the context of your request.
- If a single policy has a deny action IAM denies the request and stops evaluating (explicit deny).
- Evaluation logic:
    - By default all requests are denied (implicit deny).
    - An explicit allow overrides the implicit deny.
    - An explicit deny overrides any explicit allows.
- Only the root user has access to all resources in the account by default.

Actions:

- Actions are defined by a service.
- Actions are the things you can do to a resource such as viewing, creating, editing, deleting.
- Any actions on resources that are not explicitly allowed are denied.
- To allow a principal to perform an action you must include the necessary actions in a policy that applies to the principal or the affected resource.

Resources:

- A resource is an entity that exists within a service.
- E.g. EC2 instances, S3 buckets, IAM users, and DynamoDB tables.
- Each AWS service defines a set of actions that can be performed on the resource.
- After AWS approves the actions in your request, those actions can be performed on the related resources within your account.

AUTHENTICATION METHODS

Console password:

- A password that the user can enter to sign into interactive sessions such as the AWS Management Console.

- You can allow users to change their own passwords.

- You can allow selected IAM users to change their passwords by disabling the option for all users and using an IAM policy to grant permissions for the selected users.

Access Keys:

- A combination of an **access key ID** and a **secret access key.**

- You can assign two active access keys to a user at a time.

- These can be used to make programmatic calls to AWS when using the **API** in program code or at a command prompt when using the **AWS CLI** or the **AWS PowerShell** tools.

- You can create, modify, view or rotate access keys.

- When created IAM returns the access key ID and secret access key.

- The secret access is returned only at creation time and if lost a new key must be created.

- Ensure access keys and secret access keys are stored securely.

- Users can be given access to change their own keys through IAM policy (not from the console).

- You can disable a user's access key which prevents it from being used for API calls.

- Access keys are stored in:

    - Linux: ~/.aws/credentials

    - Windows: %UserProfle%\.aws\credentials

Server certificates:

- SSL/TLS certificates that you can use to authenticate with some AWS services.

- AWS recommends that you use the AWS Certificate Manager (ACM) to provision, manage and deploy your server certificates.

- Use IAM only when you must support HTTPS connections in a region that is not supported by ACM.

The following diagram shows the different methods of authentication available with IAM:

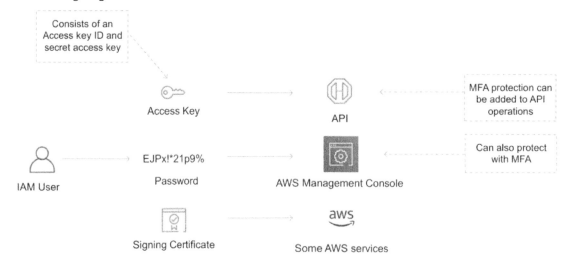

IAM USERS

An IAM user is an entity that represents a person or service.

Can be assigned:

- An access key ID and secret access key for programmatic access to the AWS API, CLI, SDK, and other development tools.
- A password for access to the management console.

By default users cannot access anything in your account.

The account root user credentials are the email address used to create the account and a password.

The root account has full administrative permissions and these cannot be restricted.

Best practice for root accounts:

- Don't use the root user credentials.
- Don't share the root user credentials.
- Create an IAM user and assign administrative permissions as required.
- Enable MFA.

IAM users can be created to represent applications and these are known as "service accounts".

You can have up to 5000 users per AWS account.

Each user account has a friendly name and an ARN which uniquely identifies the user across AWS.

A unique ID is also created which is returned only when you create the user using the API, Tools for Windows PowerShell or the AWS CLI.

You should create individual IAM accounts for users (best practice not to share accounts).

The Access Key ID and Secret Access Key are not the same as a password and cannot be used to login to the AWS console.

The Access Key ID and Secret Access Key can only be generated once and must be regenerated if lost.

A password policy can be defined for enforcing password length, complexity etc. (applies to all users).

You can allow or disallow the ability to change passwords using an IAM policy.

Access keys and passwords should be changed regularly.

GROUPS

Groups are collections of users and have policies attached to them.

A group is not an identity and cannot be identified as a principal in an IAM policy.

Use groups to assign permissions to users.

Use the principal of least privilege when assigning permissions.

You cannot nest groups (groups within groups).

ROLES

Roles are created and then "assumed" by trusted entities and define a set of permissions for making AWS service requests.

With IAM Roles you can delegate permissions to resources for users and services without using permanent credentials (e.g. user name and password).

IAM users or AWS services can assume a role to obtain temporary security credentials that can be used to make AWS API calls.

You can delegate using roles.

There are no credentials associated with a role (password or access keys).

IAM users can temporarily assume a role to take on permissions for a specific task.

A role can be assigned to a federated user who signs in using an external identity provider.

Temporary credentials are primarily used with IAM roles and automatically expire.

Roles can be assumed temporarily through the console or programmatically with the **AWS CLI**, **Tools for Windows PowerShell** or **API.**

IAM roles with EC2 instances:

- IAM roles can be used for granting applications running on EC2 instances permissions to AWS API requests using instance profiles.

- Only one role can be assigned to an EC2 instance at a time.

- A role can be assigned at the **EC2 instance creation time or at any time afterwards.**

- When using the AWS CLI or API instance profiles must be created manually (it's automatic and transparent through the console).

- Applications retrieve temporary security credentials from the instance metadata.

Role Delegation:

- Create an IAM role with two policies:
    - Permissions policy – grants the user of the role the required permissions on a resource.

- Trust policy – specifies the trusted accounts that are allowed to assume the role.
- Wildcards (*) cannot be specified as a principal.
- A permissions policy must also be attached to the user in the trusted account.

POLICIES

Policies are documents that define permissions and can be applied to users, groups and roles.

Policy documents are written in JSON (key value pair that consists of an attribute and a value).

All permissions are implicitly denied by default.

The most restrictive policy is applied.

The IAM policy simulator is a tool to help you understand, test, and validate the effects of access control policies.

The Condition element can be used to apply further conditional logic.

The diagram below provides some more information on the relationship between IAM roles, users, groups and policies.

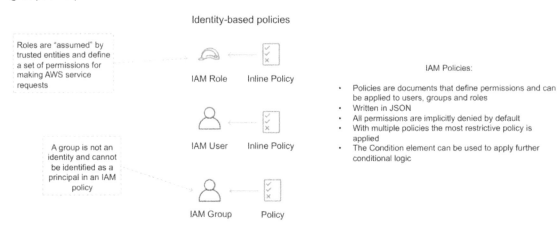

INLINE POLICIES VS MANAGED POLICIES

There are 3 types of policies:

- Managed policies.
- Customer managed policies.
- Inline policies.

Managed Policy:

- Created and administered by AWS.
- Used for common use cases based on job function.
- Save you having to create policies yourself.
- Can be attached to multiple users, groups, or roles within and across AWS accounts.
- Cannot change the permissions assigned.

Customer Managed Policy:

- Standalone policy that you create and administer in your own AWS account.
- Can be attached to multiple users, groups, and roles – but only within your own account.
- Can be created by copying an existing managed policy and then customizing it.
- Recommended for use cases where the existing AWS Managed Policies don't meet the needs of your environment.

Inline Policy:

- Inline policies are embedded within the user, group or role to which it is applied.
- Strict 1:1 relationship between the entity and the policy.
- When you delete the user, group or role in which the inline policy is embedded, the policy will also be deleted.
- In most cases, AWS recommends using Managed Policies instead of inline policies.
- Inline policies are useful when you want to be sure that the permissions in a policy are not inadvertently assigned to any other user, group, or role.

AWS MANAGED AND CUSTOMER MANAGED POLICIES

An AWS managed policy is a standalone policy that is created and administered by AWS.

Standalone policy means that the policy has its own Amazon Resource Name (ARN) that includes the policy name.

AWS managed policies are designed to provide permissions for many common use cases.

You cannot change the permissions defined in AWS managed policies.

Some AWS managed policies are designed for specific job functions.

The job-specific AWS managed policies include:

- Administrator.
- Billing.
- Database Administrator.
- Data Scientist.
- Developer Power User.
- Network Administrator.
- Security Auditor.
- Support User.
- System Administrator.
- View-Only User.

You can create standalone policies that you administer in your own AWS account, which we refer to as customer managed policies.

You can then attach the policies to multiple principal entities in your AWS account.

When you attach a policy to a principal entity, you give the entity the permissions that are defined in the policy.

IAM POLICY EVALUATION LOGIC

By default, all requests are implicitly denied. (Alternatively, by default, the AWS account root user has full access.)

An explicit allow in an identity-based or resource-based policy overrides this default.

If a permissions boundary, Organizations SCP, or session policy is present, it might override the allow with an implicit deny.

An explicit deny in any policy overrides any allows.

A few concepts should be known to understand the logic:

- **Identity-based policies** – Identity-based policies are attached to an IAM identity (user, group of users, or role) and grant permissions to IAM entities (users and roles).

- **Resource-based policies** – Resource-based policies grant permissions to the principal (account, user, role, or federated user) specified as the principal.

- **IAM permissions boundaries** – Permissions boundaries are an advanced feature that sets the maximum permissions that an identity-based policy can grant to an IAM entity (user or role).

- **AWS Organizations service control policies (SCPs)** – Organizations SCPs specify the maximum permissions for an organization or organizational unit (OU). Session policies – Session policies are advanced policies that you pass as parameters when you programmatically create a temporary session for a role or federated user.

The following flowchart details the IAM policy evaluation logic:

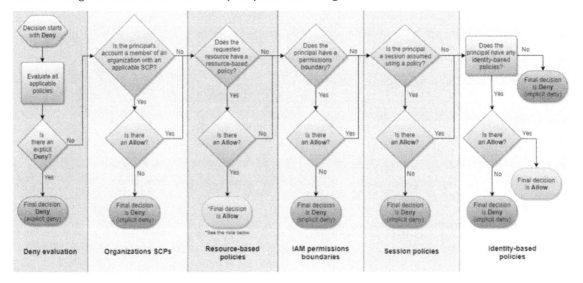

IAM INSTANCE PROFILES

An instance profile is a container for an IAM role that you can use to pass role information to an EC2 instance when the instance starts.

An instance profile can contain only one IAM role, although a role can be included in multiple instance profiles.

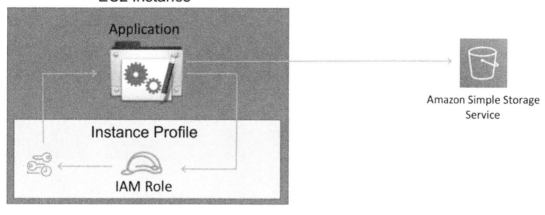

You can use the following AWS CLI commands to work with instance profiles in an AWS account:

- Create an instance profile: aws iam create-instance-profile
- Add a role to an instance profile: aws iam add-role-to-instance-profile
- List instance profiles: aws iam list-instance-profiles, aws iam list-instance-profiles-for-role
- Get information about an instance profile: aws iam get-instance-profile
- Remove a role from an instance profile: aws iam remove-role-from-instance-profile
- Delete an instance profile: aws iam delete-instance-profile

AWS SECURITY TOKEN SERVICE

The AWS Security Token Service (STS) is a web service that enables you to request temporary, limited-privilege credentials for IAM users or for users that you authenticate (federated users).

By default, AWS STS is available as a global service, and all AWS STS requests go to a single endpoint at https://sts.amazonaws.com

You can optionally send your AWS STS requests to endpoints in any region (can reduce latency).

All regions are enabled for STS by default but can be disabled.

The region in which temporary credentials are requested must be enabled.

Credentials will always work globally.

STS supports AWS CloudTrail, which records AWS calls for your AWS account and delivers log files to an S3 bucket.

Temporary security credentials work almost identically to long-term access key credentials that IAM users can use, with the following differences:

- Temporary security credentials are short-term.
- They can be configured to last anywhere from a few minutes to several hours.
- After the credentials expire, AWS no longer recognizes them or allows any kind of access to API requests made with them.
- Temporary security credentials are not stored with the user but are generated dynamically and provided to the user when requested.

- When (or even before) the temporary security credentials expire, the user can request new credentials, as long as the user requesting them still has permission to do so.

Advantages of STS are:

- You do not have to distribute or embed long-term AWS security credentials with an application.
- You can provide access to your AWS resources to users without having to define an AWS identity for them (temporary security credentials are the basis for IAM Roles and ID Federation).
- The temporary security credentials have a limited lifetime, so you do not have to rotate them or explicitly revoke them when they're no longer needed.
- After temporary security credentials expire, they cannot be reused (you can specify how long the credentials are valid for, up to a maximum limit).

The AWS STS API action returns temporary security credentials that consist of:

- An access key which consists of an access key ID and a secret ID.
- A session token.
- Expiration or duration of validity.
- Users (or an application that the user runs) can use these credentials to access your resources.

With STS you can request a session token using one of the following APIs:

- AssumeRole – can only be used by IAM users (can be used for MFA).
- AssumeRoleWithSAML – can be used by any user who passes a SAML authentication response that indicates authentication from a known (trusted) identity provider.
- AssumeRoleWithWebIdentity – can be used by an user who passes a web identity token that indicates authentication from a known (trusted) identity provider.
- GetSessionToken – can be used by an IAM user or AWS account root user (can be used for MFA).
- GetFederationToken – can be used by an IAM user or AWS account root user.

STS AssumeRoleWithWebIdentity:

- Assume-role-with-web-identity is an API provided by STS (Security Token Service).
- Returns temporary security credentials for users authenticated by a mobile or web application or using a Web ID Provider like Amazon, Facebook or Google.
- For mobile applications, Cognito is recommended.
- Regular web applications can use the STS assume-role-with-web-identity API.

AWS recommends using Cognito for identity federation with Internet identity providers.

Users can come from three sources:

Federation (typically AD)

- Uses SAML 2.0.
- Grants temporary access based on the users AD credentials.
- Does not need to be a user in IAM.
- Single sign-on allows users to login to the AWS console without assigning IAM credentials.

Federation with Mobile Apps

- Use Facebook/Amazon/Google or other OpenID providers to login.

There are a couple of ways STS can be used

Scenario 1:

1. Develop an Identity Broker to communicate with LDAP and AWS STS.

2. Identity Broker always authenticates with LDAP first, then with AWS STS.

3. Application then gets temporary access to AWS resources.

Scenario 2:

1. Develop an Identity Broker to communicate with LDAP and AWS STS.

2. Identity Broker authenticates with LDAP first, then gets an IAM role associated with the user.

3. Application then authenticates with STS and assumes that IAM role.

4. Application uses that IAM role to interact with the service.

CROSS ACCOUNT ACCESS

Useful for situations where an AWS customer has separate AWS account – for example for development and production resources.

Cross Account Access makes is easier to work productively within a multi-account (or multi-role) AWS environment by making is easy to switch roles within the AWS Management Console.

Can sign-in to the console using your IAM user name and then switch the console to manage another account without having to enter another user name and password.

Lets users from one AWS account access resources in another.

To make a request in a different account the resource in that account must have an attached resource-based policy with the permissions you need.

Or you must assume a role (identity-based policy) within that account with the permissions you need.

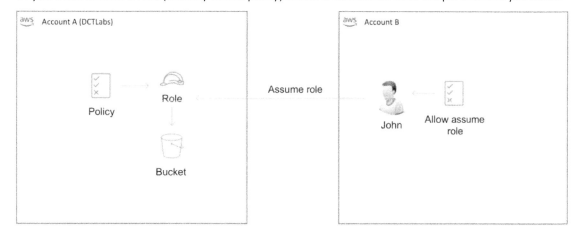

IAM BEST PRACTICES

- Lock Away Your AWS Account Root User Access Keys.

- Create Individual IAM Users.

- Use Groups to Assign Permissions to IAM Users.

- Grant Least Privilege.

- Get Started Using Permissions with AWS Managed Policies.
- Use Customer Managed Policies Instead of Inline Policies.
- Use Access Levels to Review IAM Permissions.
- Configure a Strong Password Policy for Your Users.
- Enable MFA.
- Use Roles for Applications That Run on Amazon EC2 Instances.
- Use Roles to Delegate Permissions.
- Do Not Share Access Keys.
- Rotate Credentials Regularly.
- Remove Unnecessary Credentials.
- Use Policy Conditions for Extra Security.
- Monitor Activity in Your AWS Account.

AWS COGNITO

GENERAL AMAZON COGNITO CONCEPTS

Amazon Cognito lets you add user sign-up, sign-in, and access control to your web and mobile apps quickly and easily.

Amazon Cognito provides authentication, authorization, and user management for your web and mobile apps.

Your users can sign in directly with a user name and password, or through a third party such as Facebook, Amazon, or Google.

WEB IDENTITY FEDERATION

AWS Cognito works with external identity providers that support SAML or OpenID Connect, social identity providers (such as Facebook, Twitter, Amazon)

Federation allows users to authenticate with a Web Identity Provider (e.g. Google, Facebook, Amazon).

The user authenticates first with the Web ID provider and receives an authentication token, which is then exchanges for temporary AWS credentials allowing them to assume an IAM role allowing access to the required resources.

Cognito is an Identity Broker which handles interaction between your applications and the Web ID provider (you don't need to write your own code to do this).

You can use Amazon, Facebook, Twitter, Digits, Google and any other OpenID Connect compatible identity provider.

You can also integrate your own identity provider.

USER POOLS AND IDENTITY POOLS

The two main components of AWS Cognito are user pools and identity pools:

- User pools are user directories that provide sign-up and sign-in options for your app users.
- Identity pools enable you to grant your users access to other AWS services.

You can use identity pools and user pools separately or together.

No need for the application to embed or store AWS credentials locally on the device and it gives users a seamless experience across all mobile devices.

Cognito Identity provides temporary security credentials to access your app's backend resources in AWS or any service behind Amazon API Gateway.

Cognito exposes server-side APIs.

Users can sign-up and sign-in using email, phone number, or user name.

End users of an application can also sign in with SMS-based MFA.

There is an import tool for migrating users into an Amazon Cognito User Pool.

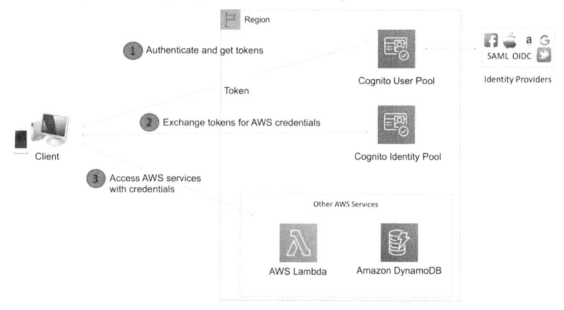

USER POOLS

Cognito User Pools are user directories used to manage sign-up and sign-in functionality for mobile and web applications.

With a user pool, users can sign in to your web or mobile app through Amazon Cognito.

Users can also sign in through social identity providers like Facebook or Amazon, and through SAML identity providers.

Whether users sign-in directly or through a third party, all members of the user pool have a directory profile that you can access through an SDK.

Cognito acts as an Identity Broker between the ID provider and AWS.

User pools provide:

- Sign-up and sign-in services.
- A built-in, customizable web UI to sign in users.

- Social sign-in with Facebook, Google, and Login with Amazon, as well as sign-in with SAML identity providers from your user pool.

- User directory management and user profiles.

- Security features such as multi-factor authentication (MFA), checks for compromised credentials, account takeover protection, and phone and email verification.

- Customized workflows and user migration through AWS Lambda triggers.

After successfully authenticating a user, Amazon Cognito issues JSON web tokens (JWT) that you can use to secure and authorize access to your own APIs, or exchange for AWS credentials.

IDENTITY POOLS

Identity Pools enable you to create unique identities for your users and authenticate them with identity providers.

With an identity, you can obtain temporary, limited-privilege AWS credentials to access other AWS services.

Cognito tracks the association between user identity and the various different devices they sign-in from.

In order to provide a seamless user experience for your application, Cognito uses Push Synchronization to push updates and synchronize user data across multiple devices.

Amazon SNS is used to send a silent push notification to all the devices whenever data stored in the cloud changes.

Amazon Cognito identity pools support the following identity providers:

- Public providers: Login with Amazon (Identity Pools), Facebook (Identity Pools), Google (Identity Pools).

- Amazon Cognito User Pools.

- Open ID Connect Providers (Identity Pools).

- SAML Identity Providers (Identity Pools).

- Developer Authenticated Identities (Identity Pools).

Exam tip: To make it easier to remember the different between User Pools and Identity Pools, think of Users Pools as being similar to IAM Users or Active Directory and an Identity Pools as being similar to an IAM Role.

AMAZON COGNITO SYNC

Amazon Cognito Sync is an AWS service and client library that enables cross-device syncing of application-related user data.

You can use it to synchronize user profile data across mobile devices and the web without requiring your own backend.

The client libraries cache data locally so your app can read and write data regardless of device connectivity status.

When the device is online, you can synchronize data, and If you set up push sync, notify other devices immediately that an update is available.

Exam tip: AWS AppSync is a similar service that has additional capabilities. With AppSync you can synchronize mobile app data across devices and users (Cognito Sync cannot synchronize across users, only devices), it has support for additional devices and data types, and is based on GraphQL.

AMAZON INSPECTOR

GENERAL AMAZON INSPECTOR CONCEPTS

Amazon Inspector is an automated security assessment service that helps improve the security and compliance of applications deployed on AWS.

Amazon Inspector automatically assesses applications for exposure, vulnerabilities, and deviations from best practices.

After performing an assessment, Amazon Inspector produces a detailed list of security findings prioritized by level of severity.

These findings can be reviewed directly or as part of detailed assessment reports which are available via the Amazon Inspector console or API.

Amazon Inspector security assessments help you check for unintended network accessibility of your Amazon EC2 instances and for vulnerabilities on those EC2 instances.

Amazon Inspector assessments are offered to you as pre-defined rules packages mapped to common security best practices and vulnerability definitions.

Examples of built-in rules include checking for access to your EC2 instances from the internet, remote root login being enabled, or vulnerable software versions installed.

These rules are regularly updated by AWS security researchers.

AWS KMS

GENERAL AWS KMS CONCEPTS

AWS Key Management Store (KMS) is a managed service that enables you to easily encrypt your data.

AWS KMS provides a highly available key storage, management, and auditing solution for you to encrypt data within your own applications and control the encryption of stored data across AWS services.

AWS KMS allows you to centrally manage and securely store your keys. These are known as customer master keys or CMKs.

CUSTOMER MASTER KEYS (CMK'S)

A Customer Master Key (CMK) consists of:

- Alias.
- Creation date.
- Description.
- Key state.
- Key material (either customer provided or AWS provided).

Customer master keys are the primary resources in AWS KMS.

The CMK includes metadata, such as the key ID, creation date, description, and key state.

The CMK also contains the key material used to encrypt and decrypt data.

AWS KMS supports symmetric and asymmetric CMKs.

CMKs are created in AWS KMS. Symmetric CMKs and the private keys of asymmetric CMKs never leave AWS KMS unencrypted.

By default, AWS KMS creates the key material for a CMK.

A CMK can encrypt data up to 4KB in size.

A CMK can generate, encrypt and decrypt Data Encryption Keys (DEKs).

A CMK can never be exported from KMS (CloudHSM allows this).

AWS Managed CMKs:

- CMKs managed by AWS are used by AWS services that interact with KMS to encrypt data.

- They can only be used by the service that created them within a particular region.

- They are created on the first time you implement encryption using that service.

Customer managed CMKs:

- These provide the ability to implement greater flexibility.

- You can perform rotation, governing access and key policy configuration.

- You are able to enable and disable the key when it is no longer required.

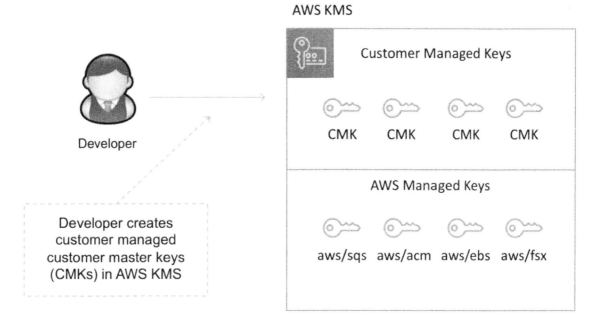

CUSTOMER MANAGED CMK'S

Customer managed CMKs are CMKs in your AWS account that you create, own, and manage.

You have full control over these CMKs, including establishing and maintaining their key policies, IAM policies, and grants, enabling and disabling them, rotating their cryptographic material, adding tags, creating aliases that refer to the CMK, and scheduling the CMKs for deletion.

Customer managed CMKs incur a monthly fee and a fee for use in excess of the free tier.

AWS MANAGED CMK'S

AWS managed CMKs are CMKs in your account that are created, managed, and used on your behalf by an AWS service that is integrated with AWS KMS.

You cannot manage these CMKs, rotate them, or change their key policies.

You also cannot use AWS managed CMKs in cryptographic operations directly; the service that creates them uses them on your behalf.

You do not pay a monthly fee for AWS managed CMKs. They can be subject to fees for use in excess of the free tier, but some AWS services cover these costs for you.

AWS OWNED CMK'S

AWS owned CMKs are a collection of CMKs that an AWS service owns and manages for use in multiple AWS accounts.

Although AWS owned CMKs are not in your AWS account, an AWS service can use its AWS owned CMKs to protect the resources in your account.

You do not need to create or manage the AWS owned CMKs.

However, you cannot view, use, track, or audit them.

You are not charged a monthly fee or usage fee for AWS owned CMKs and they do not count against the AWS KMS quotas for your account.

DATA ENCRYPTION KEYS

Data keys are encryption keys that you can use to encrypt data, including large amounts of data and other data encryption keys.

You can use AWS KMS customer master keys (CMKs) to generate, encrypt, and decrypt data keys.

AWS KMS does not store, manage, or track your data keys, or perform cryptographic operations with data keys.

You must use and manage data keys outside of AWS KMS.

The GenerateDataKey API can be used to create a data encryption key using a CMK:

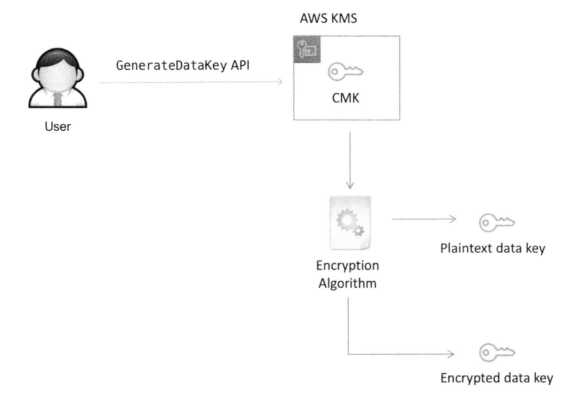

KMS DETAILS

You set usage policies on the keys that determine which users can use them to encrypt and decrypt data and under which conditions.

Key material options:

- KMS generated.
- Import your own.

You can generate CMKs in KMS, in an AWS CloudHSM cluster, or import them from your own key management infrastructure.

These master keys are protected by hardware security modules (HSMs) and are only ever used within those modules.

You can submit data directly to KMS to be encrypted or decrypted using these master keys.

KMS now has the option for symmetric and asymmetric keys.

KMS is for encryption at rest only (not in transit, use SSL).

KMS is tightly integrated into many AWS services like Lambda, S3, EBS, EFS, DynamoDB, SQS etc.

Data keys are not retained or managed by KMS.

AWS services encrypt your data and store an encrypted copy of the data key along with the data it protects.

When a service needs to decrypt your data they request KMS to decrypt the data key using your master key.

If the user requesting data from the AWS service is authorized to decrypt under your master key policy, the service will receive the decrypted data key from KMS with which it can decrypt your data and return it in plaintext.

All requests to use your master keys are logged in AWS CloudTrail so you can understand who used which key under which context and when they used it.

You can control who manages and accesses keys via IAM users and roles.

You can audit the use of keys via CloudTrail.

KMS differs from Secrets Manager as its purpose-built for encryption key management.

KMS is validated by many compliance schemes (e.g. PCI DSS Level 1, FIPS 140-2 Level 2).

Exam tip: Encryption keys are regional.

KEY MANAGEMENT WITH KMS

You can perform the following key management functions in AWS KMS:

- Create keys with a unique alias and description.
- Import your own key material.
- Define which IAM users and roles can manage keys.
- Define which IAM users and roles can use keys to encrypt and decrypt data.
- Choose to have AWS KMS automatically rotate your keys on an annual basis.

- Temporarily disable keys so they cannot be used by anyone.

- Re-enable disabled keys.

- Delete keys that you no longer use.

- Audit use of keys by inspecting logs in AWS CloudTrail.

- Create custom key stores*.

- Connect and disconnect custom key stores*.

- Delete custom key stores*.

* The use of custom key stores requires CloudHSM resources to be available in your account.

DATA ENCRYPTION SCENARIOS

Typically, data is encrypted in one of the following three scenarios:

1. You can use KMS APIs directly to encrypt and decrypt data using your master keys stored in KMS.

2. You can choose to have AWS services encrypt your data using your master keys stored in KMS. In this case data is encrypted using data keys that are protected by your master keys in KMS.

3. You can use the AWS Encryption SDK that is integrated with AWS KMS to perform encryption within your own applications, whether they operate in AWS or not.

CUSTOM KEY STORE

The AWS KMS custom key store feature combines the controls provided by AWS CloudHSM with the integration and ease of use of AWS KMS.

You can configure your own CloudHSM cluster and authorize KMS to use it as a dedicated key store for your keys rather than the default KMS key store.

When you create keys in KMS you can chose to generate the key material in your CloudHSM cluster. Master keys that are generated in your custom key store never leave the HSMs in the CloudHSM cluster in plaintext and all KMS operations that use those keys are only performed in your HSMs.

In all other respects master keys stored in your custom key store are consistent with other KMS CMKs.

KEY DELETION

You can schedule a customer master key and associated metadata that you created in AWS KMS for deletion, with a configurable waiting period from 7 to 30 days.

This waiting period allows you to verify the impact of deleting a key on your applications and users that depend on it.

The default waiting period is 30 days.

You can cancel key deletion during the waiting period.

LIMITS

You can create up to 1000 customer master keys per account per region.

As both enabled and disabled customer master keys count towards the limit, AWS recommend deleting disabled keys that you no longer use.

AWS managed master keys created on your behalf for use within supported AWS services do not count against this limit.

There is no limit to the number of data keys that can be derived using a master key and used in your application or by AWS services to encrypt data on your behalf.

AWS KMS API'S

The following APIs are useful to know for the exam:

Encrypt (aws kms encrypt):

- Encrypts plaintext into ciphertext by using a customer master key (CMK).
- You can encrypt small amounts of arbitrary data, such as a personal identifier or database password, or other sensitive information.
- You can use the Encrypt operation to move encrypted data from one AWS region to another.

Decrypt (aws kms decrypt):

- Decrypts ciphertext that was encrypted by a AWS KMS customer master key (CMK) using any of the following operations:
    - Encrypt
    - GenerateDataKey
    - GenerateDataKeyPair
    - GenerateDataKeyWithoutPlaintext
    - GenerateDataKeyPairWithoutPlaintext

Re-encrypt (aws kms re-encrypt):

- Decrypts ciphertext and then re-encrypts it entirely within AWS KMS.
- You can use this operation to change the customer master key (CMK) under which data is encrypted, such as when you manually rotate a CMK or change the CMK that protects a ciphertext.
- You can also use it to re-encrypt ciphertext under the same CMK, such as to change the encryption context of a ciphertext.

Enable-key-rotation:

- Enables automatic rotation of the key material for the specified symmetric customer master key (CMK).
- You cannot perform this operation on a CMK in a different AWS account.

GenerateDataKey (aws kms generate-data-key):

- Enables automatic rotation of the key material for the specified symmetric customer master key (CMK).
- You cannot perform this operation on a CMK in a different AWS account.

GenerateDataKeyWithoutPlaintext (generate-data-key-without-plaintext):

- Generates a unique symmetric data key.

- This operation returns a data key that is encrypted under a customer master key (CMK) that you specify.

- To request an asymmetric data key pair, use the GenerateDataKeyPair or GenerateDataKeyPairWithoutPlaintext operations.

KMS ENVELOPE ENCRYPTION

AWS KMS is integrated with AWS services and client-side toolkits that use a method known as envelope encryption to encrypt your data.

Under this method, KMS generates data keys which are used to encrypt data and are themselves encrypted using your master keys in KMS:

- A CMK is used to encrypt the data key (envelope key).

- The envelope key is used to decrypt the data.

SECURITY, IDENTITY AND COMPLIANCE QUIZ QUESTIONS

Question 1: A Developer has run aws configure on an Amazon EC2 Linux instance. Where would the access keys be stored on the filesystem?

1. ~/.aws/credentials

2. %UserProfle%\.aws\credentials

3. ~/.aws/config

Question 2: What is the best practice for applying permissions to many users who perform the same job role?

1. Apply a permissions policy to an IAM Role and allow the users to assume the role

2. Add the users to an IAM Group and apply a permissions policy to the group

3. Add an inline permissions policy to each individual IAM user

Question 3: What container is used for applying an IAM Role to an Amazon EC2 instance?

1. A Docker container

2. The AWS Security Token Service (STS)

3. An Instance Profile

Question 4: An organization has separate production and development accounts. What's the most efficient way to enable a Developer with a user account in the development account permissions to deploy AWS services into the production account?

1. Use a Lambda authorizer

2. Allow the user to assume a role in the production account that has the necessary permissions

3. Allow the user to login with separate credentials to the production account

4. Enable access to the resources in the production account through an IAM permissions policy in the development account

Question 5: Which element of an IAM policy document can be used to specify that a policy should take effect only if the caller is coming from a specific source IP address?

1. Action

2. Resource

3. Effect

4. Condition

Question 6: Which of the following is NOT an IAM best practice?

1. Use Groups to Assign Permissions to IAM Users

2. Configure a Strong Password Policy for Your Users

3. Do Not Share Access Keys

4. Rotate Credentials Regularly

Question 7: Which of the following is an example of encryption in-transit?

1. KMS encryption of an Amazon S3 bucket

2. An encrypted EBS volume

3. An encrypted Amazon RDS database snapshot

4. An Elastic Load Balancer with an SSL listener

Question 8: What type of AWS KMS key can be used for encrypting a 1 GB file with the AWS CLI?

1. AWS KMS customer master key (CMK)

2. AWS Managed Keys

3. A Data Encryption Key (DEK)

Question 9: A Developer needs to securely store a database connection string that must be accessible from an AWS Lambda function. Which service can a Developer use to store the connection string as ciphertext MOST cost-effectively?

1. AWS Systems Manager Parameter Store

2. AWS Secrets Manager

Question 10: Which AWS Cognito feature allows an authenticated user to gain temporary security credentials for accessing AWS services?

1. A Cognito User Pool

2. A Cognito Identity Pool

3. A Cognito Token-Based Authorizer

Question 11: A customer needs to encrypt data on-premises before uploading it to Amazon S3. Which encryption option should be used?

1. Server-side encryption with S3 managed keys

2. Server-side encryption with client provided keys

3. Client-side encryption

4. Server-side encryption with AWS KMS managed keys

Question 12: Which AWS service provides a dedicated single-tenant managed service for securely creating and managing encryption keys?

1. AWS KMS

2. AWS CloudHSM

3. AWS Certificate Manager

SECURITY, IDENTITY AND COMPLIANCE - QUIZ QUESTIONS & ANSWERS

Question 1, Answer 1

Explanation:

1 is correct. This is the correct path to the credentials file which will have the access keys stored in plaintext.

2 is incorrect. This is the correct path to the credentials file on a Windows operating system.

3 is incorrect. This config file does not contain the access keys.

Question 2: What is the best practice for applying permissions to many users who perform the same job role?

1. Apply a permissions policy to an IAM Role and allow the users to assume the role

2. Add the users to an IAM Group and apply a permissions policy to the group

3. Add an inline permissions policy to each individual IAM user

Question 2, Answer 2

Explanation:

1 is incorrect. This is not a best practice.

2 is correct. The best practice is to put users into a group and apply a permissions policy to the group.

3 is incorrect. This is not a best practice as it would be extremely difficult to manage.

Question 3: What container is used for applying an IAM Role to an Amazon EC2 instance?

1. A Docker container

2. The AWS Security Token Service (STS)

3. An Instance Profile

Question 3, Answer 3

Explanation:

1 is incorrect. Docker containers do not apply roles to EC2 instances.

2 is incorrect. The AWS Security Token Service (STS) is a web service that enables you to request temporary, limited-privilege credentials for AWS Identity and Access Management (IAM) users or for users that you authenticate (federated users).

3 is correct. An instance profile is a container for an IAM role that you can use to pass role information to an EC2 instance when the instance starts.

Question 4: An organization has separate production and development accounts. What's the most efficient way to enable a Developer with a user account in the development account permissions to deploy AWS services into the production account?

1. Use a Lambda authorizer

2. Allow the user to assume a role in the production account that has the necessary permissions

3. Allow the user to login with separate credentials to the production account

4. Enable access to the resources in the production account through an IAM permissions policy in the development account

Question 4, Answer 2

Explanation:

1 is incorrect. A Lambda authorizer (formerly known as a custom authorizer) is an API Gateway feature that uses a Lambda function to control access to an API.

2 is correct. This is also known as cross-account access and is the most efficient way to provide the required access.

3 is incorrect. This is not a very efficient way to provide access as the Developer must log out and back in again and manage multiple user accounts.

4 is incorrect. This is not possible as you cannot add permissions to the resources from the production account to the permissions policy in the development account.

Question 5: Which element of an IAM policy document can be used to specify that a policy should take effect only if the caller is coming from a specific source IP address?

1. Action

2. Resource

3. Effect

4. Condition

Question 5, Answer 4

Explanation:

1 is incorrect. The Action element describes the specific action or actions that will be allowed or denied.

2 is incorrect. The Resource element specifies the object or objects that the statement covers.

3 is incorrect. The Effect element is required and specifies whether the statement results in an allow or an explicit deny.

4 is correct. The Condition element (or Condition block) lets you specify conditions for when a policy is in effect.

Question 6: Which of the following is NOT an IAM best practice?

1. Use Groups to Assign Permissions to IAM Users

2. Configure a Strong Password Policy for Your Users

3. Do Not Share Access Keys

4. Rotate Credentials Regularly

Question 6, Answer 4

Explanation:

1 is incorrect. This is an IAM best practice.

2 is incorrect. This is an IAM best practice.

3 is incorrect. This is an IAM best practice.

4 is correct. This is an IAM best practice.

Question 7: Which of the following is an example of encryption in-transit?

1. KMS encryption of an Amazon S3 bucket

2. An encrypted EBS volume

3. An encrypted Amazon RDS database snapshot

4. An Elastic Load Balancer with an SSL listener

Question 7, Answer 4

Explanation:

1 is incorrect. This is an example of encryption at rest.

2 is incorrect. This is an example of encryption at rest.

3 is incorrect. This is an example of encryption at rest.

4 is correct. This is an example of encryption in-transit.

Question 8: What type of AWS KMS key can be used for encrypting a 1 GB file with the AWS CLI?

1. AWS KMS customer master key (CMK)

2. AWS Managed Keys

3. A Data Encryption Key (DEK)

Question 8, Answer 3

Explanation:

1 is incorrect. A CMK can encrypt data up to 4KB in size. For anything bigger a data encryption key must be generated from the CMK.

2 is incorrect. You cannot use AWS managed keys on the AWS CLI. These are used by AWS for encryption operations on AWS services.

3 is correct. A CMK can generate, encrypt and decrypt Data Encryption Keys (DEKs). These keys can be used for encrypting large amounts of data.

Question 9: A Developer needs to securely store a database connection string that must be accessible from an AWS Lambda function. Which service can a Developer use to store the connection string as ciphertext MOST cost-effectively?

1. AWS Systems Manager Parameter Store

2. AWS Secrets Manager

Question 9, Answer 1

Explanation:

1 is correct. This service can be used to store parameters as ciphertext which can then be accessed from services such as AWS Lambda. This service is also free to use for standard parameters.

2 is incorrect. This service does provide the functionality required but there is a small cost per secret so it's not the most cost-effective option.

Question 10: Which AWS Cognito feature allows an authenticated user to gain temporary security credentials for accessing AWS services?

1. A Cognito User Pool

2. A Cognito Identity Pool

3. A Cognito Token-Based Authorizer

Question 10, Answer 2

Explanation:

1 is incorrect. A Cognito user pool uses JSON web tokens, it does not provide temporary security credentials for AWS services.

2 is correct. Cognito Identity pools provide temporary security credentials to access your app's backend resources in AWS or any service behind Amazon API Gateway.

3 is incorrect. A token is different to temporary security credentials.

Question 11: A customer needs to encrypt data on-premises before uploading it to Amazon S3. Which encryption option should be used?

1. Server-side encryption with S3 managed keys

2. Server-side encryption with client provided keys

3. Client-side encryption

4. Server-side encryption with AWS KMS managed keys

Question 11, Answer 3

Explanation:

1 is incorrect. With this option the data is encrypted on Amazon S3 with keys managed by S3.

2 is incorrect. With this option the data is encrypted on Amazon S3 with key provided by the client.

3 is correct. With this option all encryption and decryption happens on the client side without any involvement of Amazon S3. This should be used to encrypt the data before uploading.

4 is incorrect. With this option the data is encrypted on Amazon S3 with keys managed by KMS.

Question 12: Which AWS service provides a dedicated single-tenant managed service for securely creating and managing encryption keys?

1. AWS KMS

2. AWS CloudHSM

3. AWS Certificate Manager

Question 12, Answer 2

Explanation:

1 is incorrect. This is a multi-tenant solution.

2 is correct. Only AWS CloudHSM is single-tenant.

3 is incorrect. This service is used for creating SSL/TLS certificates, not encryption keys.

AWS APPLICATION INTEGRATION

AMAZON SNS

GENERAL AMAZON SNS CONCEPTS

Amazon SNS is a web service that is used to setup, operate and send notifications from the cloud.

Push notifications can go to Apple, Google, Fire OS, and Windows devices as well as Android devices in China with Baidu Cloud Push.

SNS can also send notifications via SMS text message, email, SQS queues or to any HTTP endpoint.

SNS notifications can also trigger Lambda functions.

Inexpensive, pay-as-you-go model with no upfront costs.

Pub-sub model whereby users subscribe to topics.

Publisher systems can fan out messages to a large number of subscriber endpoints:

Endpoints include:

- Amazon SQS queues.
- AWS Lambda functions.
- HTTP/S webhooks.
- Mobile push.
- SMS.
- Email.

Sending messages to many receivers:

- The event producer only sends message to one SNS topic.
- As many event receivers (subscriptions) as we want listen for notifications.
- Each subscriber will get all the messages.
- Can filter messages.
- Up to 10,000,000 subscriptions per topic.
- Limit of 100,000 topics.

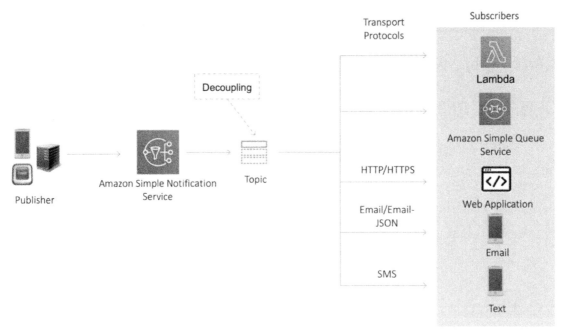

Multiple recipients can be grouped using Topics.

A topic is an "access point" for allowing recipients to dynamically subscribe for identical copies of the same notification.

One topic can support deliveries to multiple endpoint types.

All messages are stored redundantly across multiple availability zones.

Instantaneous, push-based delivery.

Simple APIs and easy integration with applications.

Flexible message delivery over multiple transport protocols.

SNS + SQS FAN OUT

You can subscribe one or more Amazon SQS queues to an Amazon SNS topic from a list of topics available for the selected queue.

Amazon SQS manages the subscription and any necessary permissions.

When you publish a message to a topic, Amazon SNS sends the message to every subscribed queue.

SNS topic pushes once to multiple SQS queues.

Fully decoupled.

No data loss.

Ability to add receivers later.

SQS allows for delayed processing.

SQS allows for retries of work.

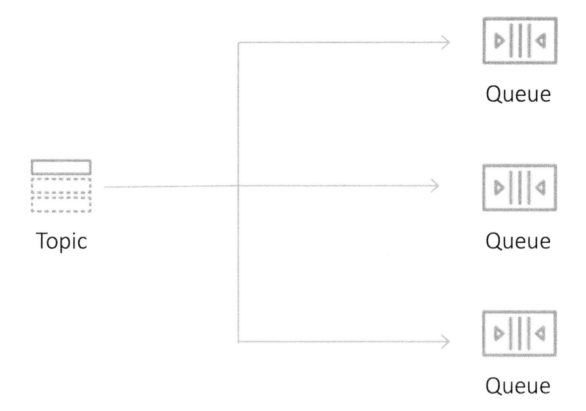

Topic

Queue

Queue

Queue

AMAZON SQS

GENERAL AMAZON SQS CONCEPTS

Amazon Simple Queue Service (SQS) is a fully managed message queuing service that enables you to decouple and scale microservices, distributed systems, and serverless applications.

SQS eliminates the complexity and overhead associated with managing and operating message oriented middleware, and empowers developers to focus on differentiating work.

Using SQS, you can send, store, and receive messages between software components at any volume, without losing messages or requiring other services to be available.

SQS is a distributed queue system that enables web service applications to quickly and reliably queue messages that one component in the application generates to be consumed by another component.

A queue is a temporary repository for messages that are awaiting processing.

The queue acts as a buffer between the component producing and saving data, and the component receiving the data for processing.

This means the queue resolves issues that arise if the producer is producing work faster than the consumer can process it, or if the producer or consumer are only intermittently connected to the network.

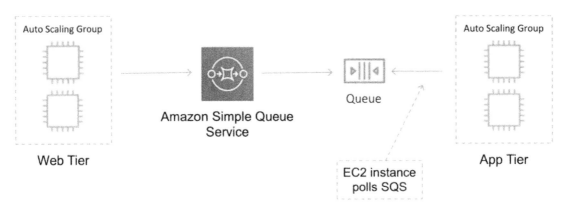

This is known as decoupling / loose coupling.

Helps enable elasticity for your application.

KEY FACTS

SQS is pull-based, not push-based (like SNS).

Messages are up to 256KB in size.

Messages can be kept in the queue from 1 minute to 14 days.

Default retention period is 4 days.

SQS guarantees that your messages will be processed at least once.

QUEUES

There are two types of queue – standard queues and FIFO queues.

STANDARD

Default queue type.

Nearly unlimited transactions per second.

Guarantee that a message is delivered at least once.

Occasionally more than one copy of a message might be delivered out of order.

Provides best-effort ordering which ensures that messages are generally delivered in the same order as they are sent.

FIRST IN FIRST OUT (FIFO)

Delivers exactly-once processing.

The order in which messages are sent and received is strictly preserved and a message is delivered once and remains available until a consumer processes and deletes it.

Duplicates are not introduced into the queue.

FIFO queues also support message groups that allow multiple ordered message groups within a single queue.

Limited to 300 transactions per second (TPS), but have all the capabilities of standard queues.

Deduplication with FIFO queues:

- Provide a MessageDeduplicationId with the message.

- The de-duplication interval is 5 minutes.

- Content based duplication – the MessageDeduplicationId is generated as the SHA-256 with the message body.

Sequencing with FIFO queues:

- To ensure strict ordering between messages, specify a MessageGroupId.

- Messages with a different Group ID may be received out of order.

- Messages with the same Group ID are delivered to one consumer at a time.

FIFO queues require the Message Group ID and Message Deduplication ID parameters to be added to messages.

Message Group ID:

- The tag that specifies that a message belongs to a specific message group. Messages that belong to the same message group are guaranteed to be processed in a FIFO manner.

Message Deduplication ID:

- The token used for deduplication of messages within the deduplication interval.

The following table provides a side-by-side comparison of standard and FIFO queues:

Standard Queue	FIFO Queue
Unlimited Throughput: Standard queues support a nearly unlimited number of transactions per second (TPS) per API action.	High Throughput: FIFO queues support up to 300 messages per second (300 send, receive, or delete operations per second). When you batch 10 messages per operation (maximum), FIFO queues can support up to 3,000 messages per second
Best-Effort Ordering: Occasionally, messages might be delivered in an order different from which they were sent	First-In-First-out Delivery: The order in which messages are sent and received is strictly preserved
At-Least-Once Delivery: A message is delivered at least once, but occasionally more than one copy of a message is delivered	Exactly-Once Processing: A message is delivered once and remains available until a consumer processes and deletes it. Duplicates are not introduced into the queue

VISIBILITY TIMEOUT

The amount of time a message is invisible in the queue after a reader picks it up.

Provided the job is processed before the visibility timeout expires, the message will then be deleted from the queue.

If the job is not processed within the visibility timeout, the message will become visible again and another reader will process it.

This could result in the same message being delivered twice.

The default visibility timeout is 30 seconds.

Increase it if your task takes >30 seconds.

The maximum is 12 hours.

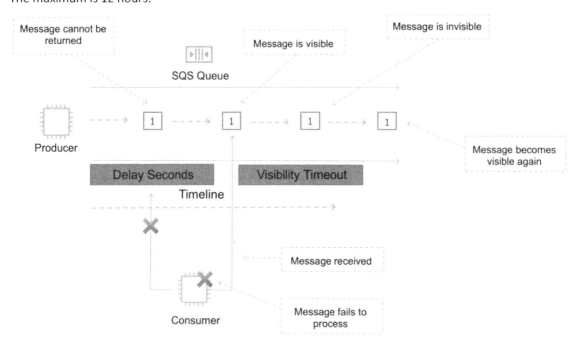

LONG POLLING VS SHORT POLLING

Amazon SQS long polling is a way to retrieve messages from SQS queues.

While the regular short polling returns immediately (even if the message queue is empty), long polling doesn't return a response until a message arrives in the message queue or the long poll times out.

Long polling can lower costs

Long polling can be enabled at the queue level or at the API level using WaitTimeSeconds.

Long polling is in effect when the Receive Message Wait Time is a value greater than 0 seconds and up to 20 seconds.

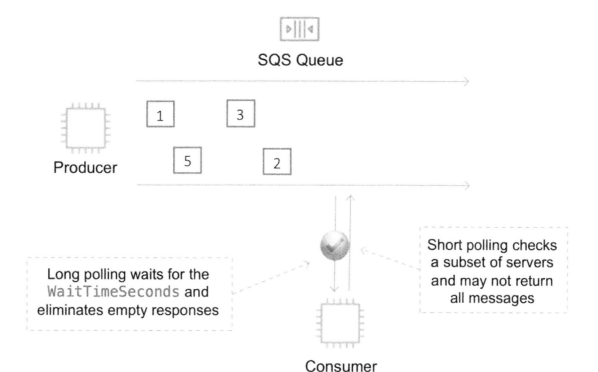

DEAD-LETTER QUEUE

The main task of a dead-letter queue is handling message failure.

A dead-letter queue lets you set aside and isolate messages that can't be processed correctly to determine why their processing didn't succeed.

It is not a queue type, it is a standard or FIFO queue that has been specified as a dead-letter queue in the configuration of another standard or FIFO queue.

Messages are moved to the dead-letter queue when the ReceiveCount for a message exceeds the maxReceiveCount for a queue.

Dead-letter queues should not be used with standard queues when your application will keep retrying transmission.

Dead-letter queues will break the order of messages in FIFO queues.

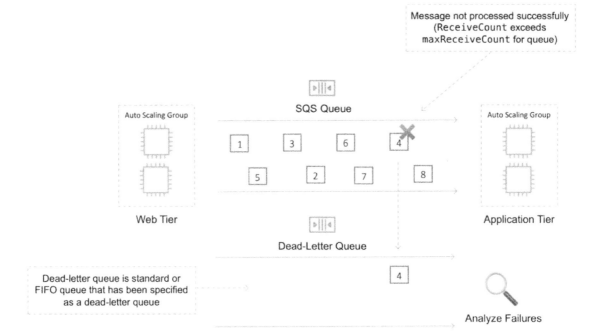

Message not processed successfully
(ReceiveCount exceeds
maxReceiveCount for queue)

SQS Queue

Auto Scaling Group

Web Tier

Auto Scaling Group

Application Tier

Dead-Letter Queue

Dead-letter queue is standard or
FIFO queue that has been specified
as a dead-letter queue

Analyze Failures

SQS DELAY QUEUES

A delay queue postpones delivery of new messages to a queue for a number of seconds.

Messages sent to the Delay Queue remain invisible to consumers for the duration of the delay period.

Default delay is 0 seconds, maximum is 900 seconds (15 minutes).

For standard SQS queues, changing this setting doesn't affect the delay of messages already in the queue, only new messages.

For FIFO queues, this affects the delay of messages already in the queue.

When to use a delay queue:

- Large distributed applications which may need to introduce a delay in processing.

- You need to apply a delay to an entire queue of messages.

- For example adding a delay of a few seconds to allow updates to sales or stock control databases before sending a notification to a customer confirming an online transaction.

DLQs must be the same type as the source.

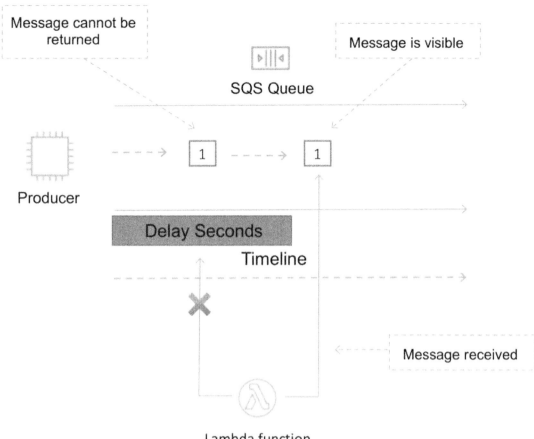

Producer

SQS Queue

Message cannot be returned

Message is visible

Delay Seconds

Timeline

Message received

Lambda function

SQS EXTENDED CLIENT

The maximum message size in SQS is 256 KB.

You can use Amazon S3 and the Amazon SQS Extended Client Library for Java to manage Amazon SQS messages.

Useful for storing and consuming messages up to 2 GB in size.

You can use the Amazon SQS Extended Client Library for Java library to do the following:

- Specify whether messages are always stored in Amazon S3 or only when the size of a message exceeds 256 KB.

- Send a message that references a single message object stored in an Amazon S3 bucket.

- Get the corresponding message object from an Amazon S3 bucket.

- Delete the corresponding message object from an Amazon S3 bucket.

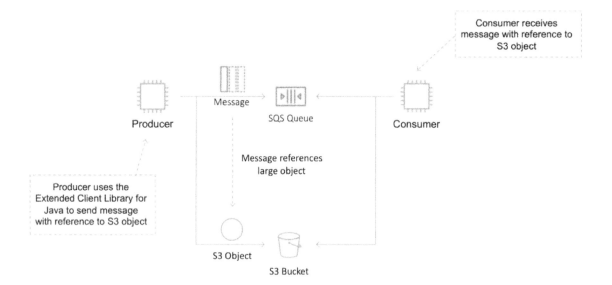

SECURITY

In-flight security is provided using HTTPS.

Can enable server-side encryption (SSE) using KMS.

- Can set the CMK you want to use.
- Can set the data key reuse period.
- SSE only encrypts the message body not the message attributes.

IAM policy must allow usage of SQS.

Can also specify permissions in an SQS queue access policy:

- Providers finer grained control.
- Control over the requests that come in.

There is no VPC endpoint for SQS (must have Internet access).

AMAZON SQS API'S

APIs you should know for the exam:

CreateQueue (aws sqs create-queue):

- Creates a new standard or FIFO queue. You can pass one or more attributes in the request.

DeleteQueue (aws sqs delete-queue):

- Deletes the queue specified by the QueueUrl , regardless of the queue's contents.
- If the specified queue doesn't exist, Amazon SQS returns a successful response.

PurgeQueue (aws sqs purge-queue):

- Deletes the messages in a queue specified by the QueueURL parameter.

SendMessage (aws sqs send-message):

- Delivers a message to the specified queue.

ReceiveMessage (aws sqs receive-messsage):

- Retrieves one or more messages (up to 10), from the specified queue.
- Using the WaitTimeSeconds parameter enables long-poll support.

DeleteMessage (aws sqs delete-message):

- Deletes the specified message from the specified queue.
- To select the message to delete, use the ReceiptHandle of the message (not the MessageId which you receive when you send the message).

ChangeMessageVisibility (aws sqs change-message-visibility):

- Changes the visibility timeout of a specified message in a queue to a new value.
- The default visibility timeout for a message is 30 seconds.
- The minimum is 0 seconds.
- The maximum is 12 hours.

To reduce costs or manipulate up to 10 messages with a single action, you can use the following actions:

- SendMessageBatch
- DeleteMessageBatch
- ChangeMessageVisibilityBatch

AMAZON STEP FUNCTIONS

GENERAL AWS STEP FUNCTIONS CONCEPTS

AWS Step Functions makes it easy to coordinate the components of distributed applications as a series of steps in a visual workflow.

You can quickly build and run state machines to execute the steps of your application in a reliable and scalable fashion.

How it works:

1. Define the steps of your workflow in the JSON-based Amazon States Language. The visual console automatically graphs each step in the order of execution.

2. Start an execution to visualize and verify the steps of your application are operating as intended. The console highlights the real-time status of each step and provides a detailed history of every execution.

3. AWS Step Functions operates and scales the steps of your application and underlying compute for you to help ensure your application executes reliably under increasing demand.

Managed workflow and orchestration platform.

Scalable and highly available.

Define your app as a state machine.

Create tasks, sequential steps, parallel steps, branching paths or timers.

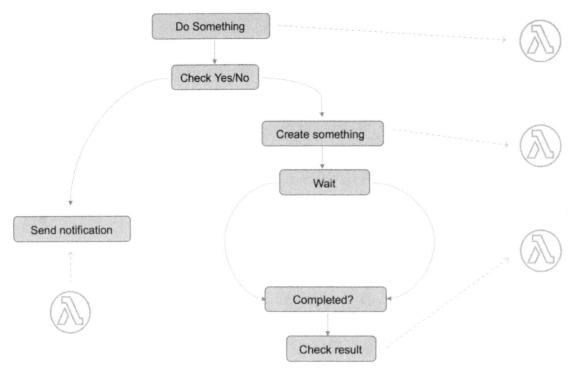

Uses the Amazon State Language declarative JSON.

Apps can interact and update the stream via Step Function API.

Visual interface describes flow and real-time status.

Detailed logs of each step execution.

Uses AWS Lambda functions

Can do sequential, branching or parallel steps.

Can visualize the serverless application.

Step Functions automatically triggers and tracks each step.

Logs the state of each step so if something goes wrong you can track what went wrong and where.

AWS APPLICATION INTEGRATION QUIZ QUESTIONS

Question 1: Applications are taking a long time to process messages from an Amazon SQS queue and there have been incidents of messages being processed multiple times. How can the queue be configured to prevent this from occurring?

1. Configure a delay queue

2. Use long polling

3. Increase the visibility timeout

Question 2: How can a notification be sent to multiple Amazon SQS queues?

1. Use Amazon SNS and SQS fan-out

2. Use an Amazon SQS FIFO queue

to multiple queues.

Question 3: Which Amazon SQS queue type provides deduplication of messages?

1. Amazon SQS Standard Queue

2. Amazon SQS Delay Queue

3. Amazon SQS FIFO Queue

Question 4: Several legacy batch processes have been refactored into AWS Lambda functions. The functions call each other. Which services can be used to configure the functions into an orchestrated serverless workflow?

1. Amazon SQS

2. AWS Step Functions

3. Amazon SWF

4. AWS CloudFormation

Question 5: A company operates a number of IoT devices placed in manufacturing facilities. The devices send streaming data that is being received in an Amazon Kinesis Data Stream. The volume of data has been increasing and the stream has reached capacity. How can the Data Stream be scaled?

1. Merge existing shards to increase the capacity of the stream

2. Add more shards to increase the capacity of the stream

3. Increase the number of consumers

4. Increase the capacity of the stream by increasing the number of put records allowed per shard

Question 6: Which AWS service is best suited to receive streaming data and load the data into an Elasticsearch cluster?

1. Amazon Kinesis Data Streams

2. Amazon Kinesis Data Analytics

3. Amazon Kinesis Data Firehose

4. Amazon SQS

AWS APPLICATION INTEGRATION - QUIZ QUESTIONS & ANSWERS

Question 1: Applications are taking a long time to process messages from an Amazon SQS queue and there have been incidents of messages being processed multiple times. How can the queue be configured to prevent this from occurring?

1. Configure a delay queue

2. Use long polling

3. Increase the visibility timeout

Question 1, Answer 3

Explanation:

1 is incorrect. This postpones delivery of new messages to a queue for a number of seconds and will not help in this scenario as it will not prevent messages from becoming visible whilst still being processed.

2 is incorrect. Amazon SQS long polling is a way to retrieve messages from SQS queues. It can assist with reducing cost but will not help to prevent messages from being processed multiple times.

3 is correct. The amount of time a message is invisible in the queue after a reader picks it up. Provided the job is processed before the visibility timeout expires, the message will then be deleted from the queue. Increasing the visibility timeout will provide more time for the applications to process and delete the messages.

Question 2: How can a notification be sent to multiple Amazon SQS queues?

1. Use Amazon SNS and SQS fan-out

2. Use an Amazon SQS FIFO queue

Question 2, Answer 1

Explanation:

1 is correct. With this configuration an SNS topic pushes a notification once to multiple SQS queues.

2 is incorrect. This is just a queue type that provides first-in-first-out processing. It will not send messages to multiple queues.

Question 3: Which Amazon SQS queue type provides deduplication of messages?

1. Amazon SQS Standard Queue

2. Amazon SQS Delay Queue

3. Amazon SQS FIFO Queue

Question 3, Answer 3

Explanation:

1 is incorrect. Guarantee that a message is delivered at least once. Occasionally more than one copy of a message might be delivered out of order.

2 is incorrect. A queue configured as a delay queue postpones delivery of new messages for a number of seconds. Messages sent to the Delay Queue remain invisible to consumers for the duration of the delay period.

3 is correct. FIFO queues also support message groups that allow multiple ordered message groups within a single queue. You can configure a MessageDeduplicationId with the message that allows for deduplication.

Question 4: Several legacy batch processes have been refactored into AWS Lambda functions. The functions call each other. Which services can be used to configure the functions into an orchestrated serverless workflow?

1. Amazon SQS

2. AWS Step Functions

3. Amazon SWF

4. AWS CloudFormation

Question 4, Answer 2

Explanation:

1 is incorrect. Amazon SQS is used for decoupling, not orchestrating serverless workflows.

2 is correct. AWS Step Functions makes it easy to coordinate the components of distributed applications as a series of steps in a visual workflow.

3 is incorrect. Amazon Simple Workflow Service (SWF) is used for human-enabled workflows and other use cases, but not serverless workflows.

4 is incorrect. AWS CloudFormation is used for launching infrastructure on AWS but not orchestrating serverless workflows.

Question 5: A company operates a number of IoT devices placed in manufacturing facilities. The devices send streaming data that is being received in an Amazon Kinesis Data Stream. The volume of data has been increasing and the stream has reached capacity. How can the Data Stream be scaled?

1. Merge existing shards to increase the capacity of the stream

2. Add more shards to increase the capacity of the stream

3. Increase the number of consumers

4. Increase the capacity of the stream by increasing the number of put records allowed per shard

Question 5, Answer 2

Explanation:

1 is incorrect. Merging shards decreases the capacity of the stream.

2 is correct. This will increase the total capacity of the stream as the total capacity of the stream is the sum of the capacities of its shards.

3 is incorrect. This will not increase the capacity of the data stream.

4 is incorrect. You cannot do this. You need to add more shards to the stream to add additional capacity.

Question 6: Which AWS service is best suited to receive streaming data and load the data into an Elasticsearch cluster?

1. Amazon Kinesis Data Streams

2. Amazon Kinesis Data Analytics

3. Amazon Kinesis Data Firehose

4. Amazon SQS

Question 6, Answer 3

Explanation:

1 is incorrect. Data Streams does not load data directly into a destination. The data is stored in shards that are processed by consumers.

2 is incorrect. This service is used to run SQL queries on streaming data in a stream.

3 is correct. This service loads data directly into a destination such as Elasticsearch.

4 is incorrect. This service is a message queueing service. The messages are not sent to a destination they are pulled by consumers and processed.

CONCLUSION

We trust that these training notes have helped you to gain a complete understanding of the facts you need to know to pass the AWS Certified Developer Associate exam first time.

The exam covers a broad set of technologies. It's vital to ensure you are armed with the knowledge to answer whatever questions come up in your certification exam. We recommend reviewing these training notes until you're confident in all areas.

BEFORE TAKING THE AWS EXAM

Familiarize yourself with the AWS platform

AWS certification exams such as the Developer Associate test your experience with the AWS platform. It's therefore super important to have some hands-on experience before you sit the exam.

Our AWS Certified Developer Associate Hands-On Labs course provides a practical approach to learning. Through over 28 hours of videos you will learn how to architect and build solutions on Amazon Web Services. By the end of the course you will have a strong experience-based skillset. This is the best way to develop strong hands-on skills and will really help you when it comes time to answer exam questions.

Assess your exam readiness with the online Exam Simulator from digital cloud training

These 390 unique practice questions are the closest to the actual exam question format and the only exam-difficulty questions on the market. If you can pass these mock exams, you're well set to ace the real thing! To learn more, visit:

AWS Certified Developer Associate Practice Exams

Reach out with any questions you may have

If anything is not 100% to your liking, please email us at feedback@digitalcloud.training. We promise to address all questions and concerns. For technical support, contact us at:

support@digitalcloud.training.

Also, remember to join our private Facebook group to ask questions and share knowledge and exam tips with the AWS community:

https://www.facebook.com/groups/awscertificationqa

BONUS OFFER

To gain access to your **free practice exam with 65 exam-difficulty questions** on the interactive online exam simulator from digital cloud training, visit https://digitalcloud.training/aws-practice-questions-for-the-certified-developer-associate or scan this QR code. You then click "Add to cart" and apply coupon code "DEV65" at checkout to get 100% off. Please reach out if you run into any difficulties in accessing your Bonus.

For those who have already purchased the full set of practice questions, please note that these 65 questions are included in the pool of 390 questions.

SMALL FAVOR

If you like reading course reviews, please consider paying it forward. It's the best way you can help us improve our courses and help your fellow students make the right choices. We celebrate every honest review and truly appreciate it. You can leave a review at any time by visiting amazon.com/ryp (or your local amazon store, e.g. amazon.co.uk/ryp).

Best wishes for your AWS certification journey!

OTHER BOOKS & COURSES BY NEAL DAVIS

AWS CERTIFIED DEVELOPER ASSOCIATE INSTRUCTOR-LED VIDEO COURSE

AVAILABLE ON DIGITALCLOUD.TRAINING

This brand-new **AWS Certified Developer Associate Exam Training** for the **AWS Certified Developer Associate certification exam** (DVA-C01) is packed with over 28 hours of comprehensive video lessons, hands-on labs, quizzes and exam-crams. With our mixture of in-depth theory, architectural diagrams and hands-on training, you'll learn how to architect and build applications on **Amazon Web Services**, fully preparing you for the **AWS Developer Certification** exam. With this complete **AWS Developer training** course, you have everything you need to comfortably pass the **AWS Developer Certification** exam at the first attempt.

How is this Course Different?

We are big believers in using practical exercises to improve memory retention and contextualize knowledge. We have included many hours of hands-on guided exercises, so you get to build a practical skillset. The course also includes many visual slides to help you understand the concepts. All practical exercises are backed by architectural diagrams so you can visualize what you're developing on Amazon Web Services. By the end of this course, you will have acquired a strong experience-based skillset on AWS along with the confidence to ace your **AWS Certified Developer Associate exam** first time!

With this **AWS Developer training**, you'll learn AWS Serverless using AWS Lambda, API Gateway, DynamoDB & Cognito, get hands-on with AWS Databases including DynamoDB, build Microservices architectures with Docker containers on Amazon ECS and create Continuous Integration and Delivery (CI/CD) pipelines with AWS CodeCommit, CodeDeploy, and CodePipeline. All of this and so MUCH more!

To learn more, visit:

https://digitalcloud.training/aws-certified-developer-associate-exam-training/

AWS CERTIFIED DEVELOPER ASSOCIATE (ONLINE) PRACTICE TESTS

AVAILABLE ON <u>DIGITALCLOUD.TRAINING</u>

Get access to the **online Exam Simulator** from Digital Cloud Training with 390 Questions in 6 sets of practice exam. All questions are unique and conform to the latest AWS DVA-C01 exam blueprint.

Our AWS Practice Tests are delivered in 3 different modes:

Simulation mode: the number of questions, time limit, and pass mark are the same as the real AWS exam. You must complete the exam before you are able to check your score and review answers and explanations.

Training mode: You are shown the answer and explanation for every question after clicking "check". Upon completion of the exam the score report shows your overall score and performance in each knowledge area.

Knowledge reviews: Collections of practice questions for a specific knowledge area. When you complete a practice exam you can use the score report to identify your strengths and weaknesses and then use the knowledge reviews to focus your efforts where they're needed most.

To learn more on how to fast-track your AWS Certified Developer Associate Exam Success, visit:

https://digitalcloud.training/aws-certified-developer-associate-practice-exams/

AWS CERTIFIED SOLUTIONS ARCHITECT ASSOCIATE VIDEO COURSE

AVAILABLE ON DIGITALCLOUD.TRAINING

This popular AWS Certified Solutions Architect Associate (SAA-C02) video course is delivered through practical AWS Hands-On Labs.

You will be looking over my shoulder and building applications on Amazon Web Services. By the end of the course , you will have a strong experience-based skillset thanks to the guided AWS Practice Labs.

We will use a process of repetition and incremental learning to ensure that you retain the knowledge as repeated practice is the best way to learn and build your cloud skills. We take you from opening your first AWS Free Tier account through to creating complex multi-tier architectures, always sticking to the **SAA-C02 exam blueprint** to ensure you're learning practical skills and also preparing for your exam.

We back the +20 hours of AWS Hands-On Labs with high-quality logical diagrams so you can visualize what you're building and check your progress.

Our AWS Hands-On Labs teach you how to design and build multi-tier web architectures with services such as EC2 Auto Scaling, Elastic Load Balancing, Route 53, ECS, Lambda, API Gateway and Elastic File System.

To learn more, visit:

https://digitalcloud.training/aws-certified-solutions-architect-associate-hands-on-course/

AWS CERTIFIED SOLUTIONS ARCHITECT ASSOCIATE (ONLINE) PRACTICE TESTS

AVAILABLE ON DIGITALCLOUD.TRAINING

Get access to the **online Exam Simulator** from Digital Cloud Training with over 500 Questions plus 6 sets of practice exams with 65 Questions each. All questions are unique, 100% scenario-based and conform to the latest AWS SAA-C02 exam blueprint.

Our AWS Practice Tests are delivered in 3 different modes:

Simulation mode: the number of questions, time limit, and pass mark are the same as the real AWS exam. You must complete the exam before you are able to check your score and review answers and explanations.

Training mode: You are shown the answer and explanation for every question after clicking "check". Upon completion of the exam the score report shows your overall score and performance in each knowledge area.

Knowledge reviews: Collections of practice questions for a specific knowledge area. When you complete a practice exam you can use the score report to identify your strengths and weaknesses and then use the knowledge reviews to focus your efforts where they're needed most.

Each exam includes questions from the four domains of the AWS exam blueprint. All questions are also available in the knowledge reviews where they are split into more than 15 categories for focused training.

To learn more on how to fast-track your AWS Certified Solutions Architect Associate Exam Success, visit:

https://digitalcloud.training/aws-certified-solutions-architect-associate-practice-tests-saa-c02/

AWS CERTIFIED SOLUTIONS ARCHITECT ASSOCIATE (OFFLINE) PRACTICE TESTS

AVAILABLE ON AMAZON ONLY

The AWS Solutions Architect Associate certification is extremely valuable in the Cloud Computing industry today and preparing to answer the difficult scenario-based questions requires a significant commitment in time and effort.

The latest **SAA-C02 exam** is composed entirely of scenario-based questions that test your knowledge and experience working with Amazon Web Services. Our practice tests are patterned to reflect the difficulty of the AWS exam and are the closest to the real AWS exam experience available anywhere.

There are **6 practice exams with 65 questions** each covering the five domains of the AWS exam blueprint. Each set of questions is repeated once without answers and explanations, and once with answers and explanations, so you get to choose from two methods of preparation:

- **To simulate the exam experience and assess your exam readiness**, use the "PRACTICE QUESTIONS ONLY" sets.

- **To use the practice questions as a learning tool**, use the "PRACTICE QUESTIONS, ANSWERS & EXPLANATIONS" sets to view the answers and read the in-depth explanations as you move through the questions.

These Practice Questions will prepare you for your AWS exam in the following ways:

- **Master the new 2020 exam pattern**: All 390 practice questions are based on the SAA-C02 exam blueprint and use the question format of the real AWS exam

- **6 sets of exam-difficulty practice questions**: Presented with and without answers so you can study or simulate an exam

- **Ideal exam prep tool that will shortcut your study time**: Assess your exam readiness to maximize your chance of passing the AWS exam first time

The exam covers a broad set of technologies and it's vital to ensure you are armed with the knowledge to answer whatever questions come up in your certification exam. We recommend reviewing these practice questions until you're confident in all areas and ready to ace your AWS exam.

To learn more, visit: https://www.amazon.com/gp/product/1079185720.

AWS CERTIFIED SOLUTIONS ARCHITECT ASSOCIATE TRAINING NOTES

AVAILABLE ON AMAZON AND DIGITAL CLOUD TRAINING

Save valuable time by getting straight to the facts you need to know to pass your AWS Certified Solutions Architect Associate exam first time!

This book is based on the 2020 SAA-C02 exam blueprint and provides a deep dive into the subject matter in a concise and easy-to-read format so you can fast-track your time to success.

AWS Solutions Architect and successful instructor, Neal Davis, has consolidated the information you need to be successful from numerous training sources and AWS FAQ pages to save you time.

In addition to the book, you are provided with access to a 65-question practice exam on an interactive exam simulator to evaluate your progress and ensure you're prepared for the style and difficulty of the real AWS exam.

This book will help you prepare for your AWS Certified Solutions Architect – Associate exam in the following ways:

• Deep dive into the SAA-C02 exam objectives with over 300 pages of detailed facts, tables and diagrams.

• Familiarize yourself with the exam question format with the practice questions included in each section.

• Use our online exam simulator to evaluate progress and ensure you're ready for the real thing.

To learn more, visit: https://digitalcloud.training/product/aws-certified-solutions-architect-associate-offline-training-notes/

AWS CERTIFIED CLOUD PRACTITIONER VIDEO COURSE

AVAILABLE ON DIGITALCLOUD.TRAINING

We have fully aligned this instructor-led video training with the AWS Certified Cloud Practitioner exam blueprint and structured the course so that you can study at a pace that suits you best. We start with some basic background to get everyone up to speed on what cloud computing is, before progressing through each knowledge domain.

Here's why this ultimate exam prep is your best chance to ace your AWS certification exam:

HIGHLY FLEXIBLE COURSE STRUCTURE: We understand that not everyone has the time to go through lengthy lectures. That's why we give you options to maximize your time efficiency and accommodate different learning styles.

6 HOURS OF THEORY LECTURES: You can move quickly through the course, focusing on the theory lectures that are 100% conform with the CLF-C01 exam blueprint - everything you need to know to pass your exam first attempt.

4 HOURS OF GUIDED HANDS-ON EXERCISES: To gain more practical experience with AWS services, you have the option to explore the guided hands-on exercises.

1 HOUR OF EXAM-CRAM LECTURES: Get through the key exam facts in the shortest time possible with the exam-cram lectures that you'll find at the end of each section.

HIGH-QUALITY VISUALS: We've spared no effort to create a highly visual training course with lots of table and graphs to illustrate the concepts. All practical exercises are backed by logical diagrams so you can visualize what we're building.

To learn more, visit: https://digitalcloud.training/aws-certified-cloud-practitioner-training-course/

AWS CERTIFIED CLOUD PRACTITIONER (ONLINE) PRACTICE TESTS

AVAILABLE ON DIGITALCLOUD.TRAINING

Get access to the online Exam Simulator from Digital Cloud Training with over 500 Practice questions plus 6 sets of practice exams with 65 Questions each. All questions are unique and conform to the latest AWS CLF-C01 exam blueprint.

Our AWS Practice Tests are delivered in 3 different modes:

Simulation mode: the number of questions, time limit and pass mark are the same as the real AWS exam. You need to complete the exam before you get to check your score and review answers and explanations.

Training mode: You are shown the answer and explanation for every question after clicking "check". Upon completion of the exam, the score report shows your overall score and performance in each knowledge area.

Knowledge reviews: Collections of practice questions for a specific knowledge area. When you complete a practice exam you can use the score report to identify your strengths and weaknesses and then use the knowledge reviews to focus your efforts where they are needed most.

To learn more on how to fast-track your AWS Certified Cloud Practitioner Exam Success, visit:

https://digitalcloud.training/aws-certified-cloud-practitioner-practice-tests/

AWS CERTIFIED CLOUD PRACTITIONER (OFFLINE) PRACTICE TESTS

AVAILABLE ON <u>AMAZON ONLY</u>

The **AWS Cloud Practitioner** exam is a foundational level exam that nonetheless includes tricky questions that test your knowledge and experience of the AWS Cloud. Our practice tests are patterned to reflect the difficulty of the AWS exam and are the closest to the real AWS exam experience available.

There are **6 practice exams with 65 questions each** covering the five domains of the AWS CLF-C01 exam blueprint. Each set of questions is repeated once without answers and explanations, and once with answers and explanations, so you get to choose from two methods of preparation:

1. To simulate the exam experience and assess your exam readiness, use the "**PRACTICE QUESTIONS ONLY**" sets.

2. To use the practice questions as a learning tool, use the "**PRACTICE QUESTIONS, ANSWERS & EXPLANATIONS**" sets to view the answers and read the in-depth explanations as you move through the questions.

These Practice Questions will prepare you for your AWS exam in the following ways:

Master the latest exam pattern: All 390 practice questions are based on the latest version of the CLF-C01 exam blueprint and use the question format of the real AWS exam

6 sets of exam-difficulty practice questions: Presented with and without answers so you can study or simulate an exam

Ideal exam prep tool that will shortcut your study time: Assess your exam readiness to maximize your chance of passing the AWS exam first time.

To learn more, visit:

https://www.amazon.com/gp/product/1081271949

AWS CERTIFIED CLOUD PRACTITIONER TRAINING NOTES

AVAILABLE ON AMAZON AND DIGITALCLOUD.TRAINING

Save valuable time by getting straight to the facts you need to know to be successful and ensure you pass your AWS Certified Cloud Practitioner exam first time!

This book is based on the CLF-C01 exam blueprint and provides a deep dive into the subject matter in a concise and easy-to-read format so you can fast-track your time to success.

The Cloud Practitioner certification is a great first step into the world of Cloud Computing and requires a foundational knowledge of the AWS Cloud, its architectural principles, value proposition, billing and pricing, key services and more.

AWS Solutions Architect and successful instructor, Neal Davis, has consolidated the information you need to be successful from numerous training sources and AWS FAQ pages to save you time.

In addition to the book, you are provided with access to a 65-question practice exam on an interactive exam simulator to evaluate your progress and ensure you're prepared for the style and difficulty of the real AWS exam.

This book can help you prepare for your AWS exam in the following ways:

• Deep dive into the CLF-C01 exam objectives with over 200 pages of detailed facts, tables, and diagrams – everything you need to know!

• Familiarize yourself with the exam question format with the practice questions included in each section.

• Use our online exam simulator to evaluate progress and ensure you're ready for the real thing.

To learn more, visit:

https://digitalcloud.training/product/aws-certified-cloud-practitioner-offline-training-notes/

ABOUT THE AUTHOR

Neal Davis is the founder of Digital Cloud Training, AWS Cloud Solutions Architect and successful IT instructor. With more than 20 years of experience in the tech industry, Neal is a true expert in virtualization and cloud computing. His passion is to help others achieve career success by offering in-depth AWS certification training resources.

Neal started **Digital Cloud Training** to provide a variety of training resources for Amazon Web Services (AWS) certifications that represent a higher standard of quality than is otherwise available in the market.

Digital Cloud Training provides **AWS Certification exam preparation resources** including instructor-led Video Courses, guided Hands-on Labs, in-depth Training Notes, Exam-Cram lessons for quick revision, Quizzes to test your knowledge and exam-difficulty Practice Exams to assess your exam readiness.

With Digital Cloud Training, you get access to highly experienced staff who support you on your AWS Certification journey and help you elevate your career through achieving highly valuable certifications. Join the AWS Community of over 70,000 happy students that are currently enrolled in Digital Cloud Training courses

Connect with Neal on social media:

digitalcloud.training/neal-davis

youtube.com/c/digitalcloudtraining

facebook.com/digitalcloudtraining

Twitter @nealkdavis

linkedin.com/in/nealkdavis

Instagram @digitalcloudtraining

Printed in Great Britain
by Amazon

42025652R00197